# ARTS TO INTELLIGENCE

# 1939 - 1946

by

## Doreen J Galvin (nee Grey)

# PREFACE

At the outset of this narrative, I intended to write 30-40 pages at the request of my two daughters, and for the future interest and amusement of my three young grandchildren. After I began what I thought would be a short task, my interest and my enthusiasm grew as I recalled one after another the incidents and situations that had been but fleeting memories in my mind for over fifty years. I do not guarantee the accuracy of every detail but my memory portrays, I believe, the actual facts and the true atmosphere of the times.

D. J G.
June 2013

# TABLE OF CONTENTS

A NEAR MISS .................................................1

THE VILLAGE OF PETT................................11

THE SUMMER AND AUTUMN OF 1940 .......23

JOINING UP .................................................37

R.A.F. SPEKE - LIVERPOOL...........................49

LEARNING PHOTO INTERPRETATION ......79

LIFE AT MEDMENHAM C.I.U........................85

WYMESWOLD & BOMBER COMMAND.....111

R.A.F. FELTWELL .......................................119

The Royal Observer Corps .........................145

MAY 3, 1943 - A DAY TO REMEMBER..........151

Marking Time.........................................164

R.A.F. TEMPSFORD .....................................171

A COLD WINTER........................................185

SPRING 1944..............................................197

D-DAY ......................................................205

A NOISY NIGHT........................................211

THE END IN SIGHT ...................................227

SUMMER AND AUTUMN 1944 .....................239

Once in a Lifetime ..................................248

R.A.F. WATERBEACH .................................253

VE-DAY AND AFTER...................................267

Preparing for Civvy Street ........................273

"Bombs Away!".........................................277

"Lost Him!" ............................................283

The First Jet ...........................................286

Surprise Sortie ........................................295

LEAVING THE RAF ....................................301

# A NEAR MISS

The German Air Force bombers crossing the East Sussex coast were passing over our village. They flew in continuous waves as they droned on their way to London. It was late October, 1940, and it was going to be another of those nights of which we had experienced so many lately.

I lay in my bed waiting to hear the last of them so that I could get an hour's sleep before their return. Tonight the Luftwaffe were out in force - for nearly half an hour they had been flying above us heading north - it was obvious that London was in for a bad time again. My mother, lying awake in her room, told me later that she was thinking exactly the same thing.

Suddenly, I heard an unfamiliar sound, which cut through the noise and deep droning of the advancing bombers. At first, it was a distant, piercing kind of sound. Almost instantaneously it grew into a loud whistle, then with accelerating speed into a shriek of rushing air, continuing with a roar that almost split my ear drums. A quick thought came to me - would I still be around to see the sunrise?

SILENCE - utter silence! It took a minute or two to regain my hearing as gradually the droning sounds returned to my ears. I was still here to tell the tale! Lying on a divan bed with no space to dive underneath, I found myself curled up with my hands protecting my face. It was an automatic reaction. I do not remember getting into that position. Jumping out of bed, I groped my way towards my mother's bedroom. In the middle of the living room, we collided in pitch darkness. We dared not infringe the blackout rules for our own safety and there was no moon, so, in blackness, we sat on the sofa and discussed the situation. Should we go to the "dug-out" shelter or stay where we were? Were we surrounded by time bombs or by duds? If we went to the bomb shelter, would we be any safer than here? We had no idea where the bombs had fallen, but the sound had indicated a salvo of them rather than an isolated one. We opted to stay in the comfort of our beds and postponed the search for the "gifts from Hitler" until daylight.

My mother's bungalow was situated close to the sea, part way up a steep hill in the village of Pett, six miles east of Hastings. We shared a three-acre garden with my uncle and aunt, Frank and Mab Earle, whose home was about fifty yards higher up the slope. We had an open and uninterrupted view from the sea in the east to the hills in the west. On each side of our garden sheep grazed in the fields. On the south side, a cart track ran beside a stream which drained the picturesque marshland in the valley below. The track connected us to the road leading to the bus stop and the beach. High up the slope at the north end of the property, our private lane entered the village road at the summit of Chick Hill, infamous for its 1 in 4 gradient. As youngsters, my cousins and I would wait at the bottom of the hill during the summer holidays, to watch unsuspecting drivers making a casual run up the gradient. We had to be ready to run out of the path of any unsuccessful car, reversing downhill out of control.

In those days, few cars could negotiate a very steep hill successfully.

My uncle had tunnelled a bomb shelter into the side of the hill in the garden next to his home, a retreat for all of us. From that vantage point, we had a magnificent view out to sea to the east and looking over the cliffs to the south. On particularly clear days, it was possible to see the far distant coastline of France across the wide expanse of the English Channel. We enjoyed a delightful rural picture of undulating hills and woodlands in the west, culminating in the distant and distinctive silhouette of Fairlight Church, with its square tower on the supposedly highest point in Sussex. From the viewpoint of our bomb shelter, we observed the Battle of Britain and all that was going on above us at the time, diving for the protection of the dugout when things happened too quickly or were too close for comfort.

The morning following our "gifts from Hitler", we rose at dawn; my uncle came to our door to see how we had fared. After the salvo of bombs had landed, he saw that our house was still standing, so guessed that we had decided to spend the night in our beds. He said, with a wry smile, "You probably did the wisest thing. We spent an uncomfortable night in the shelter and, on leaving the safety of it this morning; we saw a piece of newly upturned turf by the entrance. Judging by the angle of its entry, we spent the whole night sitting on top of an unexploded bomb!" He added," I think you and I had better go and look for the rest of them."

We both ventured out to do a survey of the garden. It was a difficult search as part of the land was under cultivation, the other area being covered with rough grass that was cut only twice a year. After searching for about ten minutes, we discovered two pieces of tell-tale turf, newly prised up from the soil. They were located no more than twenty or thirty feet from our bungalow. We continued our inspection from north to south, then criss-crossed the garden from east to west. We had every intention of discovering all the unwelcome missiles. It must have been nearly two hours before we were satisfied that we had a final count. There were eleven bombs buried in various places deep down in the garden. After a final hunt and marking the points of entry with bamboo sticks, we rang the Bomb Disposal Squad. My uncle and I thought that we had done a good job, and hoped secretly for a word of praise and immediate action from the Bomb Squad. We were a little taken aback when the voice on the other end of the 'phone answered, "They might be time bombs so we'll wait a week before doing anything." "What do we do in the meantime?" we asked. "You can just stay put, or go away if you feel nervous," came the calm reply. Terrific! So we had to live with the situation as close neighbours to a salvo of unexploded bombs - we had nowhere else to go!

There was an amusing daily incident that we saw take place at 8:25 each morning during the following week. At least four more bombs had fallen into the canal adjacent to the road leading to the bus turn-around. These missiles were discovered by deduction. Four separate splashes of mud and marshland debris had been found spread across the road next morning.

One particular man from the village was a regular traveller on the 8:30 a.m. bus to Hastings. We would watch him from our window each day as he walked towards the first muddy patch on the road. Approaching it, he would break into a fast trot, and then into a gallop, as he passed all four danger areas as quickly as possible. Gradually, then, he would resume normal walking speed with as much dignity and cool courage as he could muster. The bus was parked in full view at its terminal point at the T junction ahead of him. It was also a daily entertainment for the other commuters, who, already sitting in their seats, awaited the daily spectacle. He filled the village gossip column for quite a long time!

We, however, always walked past the same area with great courage as though nothing untoward had happened - there was nothing to lose - we were surrounded by unexploded bombs. Would it really make much difference if we hurried on our way home where, in our own garden, eleven of them awaited us? It was amazing how unconcerned one could become if there was nothing one could do about it. Such things are relative to the times.

When we got up on Saturday morning a week later, there had been no explosions. "Would the Bomb Disposal Squad live up to its promise?" we wondered. My uncle and I climbed the hill to our lane at the top of the garden and waited hopefully for the arrival of the Army. True to their word, a large truck made its way carefully along our laneway and parked in front of the garage at exactly 9 a.m. About eight or nine soldiers jumped to the ground, and soon we had shown them all the places that needed their attention. That was where our contribution ended. We were ordered to go to our respective houses and stay there until the Bomb Squad had completed its work.

Later in the morning, the first retrieved missile was brought to the surface - a healthy 100-lb. undetonated bomb. The squad hoped that the rest of them would prove to be in the same category. It would be a far safer and simpler job to blow them up in a nearby field than to defuse them on the spot.

From the kitchen window, my mother and I watched the first trophy being carried cautiously by two privates - one clutching the nose cone and the other man holding the end containing the remnants of the tail fins, as they walked with care down a long flight of steps behind our house to the patio area outside the kitchen door. They crossed the patio and continued down another equally long flight of steps to the garden gate. This opened into the sheep field. From then on, their progress was even more treacherous as they clambered down a particularly steep slope covered with a mass of ant hills, many of them over a foot high. Eventually, they laid the bomb down in the open field some way from us until the time for its detonation. The sergeant had promised that he would warn my mother and me before they began blowing things up. As I watched one of several more 100-pounders being carried past the kitchen window, a missile in the distant field went up with a tremendous explosion, vibrating throughout the house. Before the explosion, a thick cook book and a bowl of beef dripping, a small addition to our meagre fat ration, were on the kitchen table. During the blast, the bowl of dripping jumped in the air, and landed intact on top of the cook book. It was an amusing incident to an otherwise scary moment.

I then noticed the two soldiers outside putting down the bomb rather quickly beside the kitchen door. I wondered what had happened, when the private in charge of carrying the nose cone put his arms around the shoulders of his companion, hauled him into the kitchen, and sat him down on the nearest chair. "I thought we were going to be warned when you began to blow these things up," I said. "So did I!" said my friend in khaki with great emphasis. "What's wrong with your pal?" I asked. "I'm not sure," was the reply, "but I thought he was about to faint - so I made him put the thing down." His co-helper did not pass out, but his complexion was ashen and he sat there rigid, staring into space, comprehending nothing around him. We were not sure what to do.

Then the man on the chair stirred and said in a faraway voice, "Am I still alive? Am I still here?" "Why, of course you are - we are all still here," his buddy replied. Then, the seated man said with slightly more comprehension, "I thought it was *our* bomb that had just exploded. Nobody warned me that the detonating would begin yet." It took a few more minutes to convince him entirely that he was still in this world, during which time I made a cup of tea for all of us. About twenty minutes later, our shaken friend had recovered and the team of two left the house, picking up the unattended bomb which was lying by the doorstep. A tiny black and white bird, its tail bobbing wildly up and down, ran hurriedly past the soldiers as it sought the refuge of a nearby bush. The water wagtail had a natural fear of man but, of the large inanimate object on which it had been sitting, it was quite oblivious. In their muddy boots, the two privates picked their way carefully down the steps and out through the open gate into the field. Avoiding the ant hills, they continued down the slope to the level ground, and then disappeared beyond the hedge, taking their dangerous load to a safer place.

This pattern of bomb removal continued throughout the day. There were intermittent explosions, followed by tall columns of smoke rising into the air from the field in the valley. When all the unexploded bombs had been accounted for, my mother, uncle and aunt and I walked up the hill where the Bomb Disposal Truck was parked, to thank the departing crew and wish them well. As they were about to leave, we shouted, "Hey! Wait a moment. We've just found another one - it's broken through the hedge opposite the garage." The officer in charge inspected the gash in the hedge and the muddy hole beneath it, and looking at his watch, said, "Well, it's 5 o'clock. Time to go. It won't do you any harm there. The bomb is seventeen feet under the ground and, like all the others, it won't be fused." They all departed after a hard day's work and the bomb, so far as I know, is sitting there still.

For whatever reason those bombs were not fused - by ineptness on someone's part or by design on the part of a secret Allied sympathiser, I wish I could offer him or her personally a heartfelt thank you.

# THE VILLAGE OF PETT

A few years before the declaration of war on September 3, 1939, Pett, our small village, was a quiet and peaceful place. My family had left London from choice. One summer when I was a school girl, I found myself living in a bungalow six miles from the nearest town. We had exchanged all mod. con. (modern conveniences) for oil lamps and a four-burner Valor Perfection oil stove that baked some of the best cakes I have ever tasted. We even sported among other things the latest in lighting - an oil-cum-gas Aladdin lamp. This provided excellent illumination, but was a little temperamental at times. On occasion, it was "put out to grass" to burn off the flames it threw upwards, instead of concentrating its heat into the gas mantles the Instruction booklet alluded to so confidently. It was three years before electricity was available in the village.

We also boasted modern plumbing This, however, was dependent on the water tank in the loft, which was filled only by the efforts of all of us taking turns at hand pumping the precious liquid up the hill from our new well. After reaching its lofty heights for our household use, the water then deluged to its lowest depths without aid from anyone, as it flowed freely downhill through the pipes to the cesspool, carefully hidden in the centre of a mass of gorse bushes. These bushes, almost impregnable, because of their vicious thorns, were also the home of a huge rabbit warren. Here lived several generations of very hungry fluffy little animals. They had first-class taste; they became great connoisseurs of our vegetable garden as they nibbled the small succulent plants that we had sown earlier, to supplement the absence of a local greengrocer.

I took easily to the novelty of living in another age in such beautiful surroundings, rather than in a house that looked like all the others on the street. The local bus, on which I travelled daily to school in Hastings, was of a rather ancient vintage. It was the only bus in the area privately owned and belonged to a local man. It made four or five round trips to Hastings daily and had its designated stops on the way along. The driver, however, would pick up any-one anywhere, so there were many sudden halts as we rattled on our way.

The driver-cum-ticket collector would welcome pas-sengers clutching the largest and most awkward bundles, occasionally smelling of the farmyard, but thankfully he drew the line at anything to do with livestock. He even acquiesced to the wishes of one colourful character, who regularly acquired a thirst on the way home on the early evening run. As we halted outside the White Hart Inn, where we had an official five-minute wait in order to connect with the bus from Rye, our dehydrated passenger would dash out, cross the road to the pub opposite, quench his thirst, and come running back just in time for departure. On occasions when he took too long to drink his pint of bitter, a healthy blast from the horn would get him scurrying from the public bar. He would return hurriedly, brushing the back of his hand across his mouth to remove the excess froth that had accumulated in the rush to consume the last gulp of beer. With his foot barely on the bottom step of the bus, we would take off in haste to make up for the delay. Our imbiber always got a loud cheer from the passengers on these occasions. Such was the pace of life at Pett in those days.

The village at that time comprised a population of four hundred people, a 19th-century church, a good general store which housed the sub-post-office, plus a village hall - all nestled close together. As for the rest, the village was dotted with a straggling bunch of houses placed at intervals on either side of the lane which wound its way around the fields, leading first east then south towards the sea and down Chick Hill to the beach. The houses were built without much thought of symmetry, but with great care as to where the view could be most appreciated. Although our home was situated several minutes' walk from the road, we had the luxury of a visit from the butcher and the baker twice a week, plus a daily delivery of milk from a cheerful redheaded milkmaid who wore a riding jacket and britches at all times. She made the trip regularly down our grassy slope, carrying a small milk churn with a one-pint and a half-pint measure clanking against its side. We provided the jug and she filled it to our specifications. But the quiet farming existence, shared by many retired army and business people, suddenly found itself geographically in the front line of activity during the war.

Two years before war was declared, Hitler had invaded and occupied Austria, the Sudetenland and what remained of Czechoslovakia. When he set his target on Poland, he was warned by Britain that, unless he withdrew his forces from Poland's western frontier, *"a state of war would exist between Great Britain and Germany,"* as the then Prime Minister, Neville Chamberlain, put it. Unheeding, the Germans thrust forward into Poland and war was declared. After a heroic battle, Poland was forced to cease fire on September 27, 1939 - less than four weeks later. For the following eight months, very little happened, one exception being the many losses sustained by our naval and merchant ships. This period of waiting came to be known as the "Phoney War", though it was definitely an uneasy peace

One area of activity in the village provided a great challenge, entertainment, chit-chat and patience but, most of all, generosity of heart. Towards the end of September 1939, the British Government decided that, sooner or later, London would be the target of many air raids. People who had willing families or friends living in the country were advised to send their children to them to get away from the city to a safer place. But what was going to happen to the children whose families were less affluent, yet whose homes were in the most vulnerable areas of London? The solution to this problem was soon sorted out. The pupils of many city schools were evacuated and sent by bus, accompanied by their teachers to designated towns and villages in the country. We, at Pett, were informed that the children from a school not far from the docks in the East End of London would be arriving the following week. This meant that about one hundred children would need homes - quite a challenge for such a small village as ours.

We had one spare bedroom in our bungalow, so my mother and I decided that, between us, we would volunteer to take on two of the evacuees. A meeting was set up at which all the volunteers were given a general idea of the responsibilities they were about to undertake. "The children will all arrive with enough clothes to keep them going for a while and they will attend school five days a week, either in the village hall or in the village school house," they informed us. "The rest is up to you", they added, "to keep them, feed them and make them feel wanted". For this service, we would be granted a very small allowance - barely sufficient to cover the cost of the children's food with nothing left over for extras.

As we did not own a car, two little children were brought to our home by a couple of volunteers. Then, after introducing us to Alice and Ernie, the volunteers left hurriedly to take more children to their billets. We forgot to ask if they had brought a suitcase with them. Sitting Alice and Ernie down in the kitchen, we gave them some milk and biscuits. "How old are you, Alice?" my mother asked. "I'm seven and ee's six," she said, pointing to her brother. After they had consumed their snack, we showed them their room. Seeing that the children had no luggage with them, my mother said to Alice, "Have you got a suitcase with your other clothes in it, or was it left in the bus?" "Naaw!" she replied. My mother pressed on, "Perhaps your Mum packed them in a brown paper parcel and gave it to the Headmaster?" "Naaw!" said Alice again, "we wasn't given nuffink." The problem was - that we had nothing for the children either!

For the first night, they both slept in their underwear. It seemed quite normal to them. "How can we wash their clothes unless they have some sort of night attire?" we asked ourselves. It would be days before we could go to Hastings to buy any children's clothing, and we needed coupons to purchase them anyway. Instead, we made our first purchase at the local general store and bought the children a toothbrush, toothpaste and a face cloth of their own. On the second day, we looked through the linen cupboard to find what could be spared. A flannelette blanket came to light. It was white with a wide bright blue stripe at each end. "That'll do for Ernie's pyjamas," said my mother. She went to work skilfully and, by evening, Ernie was all dressed up at bedtime in what looked rather like a present-day jogging suit. He was very proud of the blue stripes on the trouser legs and the other splash of blue which was draped prominently across his chest on the pullover top. He said that it made him feel like a footballer. Alice had to wait till the following day, when we cut up one of my nightdresses and turned it into a smaller version of the same.

On their second day with us, we noticed that they each spent quite a lot of their time vigorously scratching their heads. "Is your head itchy?" I asked. "Yus!" came the reply from both of them. It was time, we thought, to take them to the bathroom and inspect those tousled heads more closely. I took charge of Alice, while my mother tackled Ernie who wriggled more than his sister. I was not sure what I was looking for, but I learned to identify the problem very quickly. Yes, there were plenty of lively little critters running back and forth, stirring up itchy feelings in the scalps of the poor little kids. Fortunately, my mother knew of a "Victorian cure". Next day, I took the bus to Hastings in search of "quasha chips", which I obtained from the chemist's shop (drugstore). On returning home, we boiled the chips in water and used the solution as a shampoo. After two or three applications, there was harmony once more in both the heads and the home. About a week later, we were given a minimal quantity of small underwear from the school's emergency supplies.

The children had been living with us for nearly a week. Their "little friends" had disappeared and the routine of our living together was beginning to fall into place. On their first Sunday with us, we decided to celebrate by inviting my uncle and aunt from next door, to join us for a midday dinner. We sat around the dining table in anticipation of sharing an excellent piece of roast beef, two green veg. and roast potatoes. What more could one ask for, with the addition of Yorkshire pudding that was just out of the oven? We adults began to eat with enthusiasm - it was delicious. But our little guests just sat and looked blankly at their plates. "Now, eat up dears while your dinner's nice and hot," my mother said. "Naaw!" Alice replied. "Do you want yours cut up into smaller pieces, Ernie, so it will be nice and easy to eat?" I asked. "Naaw!" was Ernie's reply. "It won't taste good when it's cold," my aunt added. "Don't you like it?" my mother asked. "Naaw!" said Alice. "Niver don't I!" chimed in Ernie. "Try and eat some of it," we pleaded, "or you'll be very hungry later on." "I don't wannit," said Alice pushing her plate away from her. "I don't wannit niver," echoed her little brother.

My mother decided that persuasion was getting her nowhere and, maybe, she might have more success by asking questions instead. "What do you have at home for Sunday dinner?" she asked kindly. For the first time, Alice showed some interest in the subject and in the audience sitting around the table. She drew herself up to her full height, for she was on home ground at last. She took a deep breath and, with great confidence, said in a loud voice, "*WE 'AVE BEER AN' DONUTS!*"

It took a great effort to hide the smiles on our faces, but my mother was the first to overcome the difficulty, and promised that we would all have donuts for tea next Sunday if they ate up their dinners now. However, on their first Sunday with us, they settled for bread and jam and milk instead. We began to understand the difficulties of the changing way of life these little children were going through.

For over two months, Alice and Ernie lived with us. We grew quite fond of them and I think they liked us too. Once a month, a bus came from London to bring the parents for a day's outing to be with their children. The trip was free by courtesy of the London County Council, but, alas, our two little kids were disappointed each time. Neither of their parents appeared, no reasons were given, and they did not receive any letters. It was sad having to make up excuses for their parents' neglect.

By November, the Government had a change of mind. It decided (wisely, as it turned out later) that Pett would also be an unsafe area very soon. So, with about a week's notice, the school children and their teachers were evacuated once again to somewhere in the west of England. The village returned to its normal quietness during the days of the "Phoney War". Regrettably, we never heard any more news of the little six-and seven-year olds who had begun to be part of our family.

During that first winter, the beach was still accessible. At low tide, we could walk out to the water's edge, picking our way between rocky pools and clumps of seaweed across stretches of rippled golden sand. It was part of the entertainment to collect mussels and winkles clinging to the rocks and stones as we went by. These were considered quite a delicacy by many people. At the high tide mark, the beach rose steeply away from the rocky pools and the sand became dark reddish-brown in colour. In rough weather and particularly during the January gales, this part of the beach was often strewn with all kinds of bric-a-brac.

The wind had been very strong and blustery during one of these January days. By nightfall, it had strengthened and soon reached gale force. Neither of us had much sleep that night as the full force of the gale pounded on the bungalow on the open hillside. The doors rattled and the driving rain slashed at the windows all night long. By morning, the storm had blown itself out.

After breakfast, my mother and I dressed up warmly and ventured down to the beach for some exercise and to look at the turbulent waves. On our arrival, we saw the high-tide mark scattered with large white boulder-like objects. Walking up to one of them with curiosity, we poked it with our fingers. It gave way to the touch, leaving our fingers covered with a sticky waxy substance. It was a huge lump of pure bees' wax. According to the law, no one was allowed to remove anything of value from the beach without the permission of the local Coastguard. He duly examined the washed-up cargo and decided that it was not good enough to salvage. The news spread quickly around the village and the local people came to claim their share of these heavy sticky lumps thrown up by the sea. Some pieces were acquired and taken home by car by their new owners. Most people took their salvaged wax home in wheelbarrows, on the backs of bicycles, or in sacks slung over their shoulders, and some hardy types just dragged their loads in bundles behind them. My mother and aunt each claimed a lump, but it was a family effort to drag them home. There, we scraped the sand and gravel from the outside. Then, we mixed the wax with paraffin to make furniture and floor polish, which lasted us for the rest of the war years.

A week later, an even more interesting cargo from a torpedoed ship washed up on to the shore. During our regular walk, we found dozens of tea chests lying on the beach after the tide had receded. These large strong wooden chests, lined with very heavy aluminium foil, had been thrown up on the shore in an almost undamaged condition. Once again, the people in the village soon heard of the new find. This was a particularly popular cargo as we were severely rationed for tea and, for a nation of tea drinkers, it would be especially valuable. Again, we had to wait for the Coastguard to give his O.K. before we were permitted to return to the beach with all the jars and containers we could carry to fill up with this valuable find. By discarding the first couple of inches of tea from around the outer edge of a chest, we found that the bulk of the tea had not been affected by sea water. Some chests had not been broken at all. The tea we drank for a long time afterwards was not quite as good as the ration we paid for, but it was a real windfall in a time of shortage.

Early in 1940, Pett became a bustling little community as the population grew with the arrival of the Army. A large number of engineers were sent to install defences and booby traps against a more than probable invasion of our shores. Thousands of Romney Marsh sheep, whose breed was named after the pastures on which they fed, were evacuated. Gaps were blown in the sea dykes, which had been constructed just above the high-water mark. These ran for many miles in an easterly direction along the coast line. The dykes protected the below sea-level grazing lands which were spread out for miles behind them. Within days, the fields were completely flooded a mile or more back to the cliff line of a much earlier age. The beaches above the high-tide mark were mined and covered with myriads of coils of barbed wire. Where there were obvious gaps open to the sea, the Army installed ugly concrete tank traps. From then on, we were denied the use of the beach, and visitors were forbidden to travel within ten miles of the coast.

After an eerie peace, events began to happen. Hitler's army invaded and occupied Norway and Denmark in April 1940. The following month on May 10, the Germans burst through the frontiers of Belgium and Holland, neither of which had any choice but to capitulate to the invading forces a few days later. The enemy continued to sweep across France at an alarming speed. On May 19, almost all British operational aircraft which had been stationed on French soil, were recalled to England to continue the fight from our own airfields, and, by May 30, the evacuation of Dunkirk had begun.

# THE SUMMER AND AUTUMN OF 1940

During that time, we civilians never missed the BBC news every evening, but each day's news was worse than the day before. On the night of May 24, we could see clearly the searchlights at Boulogne on the other side of the Channel, as they played and criscrossed in the sky, in their attempt to light up the German bomber force overhead. For two nights, we watched the play of searchlight beams, as they pierced the darkness above the raging fires that burned beneath them. When we went to bed, it was only with difficulty that we slept, owing to the crumps and vibrations that filtered across the sea bed and through the pillow to our ears, as the bombs exploded and the guns fired in the French port. On the third night, all was dark and quiet; Boulogne had fallen to the enemy.

Within the next few days, our own Armed Forces, which had fought alongside the French, had been cornered and surrounded in the area of Dunkirk with their backs to the sea. Their only hope of escape was by Allied shipping capable of picking them up from the open beaches. During the time of waiting, the troops were continually dive-bombed and machine-gunned as hundreds of thousands of men huddled together helplessly on the open beaches, hoping for a safe passage across the English Channel back to England.

In the meantime, as we listened to the BBC news, an unexpected request was broadcast over the radio. It was an appeal to captains of small ships, motor boats, fishing boats, pleasure craft, in fact to owners of any vessel that was capable of sailing under its own power. These men were asked to report to the appropriate local authorities immediately.

Next day, my uncle and I were scanning for convoys on the horizon through his telescope, which, on its tripod, resided permanently, protected by the roofed verandah of his house, but we were looking in the wrong place. There was little need for the telescope; from our hilltop view we saw, not far from the shore, a very large Armada of very small ships passing by in an easterly direction on its way towards Dover. On a calm sea, this panorama of little boats of all shapes, sizes, and descriptions proceeded in an orderly fashion, each spaced one from another, appropriately distanced and staggered about eight to ten abreast in a continuous stream. On the seaward side, small Naval vessels were going back and forth at a greater speed, presumably to monitor and protect the fleet of tiny craft. The bow of each little ship was set stoically towards the east as the flotilla sailed throughout the day.

During the next morning, little boats, presumably from more distant harbours and resorts, made their way in smaller numbers. They followed in the same direction as they were probably headed for Dover, one of the rallying point for small ships. On the third day, the expanse of sea was once again blue and sparkling, but deserted. The small craft, having arrived at their destination, were refuelled and their captains were briefed. The fine weather continued to hold and the sea remained calm, something extremely rare in the English Channel. On May 30th, the evacuation of Dunkirk began. The small ships made the forty mile trip across the open sea to Dunkirk. They were among the first vessels to pick up the members of the stranded British Expeditionary Force, and any other Allied men in uniform who wished to escape captivity. The crews of these little boats braved the dive-bombing, shelling and machine-gunning, as they hovered a few feet from the crowded beaches, while waiting for the men to wade out to their boats. From there, the overladen vessels would transfer the men to the larger ships waiting for them in deeper waters. The little boats then returned to the beaches to pick up more passengers, and, if necessary, taking them all the way back to Dover when the large transports were already overcrowded.

Over a period of four days, under constant air attacks from the enemy and with minimal protection from our few overworked fighters, these little ships returned again and again to the Dunkirk inferno, until all survivors on the beaches had been picked up and taken to the safety of the land that was soon to be known as the "Island Fortress". Between May 30th and June 4th, over 335,000 men were rescued, but nearly all their equipment had to be abandoned. Our fighter aircraft, already grossly outnumbered by the Luftwaffe, were pathetically low in numbers. The spirit of the British people, however, was that of thankfulness and cheerfulness, despite our being the only country in Europe (apart from a few neutrals) that was still free from Nazi occupation.

Our spirits were high but, we civilians had little or no knowledge concerning the strategies of warfare. Many of us thought that the invasion was imminent, and, as we lived beside a probable landing beach, we began to wonder what we could do to help, or if not help, at least not hinder our own troops. My mother and I came up with one practical idea only. We would put all our cans and bottled foods in waterproof bags, and bury them in the "manure hole" deep under the rotting leaves and grass cuttings in the vegetable garden. In this way, if we were forced to house the enemy, we would not have to feed them! In retrospect, I realize that it is doubtful if we, or our house, would have survived had we been invaded, but, at the time, ignorance was bliss, and our uninformed minds helped us through an otherwise frightening situation.

On June 10th, Italy invaded Southern France through the Alps and, on June 22nd, France accepted an armistice and hostilities ceased there three days later. The Nazis occupied France and, after negotiations, Vichy France in the south was allowed a puppet government.

The British civilians, though jubilant from the "success" of Dunkirk, were confused and did not know what to think or what they should do next. We needed a leader to guide and put the facts of the situation before us. The next day, the Prime Minister, Winston Churchill, who had recently formed a new coalition War Cabinet, spoke to the nation on the radio through the House of Commons, using his resolute and powerful rhetoric. It was, I think, his greatest morale-raising speech of the war. He concluded by saying the now famous words:

> "...*We shall fight on the beaches, we shall fight on the landing grounds, we shall fight in the fields and in the streets, we shall fight in the hills; we shall never surrender, and even if, which I do not for a moment believe, this island or a large part of it were subjugated and starving, then our Empire beyond the seas, armed and guarded by the British Fleet, would carry on the struggle, until, in God's good time, the new world, with all its power and might steps forth to the rescue and the liberation of the old.*"

From the most influential to the least important, Britons no longer needed to be told how to think or act; we knew exactly what was expected of us. We all needed to pitch in and do our best, however great or humble our part - there was no room or time for despair. Those inspiring words renewed our determination despite the almost impossible odds piled up against us.

Until the middle of August, life was reasonably peaceful at Pett. There was, however, one "fly in the ointment" with which everyone seemed to cope rather well. A German JU-88 light bomber flew over our area with such regularity that the people of the village were able to plan their day around the intruder's routine. Several mornings a week, the air-craft made landfall at low altitude about 11 a.m. It would fly inland along our valley, machine-gunning the local bus, cars or anything or anyone that moved, and then disappear over the hill near Fairlight Church, drop its bombs on Hastings, and retreat out to sea again. The time never varied and the Junkers could have been an easy prey, but our own fighters were too busy elsewhere to be spared for a lone raider. We learnt to stay indoors from about 10.45 a.m. until either the Junkers had passed by, or we were certain that it would not appear that morning. For the rest of the day, we felt quite safe.

Another incident seemed amusing to us at the time. The Army, encamped in the village, used to play football regularly in a large field opposite our home on the other side of the valley. The game, which they played in the morning, was usually in progress when the Junkers flew in. At the first sound of aircraft engines, the players would run for the protection of the thick hedge surrounding the meadow and hide beneath the bushes. The pilot of the enemy aircraft, seeing no activity there, would continue on his way in search of other prey. When the raider was safely out of range, the players emerged from their scattered hiding places to finish the game.

This way of life continued until the middle of August. So far, we had been spared an invasion. The sea proved to be a good ally. Then the enemy made its first massed air attack over the north-east of England and consequently suffered many losses - the Battle of Britain had begun. These raids were followed quickly by the bombing of RDF (radar) stations and airfields across the country. The next day the Luftwaffe concentrated on airfields alone in an attempt to cripple the RAF, the strategy being the preliminary to an invasion by sea. We had still not grasped the seriousness of the situation. On

August 16th, more than 1,700 German bombers and fighters penetrated our air defences. One day during this period, we saw large concentrations of JU-52's (troop-carrying aircraft), passing just east of our village above the Romney Marshes on their way to London. We had to wait until we listened to the BBC news that evening to learn that the invasion had not started. The aircraft had been carrying bombs, not troops. I think we all slept better than usual that night.

After a lull due to a few days of poor weather, Pett suddenly found itself in the centre of the battle zone again as formations of German aircraft passed overhead, only to be split up by our Hurricanes and Spitfires. Enemy squadrons flew in droves above us, and dog-fights became regular occurrences overhead as our fighters, warned by radar, met them at the coast. During the beginning of this prolonged battle from August 24th. to September 6th, over a thousand German aircraft penetrated our island daily. Our fighters, vastly inferior in numbers, were usually in the air twice in a day, the pilots landing to refuel, only to take off again to continue the fight.

Early in September, the East End of London was set ablaze. The climax of the Battle of Britain came on September 15th. The attacks trailed off to some degree by the end of the month. During these days, we spent much of our time staying close to our air raid shelter watching the dog-fights above us, often diving into the dugout with great speed. On one such occasion, when the battles overhead seemed to have dwindled to almost nothing, we were chatting over the fence to our good friends and neighbours, the Watsons and their two teen-aged sons. We were relating to each other the events we had seen during the afternoon, when suddenly we were deafened by a tremendous roar. We looked upwards towards the laneway near the brow of the hill and, in a split second, we had all thrown ourselves flat on the ground, as a Messerschmitt 110 skimmed just above the garage roof, just missing the 50 ft TV aerial on the garage roof, pointing down towards the valley and the sea beyond. The noise of machine-guns filled the air. I covered my neck with my hands, and then glanced quickly from one side to the other as a shadow passed over me. There, on either side, I saw an aircraft wing with a big black cross near its tip. It could not have been more than fifty feet above me. As I was about to rise from the grass and dust, another aircraft followed at almost as low an altitude. This time it was a Spitfire chasing the Messerschmitt, the pilot pumping lead into the foe as he followed him. After the Spitfire had passed over us, one head came up after another as each of us ventured to rise above ground level. We wanted to witness the end of the chase.

Mrs. Watson, who had thrown herself flat on the garden path under some small trees, slowly staggered to her feet. There she stood defiantly, her hair smothered in twigs and leaves, her knees showing a tinge of pink, protruding through two huge holes in her stockings - a dishevelled, indignant but smiling survivor.

The Spitfire continued to follow the Me-110, forcing it lower and lower until it plunged into the sea in a column of water and spray. The Spit. circled, and then flew back towards our valley. As it passed over us, its wings swayed gently from side to side in a "Victory Roll". We all waved our arms enthusiastically. My uncle shook his white handkerchief with a flourish, as the Spitfire headed inland towards its home base, probably for the second time that day. This pilot could still look forward to another tomorrow.

That day had been a rough one. Earlier, we had watched the air battles from a distance, where we had a panoramic view from the road at the top of Chick Hill. Much of the fighting had taken place above Winchelsea and Rye, about five to ten miles away. These two ancient and historical towns, two of the five Cinque Ports, were built on isolated hills, which rose above the expanse of the flat meadow and marshlands around them.

During one period of that day, the waves of enemy bombers were so numerous that our fighters, trying to break up their close formations, were engaged mostly in single dog fights with the enemy fighters attempting to protect the bombers. Within less than fifteen minutes, we witnessed seven fighters being shot down - too far away to identify whether they were friend or foe. Each aircraft plummeted towards the earth, followed by a ribbon of black smoke trailing behind it, before it exploded in a ball of flame on contact with the ground. Above, several white parachutes showed up clearly against the blue sky as they floated down slowly and gracefully, each supporting a small black figure below it. They drifted down quietly above the on-going dog-fights and cross-fire. We hoped that they would live, either to fight again on the morrow, or to spend the rest of the war as prisoners.

Looking back on these events makes me wonder how we could have cheered at the downing of a pilot and his aircraft as it fell into the sea. Yet, when one sums up the alternative, it seemed a natural reaction. Had the Messerschmitt not been destroyed, it would have continued on its way to London, protecting the enemy, dropping bombs on the city. So many more people would have died and others would have been injured or rendered homeless. When we were fighting against tremendous odds to preserve our freedom, there was no alternative. As it was, on that day London received a heavy concentration of bombs, and the RAF fighting force was nearing the end of its ability to fight back.

It was at that critical time when our air defences were almost exhausted that the Nazis suddenly changed their tactics. Night bombing began and our days became relatively quiet. But we at Pett paid for it by seldom enjoying an uninterrupted night's sleep. From July 10th. to the end of September, the German Luftwaffe lost 1,400 aircraft over Britain. By October 12th, the German invasion plans were shelved but that was something we did not know for many years afterwards. In the middle of October, my mother and I were pressured by the local police to vacate our home due to the possibility of invasion. We left for St. Albans to stay on a temporary basis with a friend of my mother's. Six weeks later, when the invasion had not materialized, we returned to Pett to take our chance with all the rest of the coastal residents, and to continue our lives where we had left off.

I had enjoyed a year as a full-time student at the Hastings School of Art & Architecture, but now I took my work there only one day a week for criticism. The other four days were filled creatively at home - at least that was the theory. The School had been condemned as an unsafe building in the event of an air raid, so the number of students was kept to a minimum at any one time. It was just another typical day when I took the bus to Hastings and made my way to the school with my portfolio under my arm. I walked past the doors of the Public Library on the main floor, and went up the wide stone stairs to the School of Art situated above it. As I climbed up the steps, I guessed that the staircase would probably be the only part of the structure to survive in the event of a hit, or a near-hit, by an enemy raider. It was an old building and contained a kiln for firing ceramics and several heavy printing presses on the upper floors. As usual, there would be very few people at the school today, for we represented one-fifth of the registered students, each attending, as we did, only once a week. Some of the boys from the architectural and art departments had already joined the armed services, so our numbers grew smaller. In general, it promised to be a rather dull and uninspiring day.

After the first class of the morning, with my creativity flagging, I joined two friends and we left to visit our favorite coffee shop. Our spirits revived immediately as we stepped out from the badly lit classroom into the sunlight, and breathed the fresh sea air - for the intersection on our right was only two minutes walk from the sea front. As we began strolling along the short road ahead, the tall buildings on either side restricted our vision to a narrow strip of sky above, until we reached the wide main shopping street of the town. We chatted with each other cheerfully, catching up on the week's news. Suddenly, something diverted our attention. We glanced up and saw the silhouette of a Ju-88 dive-bomber coming straight at us. It was only a short distance away and just above the rooftops. A moment later, everything was being sprayed with cannon shells; the noise deafening in the confined space of our narrow street. Having just passed the local baker's shop, the only shop on the street, we turned back hastily towards it and, one after the other, dashed through the door, and did not stop running until we had reached the far wall of the bakery. The girl behind the counter looked surprised at our sudden entry, for it had taken her a few seconds longer to realize what was happening outside. She was then, I think, quite glad to have our company. We waited until the shooting had stopped, and the sound of the aircraft engines had faded away. It was only then that the air raid siren began to wail. After the warning undulations had stopped and all was quiet, we thanked the shop assistant for temporary refuge. Then, cautiously, we went to the door, peered through the window and ventured outside once more. A moment later, we heard the noise of the returning raider. It had flown out to sea and back again, and was once more completing a circuit as it lined up for a repeat performance. We all turned round and ran like hares back to the bake shop, and burst through the door just as the shells began to ricochet off the walls of the buildings on either side of us. Breathlessly, we apologized profusely for our second uninvited entry, but we need not have bothered. The noise outside drowned out our voices, and she could not hear a word until the bomber had flown past us, up the main street and was on its way out to sea again.

This time, we waited longer until we were fairly sure that the Junkers would not return. All at once, we burst into a four-way discussion, in which we made some personal comments about the German Luftwaffe and what we thought of it! It was now, when all was quiet again, that my friends and I felt very embarrassed at having, more or less, taken over the bake shop. We each bought a cake that we did not particularly want and thanked the girl again for her hospitality. As we came out again into the street, we threw our caution to the winds as we noticed small pieces of knarled metal scattered on the ground around us. We ran all over the place, picking up souvenirs, scooping the still-warm silvery shrapnel into our hands. It was time for the next class, so, minus our coffee and with a cake in one hand and a fistful of shrapnel in the other, we turned in the direction of the Art School.

Over fifty years later, I showed the early part of this manuscript to Tony, one of the sons of the Watson family who lived next door, but higher up the hill. I asked if he had any comments or additions to make - he made just two. Referring to the German raider that used to fly regularly at low level up our valley, he said, "*From our garden, we could look down on the Ger-*

*man aircraft - we could even see the pilot in the cockpit."*
The other observation, I quote from his letter of
April 16, 1996, *"I do remember I was at Pett at the time of
the Dunkirk evacuation and remember that the miracle was in
the calm sea. It was rarely like a mill pond and then only for
a short while, but for three days there was scarcely a ripple so
that even a rowing boat could cross to France and back.
Those who knew the Channel could not believe it could be so
calm for so long and thought it must be the hand of God."*

By now, I had become increasingly disenamoured
with being a sitting duck, feeling useless and helpless
beneath the unpredictable activity from the skies
and of the threat from invasion. I wanted to be able
to do something useful and decided to "join up".

# JOINING UP

During World War I, my father designed aeroplane wings for the Handley Page Aircraft Company. My uncle, who lived next door to us, had been an Observer in the Royal Flying Corps, the predecessor of the RAF, in the First World War and now continued the tradition as an aircraft spotter in the Royal Observer Corps. I had no difficulty in choosing the Service I wished to join - it had to be the RAF.

In early November, a few weeks after the episode of the twelve unexploded bombs that landed in our garden, I volunteered to join the Women's Auxiliary Air Force (WAAF). Christmas and New Year came and went, and I received no acknowledgement of my application. January and February passed and the early garden flowers began to bloom, reminding us of Spring. I wondered if my application had been thrown into someone's waste paper basket or had been lost in transit. Maybe there was no need for more women in the RAF just now, or was it just a matter of the Civil Service taking its time? It could be that the Air Ministry was snowed under with applicants.

I thought about re-applying if nothing happened within the next month, but the problem was solved for me. Early in March 1941, four months after I had volunteered for the WAAF, I received a short, curt note from the Air Ministry. I was ordered to report to the Brighton Recruiting Centre three days later. My luggage allowance was to be no more than an overnight bag as all my needs would be supplied on arrival – where, they did not indicate.

For the next two days, I worked at turning my untidy room from a makeshift studio into a recognizable bedroom again. After saying my Goodbyes and packing the few personal belongings I was allowed, I boarded the Hastings train for Brighton. This was my first step towards becoming an A.C.W.2 (Aircraftwoman - 2nd. Class) in the RAF. Brighton is a coastal town about thirty miles west of Hastings and, in peacetime, a popular seaside resort. When I reached the Recruiting Office, situated far from the seafront and in one of the more dreary areas of town, nothing could have looked less welcoming than that cold, sparsely furnished office at 9 a.m. on a damp and chilly morning in March.

Within about fifteen minutes of my arrival, fourteen girls between the ages of about eighteen to the late twenties had turned up. Our names were checked, after which our ration books were taken from us. This really brought home the point that the RAF would provide for all our needs - it would have to now. The senior recruit was given a brown envelope containing our identity documents, plus railway warrants, for all the party. We were told to catch the next train to Victoria Station in London, then to proceed to Adastral House, Kingsway - the administrative headquarters of the RAF - where we would receive further instructions. The woman in charge of the Brighton office wished us Good Luck and off we trooped, an odd-looking collection, to the railway station.

Fortunately, we got on well together, though I doubt if even two of us had any shared interests but, being in a group, we gained a little of the confidence we needed as we began our journey in a mood of apprehension and suppressed excitement. Commuters on the train stared at us with interest, wondering what this mixed bunch of girls had in common.

We arrived at Adastral House about lunch time and, after a cursory medical examination performed by a bored doctor going through his daily routine; we received our first personal indignity. After we had been directed to another room, a nurse took us in one at a time and proceeded to pull our hair apart, peering closely into our scalps for any sign of wildlife. I felt hurt and upset by the procedure, but I tried to rationalize the operation. After all, I was only being treated in accordance with my rank, the lowliest in the RAF - A.C.W. 2 - and even this rank I had not, so far, been awarded.

Then, in no uncertain terms, the wisdom of the degrading procedure became apparent to all of us. One member of our party was harbouring biological specimens in her beautiful dark curly hair. She was detained, while the rest of us were ordered to hurry if we were to catch the next train for Gloucester. Our promise of a lunchtime meal faded into oblivion, as I was handed all the medical reports and railway warrants, and told to "Get 'em there safely". This was my first and last act of responsibility for the next nine weeks. We quickly learned to do as we were told without asking questions, however pointless the orders appeared to be.

We travelled on a slow train which stopped at every station and halt on the way along. Being famished, most of the girls decided to make the most of their last hour or two of freedom by going back to the Pullman car, three coaches behind us, for tea and biscuits. I offered to stay and keep an eye on all the small pieces of luggage, which were stacked in the racks above our heads in the two compartments we occupied. I also wanted to keep a lookout for our stop, which was just before the terminal at Gloucester. I had been put in charge so, as far as the girls were concerned, they had been relieved of all responsibility. The words "Get 'em there safely" rang in my ears. I did not want to blot my copy-book on the first day.

During the war, maps were seldom displayed anywhere and, by their absence on the train, it was difficult to know how long the journey would take. I was unfamiliar with the route, and my instructions had omitted any reference to the time of arrival. I knew only that the train was running late. Then, without warning, a guard came pushing his way through the crowd standing in the corridor, shouting that we were about to arrive at Innsworth. I was quite unprepared and, jumping up, I too had to push my way through crowded corridors to the Pullman coach behind us to collect my brood. When I reached the Pullman carriage, they looked up from their tables in dismay, for they were going to have to forgo their tea, the last little luxury they would enjoy for a long time. All I could blurt out was, "Drink up quickly and bring your food with you! We have to get out in a few minutes." They gave me the impression that it was my entire fault.

On arrival at the station, a few passengers alighted from the carriages along the platform, but to get fourteen people out of one door quickly was not an easy task. We took turns keeping one foot on the platform and the other firmly on the step of the train until all had got out. Only then did the guard blow his whistle for the train to depart. I guessed we had added a few more minutes to its already late arrival at Gloucester.

It was about 9.30 at night and very dark when we finally arrived. The station glimmered in a cold ghostly light with its shaded and low-powered electric bulbs, all that were allowed by the blackout regulations. An RAF sergeant and his driver walked up to us - they had waited a long time for us to turn up - and both looked chilled and unhappy. Once again, I expected to be told that it was my entire fault, but, instead, the sergeant smiled and accepted me as an equal, I suspect because I was still wearing civilian clothes. He and the driver helped to lift each of us up and push us, in turn, into the back of the large camouflaged truck parked in the station yard, quite a difficult feat in our tight "civvy" skirts. There, tired and hungry, we sat huddled either side of the canvas-covered vehicle on hard narrow benches as we sped away to the training camp.

The truck stopped at the gates of the newly constructed barracks and, through the canvas walls of the vehicle, we heard a few muffled words pass between the driver and the sentry at the gates. We were then spirited away along a road between recently built huts with muddy paths separating them. The view from the open rear of the truck was not very encouraging and it was starting to rain. Arriving at some central buildings, we alighted in front of the cook house and the WAAF mess. Once we were inside, a rather disgruntled-looking WAAF corporal told us to sit down at a trestle table, and gave each of us a plate of overcooked sausages and a large dollop of mashed potato. Even that looked good to us, for we were all very hungry. I stuck my fork into a sausage too enthusiastically. It reacted by jumping off the plate on to the table. I retrieved it and pushed the fork in more forcibly the second time, only to see the sausage jump higher and finish up on the floor. I left it there! The others sitting either side of the table were having the same problem. Undeniably, our "bangers" were cooked to a crisp. There was nothing more than savoury smelling charcoal on our plates to stave off our appetites. This is where (collectively) we made our first bloomer. "Please, Corporal," we said, "can we have some more sausages? We can't eat these!" "What do you expect?" she retorted vehemently, "I've kept them hot for you since six o'clock." We went to bed hungry.

In the meantime, having finished our mashed potato supper, we were marched to the sick bay to have our heads examined for the second time in one day. I wondered if the nurse knew about our first medical. Thinking that I would save both her time and ours, I enlightened her politely that we had already been through this process. I was rather naive at that stage of my career; I had a lot to learn. The nurse said pleasantly, "We always supply this service for new arrivals. One never knows!" Just to prove her point, she discovered, a moment later, that one of our group was in that embarrassing situation. Since she had sat on the Brighton train next to the girl with head lice, some of them had found their way to the more desirably clean head of hair so close to them. The girl concerned was detained at the sick-bay. We, on the other hand, were told that our hair would have to be cut to no longer than one inch above the collar once we were in uniform.

We were escorted to a newly completed sleeping hut. The WAAF corporal told us with pride that we would be the first occupants. The room was cold, damp, and had bare floors, and it was midnight. Along each side of the hut were fourteen beds, their metal bases dull with dampness. Did we have to sleep on bare springs? I had not expected things to be that bad. But the procedure was quickly explained to us by the corporal who occupied a small private room near the entrance door. We had to make our own beds every night from the odd collection of bedclothes stacked at the head of the bed. Each bed was supplied with three "biscuits", mattress-like squares which, when put beside each other, formed the mattress. There were also a pillow, two brown blankets and, joy of joys, a pair of white sheets as well! Each morning, before breakfast, we were expected to fold and stack the bedding at the head of the bed again.

After telling us to put our possessions on the bed of our choice, the corporal took us to the far end of the hut and through the door to inspect the ablutions. A dismal picture awaited us as we inspected the quality of the washing facilities. A long galvanized metal sluice ran along one side of the hut, with cold water taps protruding over it at intervals. With the aid of a stack of metal wash basins to choose from which were piled at the other end, we were expected to begin the day clean and whole-some, despite the lack of hot water in freezing tem-peratures - a bone-chilling exercise. The floor be-neath our feet, ignored by the carpenters, was a mass of muddy earth, made usable only by a series of duck boards placed over it. I doubt if any of us washed behind our ears or aspired to the excessive use of soap for the next three weeks. In low spirits, we returned to the hut, made our beds and crawled under the damp blankets, shivering. Was it really the same day that I had left Hastings? It seemed that I had left the comforts of home weeks ago.

The following morning, Service life began in ear-nest at the Equipment Section. There we were is-sued with uniforms and ugly, but warm, underwear that went with them. The strong black leather lace-up shoes were our most difficult problem, for they were the cause of many blisters during the first week.

On the second night, the girl who occupied a bed next to me broke camp. She had a great night with the boys, having left and returned unchallenged by going through a gap in the fence. She was too drunk to get into bed and so spent what was left of the night under it. Early the next morning while she was still sleeping it off, another girl from our party announced that she'd "had" the Air Force and was running away! We had already been informed that, as volunteers, we were allowed to change our minds about staying on but, after three days, it would be considered desertion, and this was the third day. She did not trust the authorities to discharge her legally, so she decided to make a quick getaway at dawn. I often wonder what happened to her!

The following twenty-one days were filled with drill on the parade ground, instructed by a sergeant who barked at us constantly. When not on the parade ground, we were sent on route marches, which grew longer and longer as the sticking plaster on our feet grew thicker and thicker. Before our first week's pay was due, we learned how to stand in line, step briskly in front of the accounts clerk, salute according to the book, shout our number - 442513 in my case - then pretend to take our weekly pittance from his hand. We usually finished doubled up with laughter. The sergeant tolerated this only on the first day. At the end of the week when I received my first ten-shilling note, I tried to keep my giggles well under control; otherwise I would have been kept waiting until the end of the pay parade to do my circus act all over again.

After the three-week initiation period, our group was split up and we were dispersed all over the country. I joined a party of about eighteen girls, all of whom had been chosen for "special duties," whatever they were. We set off in a hopeful mood, knowing that our future life could not be much more strenuous or painful than square-bashing and limping on blistered feet. I looked back on the past three weeks as an interesting experience, having shared and learned something about the lives of people whom I would otherwise never have met or known. They were a good hearted group.

We travelled to Leighton Buzzard, about thirty or forty miles north of London. By now, we appeared to be a somewhat more cohesive group, as we all wore the same Air Force blue uniform. Dusk had fallen when we alighted from the train where the inevitable lorry - as trucks were called in England - was waiting for us. As we drove through a rather uninteresting part of town, we approached our goal, a most depressing-looking building constructed of very grubby brick. Its original colour was obliterated by years of dust and dirt, and its only architectural features were two rows of small windows one above the other. These were covered with sticky tape to prevent the glass from flying during an air raid. An unprepossessing archway in the centre invited us rather grudgingly into the equally ugly quadrangle. Our sleeping quarters were on the upper floor, with an open corridor (or balcony) connecting the rooms. These were dark and the paint on the walls was brown with age. There was a small bare gas jet projecting from the wall in each room for illumination, enough to see by, but not nearly good enough for studying if we had to read at night. We were told, "Oh, yes! This place used to be a workhouse, and most of the gas power is now used to supply the factory down the road." We had six weeks to survive in this dismal industrial district!

Next morning, the same lorry driver took us a short distance, and then halted at the entrance gate to a heavily camouflaged area. Two armed guards then let the vehicle through and we dismounted outside an even more heavily camouflaged one-storey building. A couple of MPs escorted us inside and we found ourselves in another world. It was a very large room with a huge table in the centre covered with a grid map of the southern half of England. The room was a perfect replica of a Fighter Operations Room.

For several weeks, without a day off, as far as I can remember, despite the fact that the Easter week intervened, we pushed arrows around on the map as we plotted fictitious raids and air battles, until we reacted automatically to the instructions received through our earphones from the R.D.F. (Radar) lines and Observer Corps.

# R.A.F. SPEKE - LIVERPOOL

At last, the day arrived when we were considered to be qualified aircraft plotters, and we were due to be posted to a real operational station. There was some anticipation and much wild guessing. We were divided into four groups and dispersed to different parts of the country, I and four others being sent to the Fighter Command airfield at Speke, near the Garston docks at Liverpool. It was early May. After two or three quiet days and nights at Liverpool, I thought of my mother and how much she was suffering from disturbed sleep on the South Coast. Enemy aircraft were crossing overhead most nights on their way to bomb London. Though close to the sea in the north-west of England and far from the coast of France, the nights in Liverpool were quiet, and I felt relaxed in an apparently peaceful city.

Discovering a guest house not far from my billet, I booked a room immediately and wrote at once to my mother inviting her to come to Liverpool for a week's rest. My letter contained the necessary information, such as the departure and arrival times of the overnight train from London. I said that I would be at Liverpool's Lime Street Station to meet her when she arrived in the morning. The address of the guest house seemed unnecessary at the time, so unwisely I omitted to include it.

I had worked in the Operations Room for a few days where we practised plotting aircraft on the operations table on the day shifts, and were trusted with some minor enemy activity that occasionally showed up on the map at night. Very few plots of enemy aircraft, "bandits" they were called, ever appeared on our map of northern England.

The evening before my mother's arrival, I was on the night duty shift 8 p.m. - 8am. Sometime after midnight, I was plotting local activity on the map table, when a single bandit plot appeared on the southern part of our map; but that was not unusual. A few minutes later two more appeared on the east side of the map, followed by a group of about twelve. So they began to grow in numbers: 20-plus, 30-plus, even 40-plus formations of bandits. In a very short time, we could see that there was going to be a heavy raid somewhere - but where? A lot of calculating and guessing went on by the Duty officers. Coventry? No! Maybe Manchester? Could it be Liverpool? The number of bandits grew until there were 200-plus showing on our grid-map all at the same time. By then, it was obvious, even to us newcomers, that Liverpool was the target. As the enemy formations drew dangerously close, we "rookies" were relieved of our work as plotters and the more experienced girls took over. One of the officers looked at me and said, "Go and make tea for everybody; we're in for a long night".

There were about thirty personnel on duty, and I knew nothing about the whereabouts of the tea supplies. I explored and found the mugs, tea, sugar and evaporated milk in a cupboard, but where was the water tap? Three rooms further down the corridor I found a water tap over a sink, a gas ring and a kettle. That apparently was our "kitchen", all rather inadequate, but at least the brown teapot was huge.

The kettle seemed to take hours to heat and, after bringing it to the boil three times, I succeeded in filling the teapot to the brim. By this time, I could hear the crumps of exploding bombs in the distance. I staggered with the teapot to our rest room, where I had the mugs lined up on a tray. A few explosions sounded dangerously close now, as the frail wooden walls of the hut vibrated from each impact. Rumour had it that the Ops. Room and adjoining huts were constructed from packing cases, in which the partly assembled Lockheed Hudson aircraft arrived at Liverpool from Canada; the construction certainly felt flimsy enough for it to be true.

As I put the pot of steaming tea on the table, there was a sharp knocking at the window. Hurriedly I turned off the light, electricity this time, and parted the blackout curtains. One of the M.P.'s (Military Police) put his head in the half-open window and said, "Your chimney's on fire! Put it out! Quick!"

What was I to do? The water tap was along the corridor three rooms away. I could not see any fire extinguishers, and the raid was beginning to reach its peak. I took the teapot, removed the lid and emptied the complete contents into our roaring pot-bellied stove. It hissed and bubbled back at me, spewing smoke, steam and ash all over me and, within a minute or so, I was looking at a pathetically damp heap of ashes. "Aye, you've done it luv, that's grand," said the Lancashire M.P. "The fire's out; and, by the way, can you lend me a tin hat, I left mine at home?" I handed over my latest model tin chapeau through the window and wished him luck - he needed it!

Having just performed my second personally responsible act in nine weeks, I now had to go to the Ops. Room and explain to the overworked team on duty why they would have to wait another half hour before getting their hot mug of "char." Hastily, I explained the problem to an officer who was just leaving his desk. He was unimpressed and made no comments. He summoned another girl to the kitchen duties and told me to take over from the plotter at the top of the table. I was still not that familiar with the map of the north of England, and now I had to prove my abilities by working on the map with all the place names upside-down. Very soon, I overcame my trepidation by the events of the moment. Within ten minutes or so, one of the bandits that I was plotting was being followed, the co-ordinates being relayed to a Spitfire in the vicinity. The fighter was vectoring in on one of the enemy, and suddenly there was a "Tally Ho", meaning more or less, "I can see it and it's in my gun-sights." A minute later, the bandit disappeared from the RDF screen and I removed its plot from the table. That night I gained the confidence that a plotter needed, though I could not help thinking. War is such a useless waste of life.

Somewhat wearily, we returned to our billets the next morning. They were new, up-to-date and previously unoccupied houses in Woolton in the southeast suburban area of Liverpool. I had to eat hastily and then travel a few miles through the city to Lime Street Station to meet my mother who would be arriving on the night train. There were no busses or taxis on the roads. "This will have to be my debut at hitch-hiking," I thought. In several stages, with the aid of helpful drivers, I travelled past much damage and destruction. Fires were smouldering; ambulances and fire engines were still standing by the collapsed buildings. Rubble had been bulldozed to one side in an attempt to keep the thoroughfares open. Somehow I managed to reach Lime Street ten minutes before the train was due.

My mother emerged all smiles, knowing nothing of the raid on Liverpool, for the noise of the train had drowned out any sound of aircraft flying overhead. We hugged each other. Then I explained the situation and our immediate problem of transportation to the guest house. I picked up her suitcase and we walked to the nearest main road that pointed in the direction of where she was to stay. "Don't stand too close to me," I said, "By wearing uniform, I am sure to get a ride. Stay out of sight; then you can emerge at the right moment." I stood at the curb with my thumb in the air and, within a few minutes, a car drew up and the driver said, "Hop in!" I looked at him and shrank. On his sleeve, resting upon the open window ledge, I counted not one, two, three, but four blue rings. I had been offered a ride by a Group Captain, the same exalted rank as the C.O. of our RAF station at Speke, and to us *he* was almost God. I had not seen a Group Captain that close before!

Hesitantly, I asked, "Can my mother come too?" The reaction on his face is something I will not forget easily. He must have thought that the experiences of the previous night, and the tired look on my face through lack of sleep, had sent me round the bend. What should he do with me? At that moment my mother came into view, lugging her suitcase, so we both hopped in. With some embarrassment, I explained the situation and he ended up by taking us both to the front door of the guest house. It was an extremely considerate action, for his services were surely most critically needed elsewhere that day.

This was intended to be one of my mother's rare wartime holidays, but Liverpool was not a place for visitors since the nightly bombing began that continued for eight consecutive nights. No restaurants were open, and many gas and water mains had burst. On my days off, some of them during my daytime sleeping time after night duty, we made our way on foot from the centre of the city to the Birkenhead ferry, via the theatre from which we had purchased tickets for four nightly presentations of *Gilbert & Sullivan* operas. Birkenhead was hardly a holiday spot but it was on the other side of the Mersey River from Liverpool, and it was relatively undamaged. It was the closest place to Liverpool where we could obtain some sort of food, and, most of all, where we could relax together. Every morning we checked to see if the theatre was still standing. Despite some near misses, it survived all the raids. We thoroughly enjoyed all four excellent performances, which ended between 10:30 p.m. and 11 p.m., so we were both back safely in our lodgings before the bombing began again between 1 a.m. and 2 a.m. It became a regular habit for my mother to meet the other guests in the large dining room of the guest house when the raids began. There they drank tea together, ready to dive under the heavy oak table if necessary until the All Clear sounded.

After three sleepless nights, the two girls with whom I shared a room and I decided to have an early night. If we went to bed about 9:30 p.m., we reckoned that we should have the chance of about four hours of dreamless sleep before the droning noises and explosions began once again. I fell asleep as soon as my head touched the pillow - but it was not a dreamless sleep for long. I began dreaming that someone was shaking me by the shoulders, a sensation which continued to grow stronger and stronger until I awoke. Someone *was* bending over me and shaking my shoulders and, in a moment, I was wide awake.

How could I have slept through that entire racket? The anti-aircraft guns in the park behind our house were blazing away, and the room was shaking and vibrating violently after each salvo. "You are on street fire-watch duty," the voice said, and continued, shouting between the explosive noises, "You have to report at the Flight Officer's room next door in two minutes!" I made a quick calculation - I just had time to run down the corridor to "you know where," then put on my shoes, and a great coat and don my tin hat - and that is exactly what I did.

Reporting at the Admin. Office, I appeared to cause some slight amusement, as I saluted and stood there at attention awaiting orders. My greatcoat was open and a rather fancy pair of pale blue crepe-de-chine pyjamas contrasted prominently under the dark coat. The crowning glory was under my tin hat, which was perched rather precariously over a head full of unsightly hair curlers. A rather imposing looking gentleman was standing beside Flight Officer Sally Gray, the well-known film actress. She was impeccably dressed, not a blonde hair out of place, and appeared ready to play the part on camera that she was actually carrying out in reality. The impressive gentleman, an old Etonian, I heard later, was my co-partner on the first watch. I hoped that what I had in youthful energy, he would make up in the necessary wisdom probably needed during the night. Trying to disguise her amusement, the WAAF officer said, "I think it might be a good idea if you returned to your room and put on something more suitable, it may be a long night." "But," I spluttered, "I was told to report to you in two minutes. This is the best I could do."

In shame, I returned to my room to exchange the pyjamas for my warmer uniform and - horrors of horrors - when I caught sight of myself in the mirror in those awful hair curlers, my embarrassment were beyond description. For the rest of the war, I had the fear of being caught out at the wrong moment with my head covered in curlers. It turned out to be another typically noisy night, but fortunately for our suburban part of the city, most of the thunderous sounds came from our friendly guns in the park. No bombs were dropped alarmingly close, but the shrapnel from our shells was quite a hazard. My heavy and unbecoming tin hat and I became inseparable companions. It now fitted my head quite comfortably after the removal of the uncomfortable and ugly beauty aids.

Some time later when the local street warden had relieved me of my fire-watching duties, I went to bed and slept fitfully. The ack-ack (anti-aircraft) guns in the park had fired incessantly during the raid. At 7.00 a.m., feeling more asleep than awake, I got up, for I was to meet my mother at her guest house after breakfast. I went to the bedroom window and peered out. Little damage had occurred in our area during the night so I was not expecting to witness anything unusual. Nor had it been my intention to wake up the two friends who shared the room with me but, without thinking, I called automatically to the two sleeping girls, "Come and have a look at this." At first they protested mildly and then thought better of it. They got up unsteadily from beneath the blankets and came to the window.

The three of us just stood there staring. The sky was filled with sheets of white paper of all sizes, wafting and floating down gently in the breeze. Some landed in front of our house and we could see that they were pages from books, both old and new. Some bore the printed word, others fleetingly displayed coloured illustrations as they were caught up in the breeze again, to blow willy-nilly along the street in uncontrolled confusion. The papers continued to flutter down. Some were charred at the edges and others were gnarled and crumpled and as black as charcoal. These fragile pieces, having survived in the air for so long, disintegrated into patches of black dust as they touched the ground. They seemed to be playing games as they glided down and soared up again just before reaching the ground, until finally they landed. The breezes that day were strong and the updrafts were stronger still as the currents of air continued to keep the masses of papers aloft and blowing aimlessly above us all day long.

The sun penetrated through the heavy pall of smoke that hung over much of the city, and cast a ghostly light on the white fluttering objects that filled the air. The smoky haze emulated a foggy day in November; the scale and magnitude of the loss of so many valuable books and manuscripts was one more heavy blow to the people of Liverpool .The main library had been well and truly hit.

Dressing quickly and after a hasty breakfast, I called for my mother at her lodgings. She had fared even more badly than I had and had slept very little, having spent the hours during the raid in the dining room with the other guests, ready to dive under the breakfast table at the first sound of a bomb whistling down from above. It was not a good day to venture out into the centre of the city, but we had little choice. If we wanted to eat and drink, it meant taking the now familiar trip across the Mersey River to Birkenhead.

We started off well. Local busses were running again so we had a ride to the city centre but that was where our transportation stopped. After we got out of the bus, there was a smell of dirt and charred wood, plus a faint aroma of gas in the air. It made us want to get out of Liverpool as soon as possible.

Sheets of paper were still floating in the air above us as we walked in the direction of the ferry. The damage from last night's raid became more apparent here. As we neared the centre of the highest concentration of bombing, a most peculiar odour was added to the already unpleasant smells around us, a mixture of burnt oil and bad fish. Approaching the next intersection, we were greeted with the sight of the remains of a warehouse with only three walls standing, the fourth having almost collapsed to the ground. In the centre of the building, now one large gaping hole, an enormous pile, twenty to thirty feet high, of canned sardines and other fish was still hissing and smouldering. The black column of smoke that rose from the centre of the warehouse permeated the air. Apparently, with the need for fire-fighters elsewhere, it had been considered safe to leave it in this state, as the heap slowly burnt away thousands of cans of reeking inventory.

We were about to hurry past these unpleasant reminders of another sleepless night, when we noticed four small children between about four and six years old, each walking idly up and down the centre of the road. The sides of the street were piled with bricks and rubble, but a makeshift thoroughfare had been cleared in the centre. They shuffled along listlessly, looking dirty, tired and lost, as they gazed, without understanding, at the damage on either side of them. We guessed that they had been wandering around like this since before dawn.

Now we realized that we would have to gather them together and take them to a Centre of some sort. But where? This was an area of warehouses near the docks. There were no houses, shops or telephones, and the streets were deserted. While we were trying to decide how to handle the situation, two Red Cross workers came into view, walking in our direction from the far end of the street. They went up to the children and, bending down, said a few words to them before taking them gently by the hand. The volunteers turned round and led the little ones back in the direction from which they had just come. Our dilemma and the children's had been solved, for the moment at least.

Once more the street was quiet and deserted except for the hissing and crackling of the cans as the oil oozed out of them to ignite as small darts of flame among the charred and smouldering heap. My mother and I, our hearts saddened, hurried away from the scene towards the waterfront where, thankfully, we boarded the waiting ferry for Birkenhead. The next day, after over a week of nightly raids, the Luftwaffe left Liverpool alone. The docks and the city had been more than adequately taken care of, so the enemy looked elsewhere to carry out its destruction. After eight sleepless nights, I saw my mother off at Lime Street Station. She said what a wonderful time we had spent together! I returned to quarters trying to understand the understatement of the British.

Having had my first successful experience of hitch-hiking on the day when "My mother came too," I had found it a practical and enjoyable way of getting around. I was still not very confident in my efforts of thumbing down a vehicle, but once I had obtained a ride with a willing driver, my fears faded as the journey usually turned into a cheerful and chatty dialogue.

I enjoyed the experience of meeting and travelling with people of all walks of life from the intellectual to the barely educated, but they had one thing in common. They all made me feel welcome. They were tactful with their questions. They would ask me about myself and where I came from, but hardly ever questioned me about my work, so my stock answer of "Admin." was very seldom necessary. Travelling in this way enabled me to see many interesting places which, otherwise, it would have been impossible to visit in the short time available, and quite beyond the ability of my meagre pocket book.

Having been interested in architecture and its history as an art student, I wanted very much to see the Cathedral at Chester. I preferred not to travel on my own, so I tried to drum up business for our next day off, but there were no takers. "Whoever wants to go all that way just to see an old cathedral? They all look alike anyway," they told me. I planned therefore to go alone. How was I to know when I might be posted away and miss the opportunity?

A few days later, I hitch-hiked to the entrance of the Mersey Tunnel that runs deep under the estuary from Liverpool to Birkenhead. It was, at that time, I think, the longest tunnel in Britain. I felt rather alone as I stood there on my own, as cars and large lorries trundled past me down the steep slope to the tunnel entrance.

After a few minutes, an empty and very dirty coal lorry stopped. "Where yer making for luv'?"the clean-faced but otherwise begrimed driver asked. "Chester," I said hopefully. "Hop in," he said - just the same words as the Group Captain had used. But this time in exchange for rank and cleanliness, I could relax in friendly grubbiness where my rank made no difference at all.

"What part of Chester do you want?" he asked. "Well, somewhere near the Cathedral," I replied, not having seen a map of the city. After a little chit-chat and while I was enjoying looking at a country-side new to me, he became a little more friendly and tentatively asked me to go out with him for lunch when we arrived at Chester. He said that he knew a good hotel there. I began to see the warning signs and, flustered and, with little conviction on my part, I said, "I might be meeting a friend." He was not put off, just wanted to know where I was meeting this friend, Which street? Which cafe? as he would put me down there! He knew as well as I did that I had neither a friend nor a cafe in mind. Things were beginning to get difficult. What was more; he was strong and heavily built and was nearly old enough to be my father!

We lulled into an awkward silence for some time - we would still have more than an hour on the road together. I looked out of the window; it was a beau-tiful day in early summer. The trees were bright green with a fullness of colour found only during that early season, still free from the dirt of industry that covered their shiny leaves later in the year. In contrast to the freshness of the countryside, the damp and stale-smelling coal dust from the back of the lorry blew in through the open window, slowly but surely making me look as dirty as the man at the wheel. The dust rimmed my eyes, my face was cov-ered with smuts, and layers of dust clung to my uni-form. After an interval of silence, he had another go. "I know a good place to eat a meal. Then you can go off where you want," he said. I made the mistake of saying, "I have only about three hours or so to spare at Chester and I want to make the most of sightseeing. I have to report back at my station by 6 p.m." This was not quite true, but, if I wanted my evening meal, I would have to return by then, or starve until the following morning. Few restaurants had reopened in the city after the recent bombing, and I could not afford to go to any of them anyway.

My persistent driver then suggested by way of compromise, that he would pick me up and drive me back to Liverpool in the afternoon. "I have to get a load of coal from down the road and take it back to Liverpool to-day. I'd enjoy the company," he said almost humbly. He seemed to have changed his pitch and knew where he stood. I did need a ride back, and would accepting his offer be any more of a risk than standing by the side of the road and taking a chance with who else might pick me up?

I had to make a quick decision as we neared our destination. "O.K.," I said, "no meals on the way home but I'd enjoy the ride." He agreed and dropped me near the Cathedral, and promised to pick me up at the same place three hours later. I found a washroom nearby where I tried rather unsuccessfully to clean myself up. Then I walked into the huge memorial of stained glass and stone, built in the Middle Ages to the Glory of God.

As I walked through the west door of this one-time Benedictine monastery, the sun shone on the warm red sandstone. It had been built mainly during the

Decorated period of the 14th century. This great building looked as if it had stood there for ever. In the times that we were then living, it gave a feeling of solidity and the idea that it would be there for evermore - a consoling thought when we were uncertain of our future or the buildings in which we lived from day to day.

I sat in one of the pews and looked upwards to admire the ancient vaulting. After a few minutes the roof above me began to sway uncertainly, and then become an unclear shimmering mass. I tried to focus. No, it wasn't an earthquake! It was only a reaction to my latest injection, but I was definitely woozy. It soon passed and, as I was about to try out my shaky legs to continue a self-conducted tour, there came across the silence two or three single notes from the organ pipes. Someone was trying out the stops for effect. A few minutes later an unscheduled recital began, so I just sat back and enjoyed it. The music of Bach and Handel was indescribably beautiful, as it reverberated around the Cathedral walls. It was as if my life in uniform with its attendant rules and regulations, the bombings and the coal lorry, were non-existent for a short period of time. When the recital concluded, I continued my sightseeing tour, and saw by the discreet notices displayed around the Cathedral, that I had just listened to the final rehearsal for a concert to be given in the Cathedral on the following Saturday. There was no time left to walk the Roman walls surrounding the city, or to admire for very long some of the finest examples of half-timbered houses in England. If I wanted to keep my date for the return trip, I had to get moving quickly.

Sure enough, on the dot, the driver of the newly laden lorry arrived to pick up his passenger! Things were different this time. The lorry was very full and the smell of new coal was definitely preferable to the old coal dust I had inhaled in the morning. The driver took me at my word. We had a pleasant trip back to Liverpool; the long tunnel under the Mersey was already quite crowded with rush hour cars. It was a long distance to travel under the water and I decided that I would prefer, if I had the choice, to chance my luck above ground in an air raid, rather than risk it in the safe depths of the tunnel underneath.

I alighted from the vehicle on the Liverpool side of the tunnel exactly where I had been picked up earlier in the day. As I left, the atmosphere between us was relaxed and pleasant. I thanked him for the ride and he reciprocated by thanking me for my company. He kept his bargain and I respected him for it.

Soon after the Chester episode, we were informed that the plotters were to be evacuated to Ormskirk, a small town about forty miles north of Liverpool. A new Ops. Room was being set up at the village of Halsall, and the WAAF were to be billeted nearby at Ormskirk. Although the Ops. Room at Speke had not received any direct hits during the nightly raids, the RDF (radar) and often the Observer Corps lines had broken down. They were always repaired hastily the following day, but the RDF lines invariably went unserviceable again the next night, leaving us devoid of vital information needed to plot the enemy aircraft on the grid references on the map table.

The village hall at Halsall was commandeered by the RAF, and, by the addition of a few huts to the building, there was sufficient space for our needs. We must have been terribly unpopular with the locals as the hall was the only social centre for the people of the village. Now it was denied them until the end of hostilities.

Just prior to our departure from Liverpool, I was called into the office of the Senior Admin Officer (SAO), always referred to as the "Queen Bee". I was surprised when she said that she would like to recommend me for a commission to officer rank. After less than four months in the Air Force, I barely knew the ropes in the ranks yet. I asked tentatively what types of commissions were open to women. "They are requesting Admin. and Code & Cypher officers at the moment," she replied. As soon as she said that, I knew that I must stop things going any further. The change in my new way of life from being an art student to that of an aircraft plotter came easily and I was very happy in my work. The two alternative commissions that she suggested filled me with apprehension. I tried to explain that I would like to spend longer in the ranks first, and that the types of commissions available were not ones in which I would feel very comfortable. I think I was very naive and unwise to have said this, for I might not have a second chance. Fortunately, she was very understanding and said, "Well, we'll think about it again later."

Three months went by and I was given another opportunity to leave the ranks. Flt. Officer. Gray explained once again that Admin. and Code & Cypher commissions were still the priorities, but that a few opportunities had arisen in Intelligence. "You may not be considered for one," she said adding, "The only person I know who was successful had an Honours degree in Geography." All I had to offer was one year at the Hastings School of Art and Architecture and lots of enthusiasm. I disliked the thought of Admin. or of juggling around with strange rows of numbers in order to produce or crack a code. It should be done, I thought, by the mathematically and mechanically minded, and I was neither of these. I longed to pore over maps and charts and anything geographical, although I really had no idea of what Intelligence required. She agreed, however, to recommend me for Intelligence and said, "We'll see what transpires."

In the meantime, we had moved to Ormskirk and settled down to our duties at the Halsall Ops. Room where we were taken by bus each day. Armed guards always stood outside the front doors of the village hall, the locals passed by and wondered, and we got used to rural life, but there was one problem - the "loos". They comprised three separate one-hole privies, set side by side along an overgrown path in a field at the back of the building. The grass was knee high and thoroughly unkempt. Rather than weed and cut the grass, the authorities placed duckboards over the offending flora. But the main problem was the lack of security. These draughty and smelly little outhouses were outside the "Top Secret" area, so each time nature called, we were escorted to the loo by a sentry who waited outside, his rifle at the ready, until we emerged out of the dampness and gloom again. He then led us back solemnly to the door of the Ops. Room. We soon learned to go on these outings in twos or threes; somehow it was less embarrassing that way.

There was also another problem, a human one this time, concerning the Flt. Sgt. in charge of our watch. He was a very rude and unpleasant man, who no doubt knew his work, but not how to cope with a bunch of young girls. He took a great dislike to some of them for no reason at all, but fortunately left me alone. When the new rank of LACW (Leading Aircraft Woman) was extended to women, six of us were recommended by him - I have no idea how he chose his candidates - but we were among the first group of women to receive that rank. I never had the pleasure of sewing my insignia, a little propeller, on my sleeve, for I had received my commission in the meantime.

It was about eighteen months after my departure from Ormskirk, that a headline in the daily paper caught my eye - an RAF Flt.Sgt. was had up for bigamy. I read the news with a heavy heart. Yes! It was him all right; he had married our gentle and warm-hearted Admin. Sergeant, who was in charge of our food and comforts at Ormskirk, and who did all she could to make us feel at home when we were off duty. She had joined the WAAF after the death of her Sgt. Pilot husband, and poured her kindness on to us instead. Her new husband already had a wife and two children. How desperately lonely that lovely girl must have been to have accepted the advances of such a man, but then she had not observed his behaviour, as we had, while he was carrying out his official duties.

Our billet at Ormskirk was a large elegant house, surrounded by a beautiful garden. The girls on our watch always got on well with each other, unlike some of the other watches, but we gained little to our advantage from our example. The other WAAF were all allocated small bedrooms with no more than two or three beds in each. We, on the other hand, were given the ballroom! It was a large, light and lovely room with several big double French windows opening on to a terrace and formal garden - a perfect room to use for anything but a bedroom. Twenty-four beds were piled into it, some of which were occupied by day-shift workers. My bed and five others stood side by side in the centre of the room. Trying to sleep in the morning was a difficult exercise as the daytime workers wandered in and out for their possessions, and the expensively de-signed and well-sprung floor of the ballroom moved gently up and down each time someone entered.

We had been enjoying a few warm sunny days, something we accepted with gratitude, even in summer in the north of England. I took the oppor-tunity during a free afternoon to wander around the gardens, which sloped gently away from the house in a southerly direction towards the open fields at the far end of the landscaped area. Despite the fact that the property had been taken over by the RAF to house about sixty girls, the gardens continued to be maintained at the same standard as in the past.

I walked through the rockeries, flower beds and rose garden, stopping to read the name of a particularly spectacular rose as I passed by. In my clumsiness in trying to reach a name tag, a long thorn pricked my finger, piercing well below the surface of the skin. With a loud "Ouch!", I tried to extricate myself from the rose bush, taking the deeply embedded thorn with me. With difficulty, I began to remove it with my fingers, succeeding eventually as it came out slowly but firmly, pulling painfully against the skin until it came to the surface .With relief, I held the thorn between my nails.

I washed the puncture in salt and water, but it was soon obvious that the saline solution was not strong enough. I obtained some ointment from the Sergeant's First Aid kit, but some days later my finger was much worse. I began to feel shooting pains up my arm, and where the puncture had been, a greenish yellow blob showed under the surface of the skin. My experience of such things was minimal but this, I felt, was something that needed professional attention. I asked permission to be excused from the morning watch to attend Sick Parade. In my particular case, this was a play on words, for we were only a small group of girls and had no M.O. (Medical Officer) or sick bay. Walking into the WAAF Sergeant's office, I showed her my finger. She rang the local doctor at once and made an appointment for me in an hour's time.

During the previous couple of days, the weather had become cold and cheerless again and, on this dreary day, I walked to the doctor's house along a gravel road devoid of character. A few trees grew irregularly along the way. Small weeds and grasses struggled for existence between the paving stones, which formed the path along the side of the road. The sky was overcast and it had been drizzling since breakfast time. Everything around me at that moment seemed to echo the bleakness of spirit that was within me. After walking for about twenty minutes, I arrived at the doctor's surgery, cold and wet. Entering his dismal and unheated waiting room, I felt chilled and miserable. I sat down to wait my turn, supporting my throbbing arm in my lap with the other hand.

After a while a woman came out of the surgery, looked at me and said, "He says you are to go in now." I walked in, sat down and unwrapped the bandage and showed him my finger. He looked at it for a moment, and then said, "Huh! We'll have to lance that one." For the next two or three minutes, I watched as he opened a drawer and selected among several instruments what looked like a scalpel. He took out two small bottles of liquid and put them on his desk in front of me. He boiled the scalpel in a saucepan over a gas ring, in the meantime finding cotton wool and bandages. He turned to me and said without feeling, "I can't give you a local. I'm not allowed to as I'm on my own. There have to be two of us present for that. Hold your finger as tightly as you can, then you won't feel much. And don't move." I knew that the only way I would succeed in not moving would be to look in the opposite direction. As I did so, I felt agonizing pressure being put on the wound. When it stopped, I turned to view the results. The finger looked exactly as it had done a moment before and was hurting a lot more. Then the doctor said in an irritated voice, "That one was too blunt. I'll have to try a sharper one." He chose another unpleasant knife-like instrument and boiled it as I tightened the grip on my finger harder than ever to lessen the pain. Continuing the pressure when he was ready to begin, I looked the other way and hoped that I would not faint. There was a brief agonizing moment of piercing pain, and then a sudden relief as the pus oozed from the wound. With a gruff manner, but with gentle hands, the doctor bound up my finger, and gave me some nameless white crystals in a solution of oil for dressing the wound three times a day. He sent me out of the room, his parting words being,"Tell the next person to come in as you go." I sat in the waiting room for a few minutes, and then put on my wet greatcoat and my hat and walked out into the drizzle. By then, it was rapidly turning into rain and the pot holes in the road had started to fill with muddy water. Soon, drips from the peak of my hat began to run down my face, but I was happy. The throbbing had stopped and the cold air and the rain drops splashing on me, dispelled the feeling of faintness that had threatened me earlier in the doctor's surgery.

Early in September 1941, I travelled from Ormskirk to London to sit before the Commission Selection Board at the Air Ministry. On arrival, I settled myself on a hard bench in the hall outside the boardroom, my coat buttons and hat badge shining and my shoes impeccably polished. There, nervously, I waited my turn. A WAAF soon emerged from the boardroom, her eyes downcast and looking as though she had been through the mill. She disappeared downstairs in a great hurry - not a very reassuring sight! About ten minutes later, one of the M.P.'s escorted me to the same room and left me standing in front of a long narrow table, with seven or eight officers of varying ranks staring at me, their note pads at the ready in front of them. A civilian was sitting at the far end of the table who, I found out later, was a psychologist.

I saluted shakily and I was asked to sit down. Sinking thankfully into the only chair on my side of the table, I faced the "big chief" towering in the centre. A mass of questions were asked relating to me and my work, but, being in a real flap at the time, I cannot recall any of them now. I was severely challenged when I was informed that the war effort needed Admin. and Code & Cypher officers. "But," I interjected, "I understood that I came here to be considered for Intelligence!" "Nevertheless, Admin. and Code & Cypher are what we need now," I was told firmly. I was desperate. I mustered what little courage I had left and said, "In that case, Sir, I would prefer to go back to my job of plotting, which I enjoy!" Silence reigned. Then one of the two WAAF officers present said, "Can you tell me *why* you are not prepared to accept the commission we are offering you?" I gulped hard and replied, "Because I am not sufficiently interested in either, to feel that I would be able to do my best!" Another complete silence - and I wished the floor would swallow me up. Then the Squadron Leader sitting opposite me peered straight at me with a withering look, and said in a loud commanding voice, "YOU CAN GO!"

I retreated quickly, went to the bench, where I had left my greatcoat (military term for overcoat) and gas mask case stuffed with my pyjamas and toothbrush, and sat down. My concern now was, not so much at losing my promotion, but how I was going to tell the Queen Bee, who had so generously given me two opportunities of being considered for a commission, that I had blown it! Another WAAF was now sitting on the bench beside me awaiting her turn. She also looked nervous and all I could think was: "Surely, the Board would not fail three of us in a row. Maybe she'll be lucky".

I tried to pull myself together and had put on my coat, when the familiar M.P. approached and said, "Would you mind waiting for a few more minutes, Ma'am?" That shook me; he had corporal's stripes on his arm and mine was bare even of the little LACW propeller I was due to receive next month. I could only assume that I was being called back to be admonished for insubordinate behaviour, and that he felt sorry for me.

Five minutes or so later, he returned with a large brown envelope, plus the address of the War Office building near Horseferry Road, and a security pass for entry to the building, dated for that day only. I was instructed to take it to a Col. Churchill, whose office was three floors down, thirty feet below the surface in the large circular structure. The stout outer concrete walls of the building were what re-mained of an old disused gas-holder (incorrectly known by most people as a gasometer). My uncle, George Couper, had been responsible for its original design years before the outbreak of war, and any-thing that he designed was intended to last for gen-erations. The Government had planned to pull down the unsightly remains and replace them with something less ugly and more useful. While examining the gasholder with the intention of destroying it, it proved to be too costly to demolish. Finally, it was decided that the eyesore, with its foundations thirty feet underground, would make a perfect bomb shelter should there be a war. Consequently, an office complex was designed to fit into the empty shell. My uncle, for a long time before this, had watched with amusement from his office window nearby, the various attempts to demolish his creation. The "hole," as he always referred to it, became an ongoing family joke, as he told us of the various ways which the demolition crews had tried to tackle the problem. Then, one day, he told us with considerable delight that the powers-that-be had given up the fight. They had now begun to incorporate the old gas-holder walls into their design for a new block of offices.

Now, I was about to see inside of the reconstructed gas-holder of which I had heard so much. Security was very strict and, as I approached the entrance, I was pounced on immediately to produce my pass. An M.P. was called and I was escorted down a circular sloping passage to the Third Floor below ground. My escort ushered me in to the Colonel's office and disappeared.

What I was doing being interviewed by the Army, was beyond my comprehension. But a full Colonel sat behind the desk and welcomed me, so I guessed I was in the right place. Sitting there waiting, while he flipped through my dossier, I tried to compose myself to be ready to answer another battery of questions. After a few questions, Col. Churchill put a large aerial photograph on the desk in front of me. He wanted to know if I could see what was on it. I looked hard, but I could see almost nothing. All that appeared to be there was a long dark strip of water in the centre of the picture with some land each side. "Anything else?" he asked. "Well, the coastline is indented," I answered trying to gain time. "Look more closely at it," he said patiently, "and take your time." That last comment calmed me down and helped me to take hold of myself. He was not expecting immediate results, so I peered closely at the dark mass in the centre and tried to concentrate. Suddenly, I discovered a ship, then another, then several more, then there seemed to be dozens in that murky looking mass of water; in fact I completely lost count, for I saw ships of every description. Having little or no knowledge of nautical terms, I described them to him as large and small ones, long and short ones and thin ones and fat ones. There was even one ship which, I said bravely, was moving slowly with a white wake behind it. Then I saw some seaplanes and a square patch like a parking lot by the shore. "That could be a seaplane base," I guessed nervously. After this "remarkable" discovery, he asked only one more question. Did I know what place I was looking at? I had to reply honestly, that I hadn't the faintest idea! He then pointed out other interesting observations on the photo, and explained that I was viewing a picture of Kiel Harbour, taken two days before the invasion of Norway, and that this was a photograph of the Armada that transported the Nazi forces on their way to the invasion and occupation of that unfortunate land.

That night I spent at my uncle and aunt's home in Edgware, in north London, before returning to Ormskirk the next day. It was with the greatest difficulty that I refrained from telling him that I had been interviewed in his old gasholder that afternoon.

About a month later, I was summoned to Loughborough in Leicestershire to take part in the three-week initiation course for newly commissioned WAAF personnel. Loughborough College, a well-known boy's school, had been requisitioned by the RAF for the duration of the war. It was very pleasant there, with its spacious grounds and gracious buildings.

I arrived, dragging along my overstuffed kitbag, filled with the practical and ugly "issue" underwear provided to all other ranks. Crammed in the bag with it were some crumpled shirts and my small collection of books and other precious oddments. We soon discovered that the course that we were taking was geared to turn us into a group of efficient office managers. We battled with forms of all sizes - the larger they were, the less important they seemed to be. We listened to the intricacies of office procedures, few of which we thought would work in actual practice, and how to cope with WAAF personnel on a station. We returned once more to the parade ground and, at times, had to take over the sergeant's role of shouting orders to the assembled group. This often turned out to be a complete disaster, but we all tried hard, for it was something any of us might be asked to do without warning at our new stations.

On almost the last day of this endurance test, the tailors, who measured us for uniforms, had finished their work. By evening, we all walked around rather proudly and self-consciously wearing our new attire. Each jacket bore one very small narrow blue ring above the cuff - A.S.O. (Assistant Section Officer). This was our new rank, the equivalent of a 2nd. Lieutenant in the Army. Our old peaked caps were replaced with ones of smarter cut and better material. The RAF emblem in the centre of the hat was embroidered with gold thread. I threw away my old cap but kept the brass badge for its sentimental value - I still have it!

It was then, and only then, that we were informed of our final destinations but no information about the nature of work that each of us was to pursue. I was drafted to RAF Benson, which I discovered on arrival was an operational air reconnaissance station south of Oxford, where I was to take a six-week course in Photographic Interpretation. I could hardly believe that it was less than eight months since I was a civilian. It seemed light years away.

# LEARNING PHOTO INTERPRETATION

About six of us, a mixture of Honours Geography graduates and Art students, travelled together on the train and, on our arrival, were met by the two Squadron Leaders who were to be our instructors. Both had been recruited directly into the positions they now held in the RAF and, as University Professors, had high reputations in their particular fields of work. Each wore the white "Arctic" ribbon on his uniform, and, as far as I know, the award of this medal was very rare. I had not seen one before and have never seen one since.

Dr. Stevenson was at that time, I understand, the ultimate authority on aerial photography, and Dr. Wager, I discovered after visiting the Tensing Museum in Darjeeling in Northern India thirty-five years later, was the first man to photograph Mt. Everest from above and also the first to climb 19,000 feet up its slopes without oxygen.

That evening, we were allowed to settle in and relax, and the next morning reported at our classroom at 9 a.m. We met a surprising variety of people. There were WAAF, RAF and Army officers from a variety of regiments - tank corps, engineers, and others. There were also two naval officers taking the course. I sat down at an empty desk and I was surprised to see a U.S. Army major at the desk next to me. "What was he doing here?" I wondered, for it was about two months before the bombing of Pearl Harbour and the U.S. had not yet declared war on Germany. He kept very much to himself and seldom went beyond saying, "Good Morning" to me, or to anyone else for that matter. I was curious and wanted to find out what was going on. The explanation I received was that he would be returning to Washington to start up his own Photographic Interpretation department! The US, in those days, I understood, did not have one, but I never did discover the major's name.

After we had settled down at our desks, each instructor, in turn, gave a short welcoming address, followed by a thumbnail sketch of the objectives of his course. It was obvious from the beginning that we had exceptional teachers. We learned that we were to be trained to recognize anything and everything of importance and of a questionable nature to be found on aerial photographs. These were taken by Air Reconnaissance Spitfires from 30,000 feet, a very high altitude in those days. For example Venturas, some of our smaller daylight bombers, flew at only 13,000 feet - perfect flak height - to their detriment as I discovered some time later. The Spitfires used in this work were camouflaged in a pale metallic blue to blend with the sky. Cameras were inserted under the belly of the aircraft and overlapping pictures were taken as the pilot made a run over the target. They were then flown back to Benson (in our case) and dropped by parachute over the airfield. By the time the aircraft had landed, the photos had already been developed! Speed was the all-important factor.

After the initial talks, we were provided with small stereoscopes and slide rules, and we were all given identical pairs of overlapping pictures. The exercise was to move the two photos around under the stereoscope until they produced the correct overlap, which then showed a three-dimensional image. Then we had to interpret what we saw. I looked at my pair of photographs in dismay. I had two pictures, each with a small blackish blob, slightly more than one-half inch in diameter near the centre of the print, surrounded by dirty whitish paper, with nothing else on it as far as I could see. I remembered with what difficulty I had found the German Armada on a large picture of Kiel, and now I had to interpret an ink blot!

There was utter silence in the room. It was consoling to know that others were stumped as well. This silence continued for several minutes, when a voice suddenly piped up, breaking the tension - "I've got it!" "Got what?" I thought. Then a minute later, another voice of jubilation was followed by two or three more. I worked harder than ever pushing my two pictures around and then to my surprise and delight, I had "got it" too. Under my eyes, there appeared a steep, rocky and beautiful little island with a monastic building at its summit, towering up towards me in solid form. I even knew where it was this time - I had been there - Mont St. Michel, in Brittany. The island, I knew, was surrounded by quicksands as the picture, which was taken at low tide, clearly showed. From that moment, I never ceased to be enthralled with every photograph that came my way.

As the days and weeks went by, we learned how to identify enemy aircraft with the help of silhouette cards. These proved very useful during practice sessions when we had to list aircraft seen on photos of airfields in occupied Europe. It was a much more complicated procedure learning how to identify shipping. We studied hard, trying to recognize the German naval fleet, from the battleship *Tirpitz* and the cruisers Scharnhorst and *Gneisenau* down to the smallest "E" boat. *Jane's Fighting Ships* was the most popular book at that time and there were far too few copies to go around. The same comment went for *Jane's Merchant Ships*. Each book, with its vertical and horizontal diagrams, was invaluable. We practised identifying everything from the largest passenger ship and oil tanker down to small freighters, dredgers, hoppers, tugs and self-propelled lighters.

I think I was one of the few to whom a slide rule was a new instrument. This was used mostly for measuring the length of ships and for converting from metres to feet or the other way round. In fact, we used the slide rule for everything that today would be done on a computer in a fraction of the time. It was a fascinating exercise measuring the height of a building or other structure from its shadow, and, as the photographic cover was taken only on clear days, the shadows were always there when we needed them.

The identification of industrial buildings and complexes were the most difficult. Until then, all industrial areas and buildings had looked alike to me. I saw them as depressing, untidy, dirty and smoky, and I had no desire to know anything about those unsightly blots on the landscape. Now, I found myself taking an interest in the recognition of cooling towers, coking ovens, mine shafts, turbines, electric grids and oil tanks! All these and many more gave the clue as to what went on under the roofs of these dreary looking structures and surrounding buildings. Suddenly, I was surprised to find myself greatly interested in studying photos of industrial complexes.

The alternative game of "I Spy" was a light diversion after completing my assignments. I would follow worn paths and tracks in relatively unused areas. If these terminated in a field beside a wood, there was the possibility of an ammunition dump being present under the trees, or maybe something else of importance. On the other hand, there might be nothing more than piles of firewood that had been chopped for use in the coal-hungry countryside, but my imagination was always stimulated by this type of exercise.

We studied morning, afternoon and evening, seven days a week, as far as I can remember. Anyway, with one exception, I do not recollect passing through the main gates or seeing the village during my stay. Three weeks into the course, when everyone seemed to be somewhat weary from the long hours in the classroom, we were unexpectedly given the weekend off. I stuffed my overnight bag, put my slide rule in with my gas mask, and set off once more to spend Saturday night with my aunt and uncle at Edgware. It was not too far to go and there was always a welcome at their house. What is more, I was to gain half an hour's tutoring on the slide rule and the math that I had forgotten. My uncle took me into the dining room, which was unoccupied, to give me my lesson. As always, on one end of the dining table was a large drawing board covered with intricate drawings. He was a civil engineer and did a lot of freelance work at home. I asked him what the design represented as it was meaningless to me. "It's a kind of wall," he said, puffing away at his pipe. "What sort of wall?" I asked. "A sea wall," he replied in a relaxed way. I guessed it was for some coastal resort or harbour. It did not appear to be one of his more interesting projects so I left it at that. We then got down to the more pressing business of the moment, a lesson on the slide rule. One day, several years after the war, I recalled that evening - and wondered. But that belongs to a later story.

During our final week at Benson, we were treated to an evening of light relief when our "professors" gave a slide show, featuring themselves on a expedition in the Canadian North. The shots of them mastering the art of paddling the kayak were hilarious, a great source of entertainment and relaxation to us all. Little did I dream that some years later I would be a Canadian citizen.

Six weeks after my first confrontation with the "ink blot", I graduated. A few of the Army officers preferred to return to their regiments, for they were young and wished to fight with their men. Our American friend returned to Washington to start up his own U.S. Photographic Interpretation Department. The rest of us were posted to the C.I.U. (Central Interpretation Unit) at RAF Medmenham, near Marlow on the River Thames.

# LIFE AT MEDMENHAM C.I.U.
## (Central Interpretation Unit)

The WAAF officers were housed at Phyllis Court, the exclusive boat club at Henley-on-Thames. The gardens were lovely, with lawns stretching down to the river. A large grandstand stood on the west side, which in peacetime provided for the rich and privileged the finest view of the annual Henley Regatta. On the east side was a large boathouse well stocked with canoes and skiffs. I wondered how many of the past members were now sailing the Atlantic. This beautiful and peaceful place seemed a thousand miles from wartime Britain, and in a different world from the top-secret activities taking place at Medmenham, near Marlow, a few miles down the river. On our days off, we took advantage of the facilities offered to us, and I became quite deft at rowing and feathering my oars on the skiff, and paddling a canoe in a passably straight line. The joy of living in such idyllic surroundings was curtailed only three months after my arrival, when we were moved and sent to live in the recently built standard huts hidden in the dense woods at Medmenham. I look back at that time with pleasure, and recall fondly one of the WAAF officers who always travelled with us on the bus from Henley to Medmenham for the day-shift duties.

"Lady B.C." we affectionately called her - Lady Charlotte Bonham-Carter was a memorable character, whose presence always exuded a cheerfulness and diversity from RAF protocol. She was older than the rest of us, probably by twenty to twenty-five years. This could not have made her more than about forty-five years old, but with her greying hair and kindly, cheerful and approachable manner, she became a Mother Figure in the mess. The grand piano she had lent to us stood in solitary splendour in the upstairs balcony area at Phyllis Court. It was there for the use and pleasure of everyone. We budding and not-so-budding musicians were encouraged to pursue our keyboard ambitions and achievements anytime we wished.

When we were catching the RAF bus which ferried us between our living quarters and our work, Lady B.C. was usually one of the later arrivals. She would hurry along carrying a wicker basket crammed with personal correspondence. These letters she always took with her in the hope of answering some of the mail during the lunch-hour break. She must have had a large circle of friends, for the basket was always full. She did not want to lose touch with her family and acquaintances just because she was away from home and serving in the WAAF. There was always a pair of moccasins stuffed in the basket with the collection of correspondence. She said that she felt so much more comfortable in slippers while working in the office. It sounded like an excellent idea, but only Lady B.C. would ever get away with anything like that.

When I left Medmenham nearly a year later, Lady B.C.'s personal correspondence basket was even more full with letters from her ever-increasing circle of friends, as it was on the day when we first met. The moccasins were always tucked in amongst the collection of mail waiting to be answered. I wondered where these slippers had come from. Such luxuries were unobtainable in England at the time, but maybe one of her close correspondents happened to live in Canada.

The men were already living in the huts at Medmenham; now more had been constructed to house the WAAF officers as well. There were, however, consolations in moving to this location from Phyllis Court. The daily bus trip had been eliminated, so there was time to enjoy a stroll in the peaceful gardens surrounding the enormous house which was our headquarters. It was perched high up on a hill overlooking the River Thames. Trees, ornamental shrubs, rock and herb gardens swept down the slope to the river's edge. I remember with nostalgia the perfume of wisteria on a warm summer night, as it wafted through the large open windows of the Elizabethan-style refectory, which was the home of the Second Phase department. To sit at a desk with one's eyes glued to the stereoscope, tracking down activities going on that day in enemy-occupied Europe, was in strange contrast to the scented air blowing in at us from an English garden.

When I first arrived at Medmenham just before Christmas 1941, there were over four hundred officers working in different areas of Photo Interpretation. We represented almost every branch of the Armed Forces. Local people must have wondered as they noticed uniforms of the RAF, WAAF, Army, Navy, WREN's plus a few people who were wearing the less familiar uniforms of Allied officers who had escaped imprisonment in their own countries. We were enriched by the "direct entries", usually of Oxford Dons whose specialized knowledge in the civilian world could be used to great advantage at C.I.U. Much later in the war, yet another uniform was added to the array - that of officers from the United States who had joined the team of interpreters. These presumably were graduates of the program designed by the Major who had sat beside me on the Benson course.

In the Second Phase Section to which I was assigned, there were two Allied officers among our colleagues. One was a Polish pilot who, at the outbreak of war, had flown in the defence of Warsaw during the invasion of Poland. The other was a Norwegian. The Polish pilot, Flight Lieutenant Bieanowski, was a gracious man, older and more senior than most of us. He had escaped from Poland by making his way to the south towards Greece and, eventually by devious means, arrived in England to join the RAF. His sister had also left Poland about the same time and had reached Greece, where presumably she remained throughout the war - he had lost all contact with her. I learnt some years later that he had returned to his own country to work with the resistance movement, but I never heard if he survived.

The Norwegian was a young architect by profession and, for this reason, had been given more freedom than most people to travel in occupied Norway. He was, therefore, a valuable asset to the Underground freedom fighters. He was not suspected when challenged for his reasons for visiting a town or city far from home; there was always some building or renovation that needed his attention! Eventually the

SS got wise to his activities, and it became imperative that he disappear quickly or suffer the consequences. One dark night off the northern coast of Norway, a group of five men left for the open sea and escaped in a small but seaworthy fishing boat; they arrived off the coast of Scotland a few days later. Soon after that, one of them, Bjerke, became a member of our "watch". Each man told us his own story during the early hours of the morning watch, a time when one's resistance was at its lowest. Somehow it was much easier to be oneself, relaxed and unselfconscious at times like these. At a later date, I also met, by chance, one of his colleagues who had escaped in the same little boat.

It was rare though that we experienced quiet nights like these. On both of those occasions much of Europe had been enveloped in fog the previous day and no sorties were flown. We then filled in with back-up work, such as trying to prove by photographic evidence the authenticity of reports that had come in by agents in occupied Europe. We took this work very seriously though not quite so hurriedly. The answers we gave could make a difference to the category given to each specific agent.

The work of the interpretation of stereoscopic photographs was carried out in three phases. Interpreters at the airfields from which the reconnaissance Spitfires operated, were the first people to review the results of the missions. Their duty, the First Phase, was to look for any immediate activity taking place by the enemy at the time that the sorties were photographed. They would then bypass Medmenham and report their findings directly to London.

This work comprised mainly keeping a lookout for single enemy naval and merchant ships, flotillas and convoys at sea. On land, they searched along roadways for movements of a military nature, such as convoys of tanks and trucks, and concentrations of vehicles in open spaces, or anything else of an active and suspicious nature. Marshalling yards and railway lines also came under their scrutiny, as their trained eyes identified locomotives pulling flat cars carrying tanks, armoured cars and field guns. All these things and many more could be recognised from stereoscopic photographs. Any information on enemy movements was passed on immediately to the High Command in London. With this knowledge, the Chiefs of Staff had the opportunity of taking offensive action, should they consider it necessary. If none of these activities were seen on the photos, they left the interpretive work to be carried out in more detail by the Second Phase officers at Medmenham.

The Second Phase was where we came into the picture. Photo reconnaissance sorties were flown during the day from Wick and Leuchars, in Scotland, covering mostly Norway and Denmark. Much of Europe was photographed from the reconnaissance aircraft stationed at Benson, near Oxford. The Spitfires at St. Eval in Cornwall covered the western and the more southerly areas of France. The photos from all these sorties usually reached Medmenham before the night shift began at 8 p.m. The sets of photographs were divided among the group of about twenty to twenty-five officers, and work began at once. With only a short break at midnight for "beans and bangers", we usually worked throughout the night. The results had to be completed in readiness for the D.R. (Dispatch Rider) pick-up at 8 a.m. the next morning.

We concentrated mostly on large and small ports, airfields, and marshalling yards and railway lines that happened to be on the coverage. These pictures were compared carefully with the previous cover noting, in the case of ports, the turnover of ships and, where possible, their routes from port to port. With this information, it was possible to trace shipping routes, and sometimes make calculated guesses as to their cargoes. When covering airfields, we compared numbers and types of aircraft, noting any departures from the norm. The sudden arrival or absence of specific types of bombers or fighters might give a clue to a change in strategy on the part of the Nazi High Command. Such information was of great value to our British High Command. When all the stereo photos had been interpreted and our combined efforts had been consolidated, we proofread the results of the night's interpretations. They were then sent up to London by the D.R. in time for the daily 10 a.m. conference of the War Cabinet. At 8 a.m. in the morning, the day shift took over and we retired to the Mess for breakfast.

All the prints from the sorties that had passed through the hands of the Second Phase department during the night, were now transferred to the daytime staff of the Third Phase Section. The sorties were then divided out among the appropriate specialized departments for more detailed analysis. At this final phase of the work, specialists studied the photos in great detail. Speed by now was not usually the goal, but the minutest information on everything was of vital importance. This newly acquired knowledge was added to the existing history of each specific subject being scrutinized. In this way, dossiers were available at a moment's notice, with information that had been covered over time by the reconnaissance photos.

The Third Phase section comprised many departments and was one of the reasons for the presence of the Army, Navy and Air Force living under one roof. This group of specialists ably covered every angle of the work. Many of the direct entry professionals worked specifically in this Section. This information I learned over several months, but, at first, my knowledge was minimal and my experience non-existent.

During the first week of night duties, I was asked to interpret mostly airfield assignments which had been covered that day. It was not as difficult as I had imagined, for we always compared present coverage with that photographed a day or two before. This could be both an advantage and disadvantage for a beginner. It made the identification of specific aircraft much easier; on the other hand, one had to guard against the presumption that little or nothing had changed, except perhaps numerically. The sudden appearance of even one or two aircraft of different types could be a clue to a change in policy in the use of that particular airfield.

I was pleased with my first two assignments - full marks! Then came the third. It was a small airfield rather off the beaten track, and I had to hunt for its location on the map. It had not been photographed for quite a while. After comparing everything carefully, I gave it to "Babs" (the aircraft specialist) to check - more about her later. She soon returned with a sombre look on her face. "I think you have made a slight mistake," she said. I was mortified, and I replied, "I thought it was a Messerschmitt 262 and it is a Mark III, isn't it?" "Oh, no," she replied, " it is a Mark IV!" "What's the difference?" I asked. She put two prints under the stereoscope and told me to look more closely at the four aircraft sitting in a row on a concrete strip outside a large hangar. The parked positions of them alone would have given a more experienced interpreter reason to question further. Aircraft were always kept as far away from each other as possible and in a random and camouflaged pattern around the perimeter of the airfield. This was done to minimize losses during possible air attacks. But these were sitting close together out in the open in front of a hangar. I looked hard and then she pointed out dirty patches behind some others. "It looks like a wet and muddy field down there," I said. "Those patches behind the aircraft are scorch marks made by jet engines," she explained. "Whatever are they?" I asked even more bewildered. We had learned of nothing in that category on the Benson course. It had been my bad luck to find a seldom-photographed airfield - a factory aerodrome - that made experimental jet engines. After all, it was January at the beginning of the year 1942.

Many years after World War II, I found the following account from the book *The World's First Turbo Jet Fighter* by Heinrich Hescht:

> *"Willy Messerschmitt, designer of the ME 109, at*
> *the time the fastest fighter plane in the world, realized*
> *that he had reached the ultimate speed level possible*
> *with propeller aircraft. So, in 1938, he set out with*
> *the aid of his best designers to build his first jet air-*
> *plane. Three prototypes were ready in 1941, but due*
> *to WW II now in full swing, the German Reich Air*
> *Ministry grew less and less interested. The first ME*
> *262 took off on March 25, 1942, with a Juno*
> *210G engine and two BMW engines and with its*
> *turbines breaking down, scarcely made one circuit of*
> *the field."*

These engines were never sufficiently perfected to
be used against the Allies during the war. Uncomprehending, I had seen photographs of the first jet
aircraft a month or two before its initial flight of
one circuit of the airfield! After the episode of the
first jet engine, I learned to give more careful attention to details.

Along with all the activity of coming and going
from port to port, there was one ship that was always present in the same port. The *Ole Weger*, a
whale-oil factory ship, was under repair at Le
Havre. It was a type of vessel I had not seen before,
and I had only a vague notion of the ships that
cruised around the Arctic Circle in search of
whales, but here was one of them. Oil was very
scarce at the time, so this ship, now in the hands of
the enemy, was of great value to them. Its silhouette
made identification quite unmistakable. Every day
or two, it was towed from one berth to another
within the basin or to the adjoining basin of the
port. The repairs were nearing completion and the

Germans considered it expedient to move the ship around regularly to confuse any Allied dive bombers that might come that way. A few months after my leaving Medmenham, the existence of the *Ole Weger* once again came into my life, but that is a later story.

In the month of February, three of the largest ships of the German Navy were about to make a dash for it, or so it was indicated from the latest aerial photographs of Brest. About a month earlier, the *Tirpitz*, Hitler's only battleship still afloat, the fastest and the most powerful in the world, had been recalled from the Atlantic to Trondheim in Norway. Its purpose was to menace the Allied convoys which, under Arctic conditions and mountainous seas, were making their way to Murmansk in Russia. These ships carried armaments and supplies for use against the Nazis on the Russian Eastern Front. Now it appeared that the battle cruisers *Scharnhorst* and *Gneisenau* and the cruiser *Prince Eugen* were about to sail east too.

The port of Brest on the north-west Atlantic coast of France was photographed almost daily by our reconnaissance aircraft. For nearly a year, the *Scharnhorst* and the *Gneisenau* had been blockaded in the port by the British Navy. The cruiser *Prince Eugen* had joined them and recent photos now showed signs of life - smoke was escaping from the funnels of the ships. The Royal Navy was waiting to engage them immediately they left the shelter of the port. It was believed that these ships would attempt to sail through the English Channel to the safety of the German harbours. Preparations had been made to bomb or torpedo them and, failing that, mines awaited them near the Dutch coast.

Stereoscopic photographs probably provided some of the quickest and most accurate information. We went on night duty on February 11, 1942, and we were eager to see what the latest sorties would show. The large stone fireplace at the end of the room, and the tall and gracious Elizabethan windows spanning one side of the room were the only reminders of the purpose for which the room was originally built. It now comprised a large sprawling office cluttered with desks, tables, high stools and anglepoise lamps.

"Are they still in port?" we asked as we arrived, referring to the three ships at Brest. "Come and have a look," was the reply. The sortie covering Brest had already been interpreted. A large blow-up of the port was put on a table for us to see. It had been an almost cloudless day over France and the pictures were perfect. The reconnaissance pilot had made a comprehensive run over the port, taking in the U-Boat pens and every detail of the docks and surrounding areas. We gaped with unbelief as we picked out the battle cruiser *Gneisenau* and the heavy cruiser *Prince Eugen*. There was a small wispy cloud over the mooring of the battle cruiser *Scharnhorst*, the largest of the three ships. It was the only cloud in the entire set of pictures, making it impossible to tell if the ship was still present under that little blob of cotton wool. Probably it was there but, on the other hand, it might not be there at all. The Navy would have to wait until the next day for definite proof.

The same night the weather changed suddenly, as it does so often in that area and at that time of year. The wind rose and blew until it reached gale force. The rain came down, gradually at first, and then turned into slashing sheets of water. Visibility, combined with darkness, was reduced to almost nothing. The calm sea soon became a turbulent mass. The waves heaved and sank into troughs, to rise again in clouds of frothy spray. The weather improved the next day and, in the morning, yet another sortie was flown over Brest. The results were interpreted immediately at St. Eval - all the ships had disappeared!

> *"On the night of February 11, the two battle cruisers with the cruiser Prince Eugen, escaped from Brest and successfully made the passage of the English Channel to regain the shelter of their home ports."*
> Winston Churchill, *The Hinge of Fate*

The three ships passed through the Straits of Dover at midday in a thick mist on February 12 and reached the German ports on February 13. The patriotic British song *"Rule Britannia! Britannia Rules the Waves"* did not live up to its claim that day! Later it was discovered that the three prize ships of the German Navy did not reach home unscathed. Both the *Scharnhorst* and the *Gneisenau* were damaged by British mines and the *Scharnhorst* was out of commission for six months. By the time the war ended, the battleship *Tirpitz* had been sunk in Tromso Fjord in Norway. The battle cruiser *Scharnhorst* had been torpedoed and sank on the Russian convoy route. The *Gneisenau*, badly damaged during its escape from Brest, was later bombed in dock and never appeared to fight again in the war. The *Prince Eugen*, the only survivor of that group, was handed over to the Americans at Copenhagen at the end of hostilities, and met its fate when used in an atomic bomb test in 1947.

Spring had come when I entered our Section for another routine night duty. It had been another cloudy day over Europe and not many missions had been flown. Only a few photographs awaited us on our arrival and we quickly completed their interpretation. To fill in time, I took an earlier sortie box from the library. I wanted to look once more at the series of ramps that were springing up along the coastal areas of northern France. They were empty and there was no proof as to whether rockets would be launched from them. There was no equipment to be seen anywhere nearby. However, these ramps had one thing in common. They all pointed to the south and south-east coast of England. Specialists in that area of work had pooled their theories and suggestions, but due to lack of any photographic evidence, they were unable to prove for what purpose these ramps were intended. I guess I viewed them as an interesting challenge, rather than with any real hope of finding an answer. When I left Medmenham in late 1942, the problem was far from being solved. There had been calculated guesses, but there was no definite confirmation of anything.

I was interrupted in my musings when a collection of sortie boxes was given to us. We were asked to look for any general information before they were passed on to the appropriate departments the next day. I glanced at them and, to my surprise, discovered that one was a cover of Jersey in the Channel Islands.

These unfortunate islands were the only areas of British soil occupied by the Germans. After the fall of France, it was impossible to defend the four islands of Jersey, Guernsey, Alderney and Sark, situated so close to the French coast. The residents were warned of the difficulty, and those who wished were given only a three day period for a free but hurried boat ride to England, leaving all but their personal belongings behind. Occasionally we received photographic cover of the islands, mainly, I guess, to keep track of the defences being put up by the Germans. Jersey finished up by having the dubious distinction of being one of the most heavily fortified areas anywhere under German occupation. Gun emplacements covered practically the entire deeply indented coastline of bays and rocky cliffs. I had a particular interest in going through these pictures, for, as a small child and then as a schoolgirl, I spent all my summer holidays in Jersey. I knew almost every inch of it.

I would like to digress for a moment and go back to the days of my childhood to explain why I felt so nostalgic about the photos I had in front of me. When my parents married, they chose to run a summer-season tea garden on the sea front, which they leased from the States of Jersey at West Park, St. Helier. They spent the months of April until October running a business, where they enjoyed meeting people and the outdoor life that went with a seaside location. They would then return to London where my father, a civil engineer, took up his work again with the firm of Dorman Long, a large engineering company. My mother, sadly, was widowed when I was three years old. My father, who had been in hospital for a minor operation, returned home to recuperate and died suddenly of spinal meningitis, presumably picked up at the hospital. It was, regrettably, long before the days of antibiotics. Overnight, my mother's life changed from that of enjoying a happy marriage to the sudden realization of having to be the breadwinner with two mouths to feed. She was intelligent, but had no trained skills to offer - only too typical of a woman of her generation.

Having been self-employed, she was not eligible for any type of unemployment benefit, nor would she have accepted any, except in dire circumstances. Widow's pensions were unheard of then and my father carried no life insurance. She had to work to keep us both. She decided, therefore, to continue running the business in Jersey on her own. A month after my father's death, she returned to Jersey, accompanied by a three-year-old child for companionship, to prepare for the coming season.

She received the next blow soon after she arrived on the island. My parent's financial position had improved recently and they were in the process of remaking their wills, which were to be signed on their return to Jersey, but now it was too late and the local law took over. According to the law in Jersey, one-third of the estate was awarded to the widow and two-thirds to the child or children - she got the business and I got the money, which was tied up in War Savings Certificates until my 21st birthday.

Grudgingly, the law permitted her to receive the interest towards my upkeep. There was nothing I could do about it for eighteen years!

When she signed the first cheque from the existing joint bank account, it was promptly returned dishonoured. The bank manager refused to acknowledge their joint account as other than estate money. She was penniless! My mother had a business, no inventory and no money! After explaining her plight, she found kindness everywhere. Without exception she was given credit from well-known chocolate manufacturers, commercial travellers who represented various businesses, local merchants and food stores. They all said the same thing:" Order what you need and pay when you can." None of them went back on their word and my mother spent the summer paying off the small accounts first, and the others by the close of the season. Thanks to the trust and generosity of many people, she was once more in a viable position and able to reopen her business again the following year. Only by good luck did she decide years later, to retire earlier than anticipated. She left the island in the Autumn of 1937, less than two years before the outbreak of the Second World War.

With great interest, I studied the photos of the areas I knew so well. The Germans had dismantled my mother's tea place. This was not very surprising as it had been slated for demolition for a larger restaurant to replace it at a later date - my mother's main reason for retiring. Although she was offered the management of the proposed new restaurant, she did not wish to start again by taking over a large concern run by the States of Jersey.

It was a surprise though to see on the stereo photos, the absence of the Picket House adjacent to it. This solid building made of large granite blocks had been constructed during the First World War, beside a steep slipway leading down to the beach which led out to Elizabeth Castle, a 16th-century fortress built on a rocky island in the middle of St. Aubin's Bay. The Army garrison stationed there was marooned at the castle at high tide, but at low tide could walk to the mainland along a narrow causeway, over a mile long, badly broken up by the tides. The guard at the Picket House was stationed there for the purpose of apprehending any inebriated soldiers overnight, if he thought they might not reach the castle safely before the rising of the tide.

As it was no longer of any practical use, my mother was allowed to rent the Picket House for her inventory. The substantial building, designed to survive many centuries, comprised a guard room in which I played with my young friends and kept my toys, an outdated kitchen which we never used, and the cell, which was a large room with a small window and a raised wooden platform for a bed at the far end. A wedge of wood, at the back of the platform, at about a thirty-degree angle served for a head rest. This room was the store room for my mother's inventory as it was dry and protected from the waves that often broke over the Picket House during rough weather, and the barred window prevented break-ins. Now the entire building had disappeared. As I searched the photo again, the reason soon became obvious. The Germans had dug a huge hole into the promenade on the opposite side of the slipway leading down to the beach. I was fairly sure that it was going to be a gun emplacement and that the two buildings that had been part of my mother's life would have obstructed the gunners' line of fire.

I continued to follow along the coastline until I found the house at Millbrook where I had spent so many happy holidays with good friends of ours, a retired Naval officer, his wife and daughter. The following week another set of photographs arrived with a coverage of Jersey. I could not resist peeking again at the house where I had lived. Their daughter, Annie, now the sole occupant of the house, had been very busy during the week. In the intervening period, she had dug up the entire garden, including the flower beds, in readiness for sowing the Spring vegetables. I remembered the beautiful roses and the large colourful bushes of many varieties of fuchsia that had always lined the long gravel path from the garden gate to the front door. Food would have to be far more plentiful again before the profusion of colour pleased the eye and the perfume of roses filled the air.

Just after the end of the war, I visited Annie, who met me in style at the Harbour. There, on the dockside, her Ford 8 car was waiting as new and bright as it had looked eight years before. It was a most unexpected sight, for during the Nazi occupation, all residents had been forced to hand over all vehicles for the use of the German Army. When we returned to her house, she showed me her extra long one-car garage with pride. After the warning that the island was about to be occupied by the enemy, she had driven the car to the back of the garage and covered it with straw. Then she had erected a three-ply partition in front of the car and hurriedly bought some chickens from a nearby farm. By putting her carpentry skills to work, she had made some hen coops which occupied the front part of the garage, hiding the partition. With the muddle of straw scattered around the hen coops, and the unsavoury aroma and mess underfoot that goes with poultry keeping, the Germans never did more than a cursory inspection.

Annie also told me, with obvious amusement, how she had fooled the enemy in another way. "I heard the BBC news throughout the war, you know, "she said. I was then taken to the bathroom to inspect the built-in cupboard under the washbasin. She had put a wooden partition across the inside of the medicine cupboard. Having complied with German regulations, she had surrendered her large radio, but was one of the very few people who, in those days, owned another but smaller one. She hid the second radio behind the partition, the front of the shelf being filled with bottles and first-aid supplies to make everything look normal. By removing the partition in time for the BBC news each evening, and without causing suspicion when locking her bathroom door, she was able, in comparative safety, to hear and then pass on the news to all her friends. Had she been caught, deportation would have been the minimum punishment.

Forty years later, my husband and I visited Jersey. I showed him the place where I had spent so many summer holidays. I was particularly interested in seeing what had happened to the gun emplacement that I had discovered in the early stages of its construction. It was still there, an unsightly protuberance, gouged into the esplanade on the seaward side. It had been converted to a peacetime use worthy of its memory. On the thick concrete walls outside the bunker, two signs had been placed, one on either side. In neat blue lettering on white enamelled plaques were inscribed the words: LADIES and GENTS!

It is time to stop reminiscing about the years before and after the war, and return to the Spring of 1942. Sarah, the daughter of our illustrious Prime Minister, Winston Churchill, was a member of the team of interpreters. Although I did not know her very well, we had met on occasions when she was assigned to our watch. I remember her as a pleasant person with beautiful red hair, who fitted in easily with the members of the team. Friends who knew her better than I, told me that she took a great interest in the welfare of the group of girls, with whom she had lived previously as an airwoman at Medmenham. Sometimes, she would take several of them to London for an entertainment, and, afterwards, it was not unusual for them all to turn up at the Prime Minister's official residence, 10 Downing Street, unannounced for afternoon tea; quite a dilemma for the security police and the housekeeper, no doubt!

After a few days of fog and cloud over Europe, the weather improved considerably, and we experienced another busy night. I wandered into the powder room after finishing an assignment, in need of a break to wake myself up. It was about 2 a.m. and the canteen had long been closed. It was hot and I was thirsty, but water was the only refreshment available, and that I would have to drink through cupped hands. As I walked into the room, Sarah was the lone occupant. She too was having difficulty keeping awake. We chatted for a few minutes and then she said, "I have a problem and I don't know how to handle it." "What kind of problem?" I asked. "I received a letter today addressed to me in my married name, but, after reading the first part of it, I realized that it was not meant for me at all. It was written to someone else with the same name," she said. "Well, can't you just put it in another envelope and readdress it?" I replied, suggesting the obvious. "It's not as easy as that," she continued, "it's a very private love letter, and it could make a difference to the girl's future."

Sarah was both concerned and embarrassed. I, on the other hand, was far away enough from the problem to be able to see it impartially, despite the scanty details she gave me. At least I had enough courage to suggest a simple answer, "Then, why don't you just write the girl a handwritten note of apology and complete it with your personal signature? I'm sure she will be delighted to receive both letters." "Do you really think so?" Sarah asked, not too sure of so easy a solution. "Given the same circumstances, I know I would," I replied. She thought for a moment and then said, "Thank you, thank you for your help." Our time was up. We returned to our desks more alert from the break and, with renewed interest, began looking through the new batch of photos that awaited interpretation.

Back in the Mess, life continued normally. Every day, the race to gain possession of one of the morning papers was usually won, not by the most agile, but by the fastest eaters. I enjoyed mostly reading the news on my day off, when I could relax in the lounge and go through each copy of the paper unhindered by anyone waiting for me to turn the last page. I entered the room and settled down in one of the comfortable chairs. There was plenty of choice that day for the room was empty and quiet. I was the lone occupant.

As I read the paper with my attention on some interesting snippet of news, the silence was broken suddenly as the most glorious music filled the air. I was stunned for a minute, hesitating to look up. Lady B.C. had brought her grand piano from Phyllis Court and it now sat in a corner of the lounge. There were a few good pianists among the members of the Mess, but this - nobody at the Mess could have given anything like this performance - the music was out of this world. I glanced up furtively and, to my amazement, saw Sir Malcolm Sargent, one of Britain's most famous orchestral conductors, sitting at the piano, playing with incredible beauty and virtuosity. I remembered then that he was billed to give a piano recital with the Amadeus Quartet in the Mess that evening. Sir Malcolm was a friend of the Churchill family and Sarah had asked him to give a recital at Medmenham, but I would be on duty that night. Regretting losing the opportunity of hearing such an outstanding recital, I had deliberately tried to obliterate the forthcoming event from my mind. Little did I expect to hear the piano part played from beginning to end. I sat very quietly, hoping I had not been noticed. After about half an hour, Sir Malcolm, apparently satisfied with his rehearsal, got up quietly and walked out. He had just performed for an ecstatic audience of one!

One morning, the normal routine of the daytime watch changed suddenly. We were given some rather odd looking maps to look at. By this time I had become familiar with numerous varieties of them, but these were distinctly different. Crudely coloured maps representing almost nothing, stared back at us. We were asked to look at them for relevant details that might be of use to people who lived in the area - artesian wells, peaks, valleys, roads (almost non-existent). signs of village life, including such features as wadis, deserted forts, oases, outdoor bake ovens, and water holes. We were looking at maps that spanned large desert areas of North Africa. About a week later the project was withdrawn due to security; too many people were getting involved.

It was then decided that Sarah Churchill should give full time to the work, but where could she carry out the project in complete security and secrecy? There were no more spare rooms in this enormous house. Then someone had a brilliant idea - "How about converting one of the big bathrooms?!" About a week later, some of us asked her how the bathroom renovations were progressing, so she invited us upstairs to see her new office now that it had been completed. The carpenters had been called in and had constructed a very large desk top over the high old-fashioned claw-legged bath. She was provided with an office stool, two metal filing cabinets and two telephones, one being a direct line to No 10 Downing Street we were told. That is how C.I.U.'s research contribution to "Operation Torch", the code name for the daring invasion of North Africa, began - in a bathroom!

After I had been working at Medmenham for nearly a year, we received a notice which circulated around the department announcing that WAAF Intelligence officers were now being accepted on operational stations. If interested, we were asked to complete the attached application form. I read it with interest, but thought nothing more of it. Then after about a week had elapsed, I began to wonder if maybe, just maybe, I should consider it more seriously. It was not a thought I really cherished as I was very happy in my job. The people with whom I worked were pleasant, interesting and easy to get on with. I had made some good friends, and we lived in one of the most picturesque areas of the Thames Valley. There was only one problem; I was, and have always been a very light sleeper, and consequently I always slept very fitfully during the daytime; it was a running battle every third day. Others seemed to go to bed and sleep like logs, but I, despite, at last, having my own room, did not follow their example. A good sleep was essential after twelve hours of work with the exception of the half-hour break at midnight.

My watch comprised a cheerful group as we sat down to breakfast together. There was always a feeling of exhilaration and accomplishment after night duty. We would sit and chat over a long and relaxing breakfast; they were pleasant interludes. Then came the rub - time for bed! Most people disappeared, slept soundly, and reappeared in time for tea completely rejuvenated. I would go into my room, draw the curtains to keep the light out, shut the door to keep the people out, stuff my ears with cotton wool in an attempt to keep the noise out, and hope for the best! By that time the A.C.H. G.D's (Aircraft Hands, General Duties) were just getting going with their Hoovers, buckets and pails, etc.. People trooped up and down the uncarpeted corridors, and of course nobody wore slippers except in the bedroom.

From the windows opposite my room, noises wafted out to accompany the birds' morning song. The kitchen staffs were clattering around washing up plates and dishes from breakfast, before beginning preparations for lunch - there were no automatic dishwashers then! Such was my life and I longed for more than two consecutive nights in my bed. Therefore, I decided reluctantly to fill in the application form for Station Intelligence. I heard years later that the shift duties were changed to one week of consecutive night duties and the remainder in day duties during any one month. These changes were apparently successful, but it was too late for me. In our day there were only three watches to cover a twenty-four hour period, but with four watches spanning the same duties later on, life must have been much less fatiguing. Only three weeks after my application, I received an order to report to an airfield in the Midlands.

# WYMESWOLD & BOMBER COMMAND

The airfield was near a small village in the country, safe from the air activity still being encountered on the South coast. Wymeswold was a non-operational station - an Officers' Training Unit. Needless to say, there was very little for me to do and even less opportunity of learning much. The aircrews had almost completed their flying training and, in two or three weeks, would be sent to operational stations, after which the next batch of trainees would arrive to take their place. The Station was a hub of activity for the flying personnel, but a backwater for the Intelligence staff. I hoped that I had been sent to Wymeswold solely to learn the ropes, before moving on. So when the Code and Cypher officer asked if I would stand in for her for a day, I was more than willing to take over. She explained that she had been at Wymeswold for three months and had had scarcely any work to do, but was unable to take a day off in case something came up. There had been nobody to whom she could delegate until I arrived. I was duly initiated into the intricacies of Codes & Ciphers, after going through a dummy run about three times - just to make sure. She set off happily for a day of freedom, saying, "Don't worry, nothing ever happens!"

But it was not my day, for about an hour later a coded message arrived. Hoping I could remember the procedure, I took the books from the safe and I went through the decoding instructions five times; I came up with the same answer each time - it had to be right! The key word was the name of a flower. I then had to go through a second process to get the meaning of the key word. Only when I had repeated the exercise several times, did I pass on the message to Intelligence. The aircrews were to carry out their first operational mission. They were to fly over enemy territory to drop propaganda leaflets over a large coal-mining area in a strongly guarded Nazi-occupied zone. It was hoped that the outcome would raise the morale of the mining community, and encourage people to partake in acts of sabotage, and disrupt the every day lives of the enemy. When my Code and Cypher friend returned to the base, the aircraft were already in the air and on their way to carry out their mission. Her disappointment was obvious, but she still allowed me to stand in for her the following week. That week it was "business as usual" - nothing!

At the end of the third week, I was sent on a temporary posting to Bomber Command for six weeks. Someone was sick and I was to fill in for her in the meantime. I hoped that meant that I would not return to Wymeswold afterwards. I had no complaints as it was a friendly place and there were no problems - maybe that *was* the problem, that there *were* no problems; I just wished to be stationed where there was more action and consequently more to do. For one thing though, I was most grateful - I had spent twenty-one consecutive nights in my own bed!

Bomber Command was situated nostalgically close to Medmenham and I still missed the people and the work I did there. The Operations room and all top-secret rooms and offices at Bomber Command were constructed thirty feet underground in a thick woodland area near High Wycombe. We lived in RAF houses within the compound, about a five-minute walk to our underground fortress.

During my first morning walk to the office, I spent most of the time, not admiring the beautiful trees along the way, but saluting Air Chief Marshals, Air Marshals, Air Vice Marshals, Air Commodores and Group Captains - they seemed to be everywhere! This was a situation I was going to have to get used to but, on the first day, without a hint from anybody; it was quite an intimidating experience.

Our Intelligence office was situated quite close to the large and impressive underground operations room, which was the heartbeat of all Bomber Groups and RAF Stations throughout the British Isles. Members of our Department were allowed access to the Ops. Room when passing on pertinent information. It was an extraordinary, fascinating and vibrant centre of the RAF.

On several occasions Air Chief Marshal Harris ("Bomber Harris") was present. He was rapidly becoming a legend at the time, with his new approaches to the many problems of the day. Everyone thought that he would go a long way. He had recently been promoted from Air Commodore to Air Chief Marshal in a very short period of time. There has been strong criticism of him over the years, but that is a very easy thing to do with hindsight. I cannot judge one way or the other as to what happened during later stages of the war. I only know that, at the time I was at Bomber Command, those far senior to me said that our country could never have turned round from defensive to offensive action as quickly as it did, without the help of his brilliant mind.

Our office contained the usual desks set up with telephones and a scrambler line. There were numerous filing cabinets crammed with well-stuffed dossiers and large maps hung around the walls. Most of these maps took on an air of mystery as the "boffins", some of England's top scientists, studied them, marked them, and stuck pins and flags in selected areas. From their own quarters, they had a door that opened into our office so they came and went quite often. As to their work, it was quite beyond us. All we knew was that it had something to do with inventing precise methods for hitting a target head-on. A close concentration of bombs, for example, on a ball-bearing factory would be far more help to the war effort than scattering bombs that would kill civilians unnecessarily, and leave the factory relatively untouched. During my stay, these brilliant scientists invented, among other things, the countermeasure "Window" in no more than two or three days, when the enemy suddenly used a new radar method of pinpointing cities accurately. The German Air Force homed radio beams on chosen cities, and their aircraft followed the beams until they intersected over the target. The boffins invented the countermeasure, comprising small strips of aluminium foil. These were scattered along the German radio beams by our own aircraft, bending the beams and thereby making their chosen target difficult to find.

One of the first duties that I was given at Bomber Command was the task of reading out the morning news report over a multi-connected line to the numerous Group headquarters. It was the job of the WAAF officer on the night watch to collect information on enemy activity that had taken place around the British Isles during the previous twenty-four hours. She would then write a news report for the officer taking over the morning duty. It was my luck to have to read out this report on my first day at Bomber Command. I had not experienced being a "radio" announcer before, so I deliberately spoke a little more slowly than I would normally, pronouncing my words as clearly as possible. All went well until I was confronted with a French name. I did not know the place and wondered why it should come into our home news broadcast at all. With the best French accent I could muster, I read that bombs had been dropped at Beaulieu. A male voice on the receiving line said "Don't you mean "BEW-LEE"? "B.E.A.U.L.I.E.U" I spelt out, now feeling rather flustered. "That's right," said another voice. "It's near Southampton". "Thank you," I replied." Your pronunciation must be right. I'm afraid I'm new at this job and I didn't recognize the name". I was glad that there was no way that they could know my name either. That was the last time I ever read the news broadcast without making doubly sure, beforehand, that I could pronounce all the place names correctly.

It was early in December 1942 that I was posted to High Wycombe, so it was not long before the arrival of Christmas. The year before, I had been fortunate enough to go home for Christmas on a forty-eight hour pass. This year I was not so lucky, but at least I had the afternoon and evening free. I therefore qualified to be one of the many to celebrate the official Christmas dinner of the "Great and Small" in the main Officers' Mess. Once again, I had joined friendly people in the new office, so we went as a group to the meal. They suggested that we arrive a little early to choose our seats and relax in sight of, but well away from, the high table.

We found somewhere to sit at the far end of the hall. From there I watched fascinated as the elevated high table in the centre of the hall, filled up slowly with the highest-ranking officers of the RAF, most of whom I had been saluting regularly for the last few weeks. I have never before or since seen such an illustrious and colourful group of people sitting together at one table. I realized why my colleagues suggested sitting far away at the other end of the Mess. Only those who have worn the uniform of the Armed Services can understand the awe that junior ranks have for their seniors, and the power associated with them.

A thought came to me - what if a stray bomb hit this Christmas gathering? We were no longer thirty feet underground. What disastrous and immediate setback would it inflict on the RAF and the country in general? A bomb could have caused the annihilation of some of our greatest leaders. However, my fears were unfounded and the dinner began in a happy atmosphere after a formal grace by the padre, followed by a short welcoming speech by the Commanding Officer. We then toasted "THE KING. God bless him!" and at intervals raised a toast to lesser dignitaries. I learned to pass the port to the left and the sherry to the right - or was it the other way round? - but it was the hors d'oeuvres that were the real challenge. Rumour had gone around a few days before that there was going to be a special treat at dinner this Christmas - fresh oysters! These molluscs were an unheard-of luxury during the war and we wondered where they had come from. Most of the coastal areas and river mouths were either mined or were unapproachable by the presence of barbed wire, and were always out of bounds. It reminded me of our own beach at Pett, which was mined and sealed off from the inhabitants of the village for almost the entire war. The shoreline was protected with barbed wire and concrete tank traps and, to be doubly sure; the marshland and sheep pastures behind the beach had been deliberately flooded!

The Squadron Leader in charge of our section, a fatherly figure to us, had taken the trouble to explain to me that the Upper Crust always swallowed their oysters whole! (English oysters are large) Now the time of reckoning had come! As I plucked up courage to peer down at my plate, I was confronted with some enormous and very raw-looking oysters staring back at me. There was no way I could swallow these whole. Playing for time, I made polite conversation with the officer sitting next to me, at the same time watching the other diners for clues of etiquette. A few skilled and courageous people approached the problem and, with no effort at all, the oysters disappeared down their throats apparently in one piece. I was amazed and thought, "What a waste. I doubt if they tasted anything". I gave mine another glare; those huge oysters seemed to have grown even larger in the meantime, and they still looked just as raw. I grabbed the pepper and salt and sprinkled them liberally, then blobbed them with the appropriate sauce. I said to myself, "Who wants to be Upper Crust anyway? I am the only woman at this table. Surely I have the right to choose to do as I please?" I picked up my knife and fork and consumed the plateful in tasty bite-size pieces - they were delicious!

Only after all these gastronomical exercises had been carried out correctly or incorrectly and our plates were completely empty, did the much-anticipated traditional turkey, stuffing and all the trimmings arrive. The whole evening was a most interesting, exhilarating and unique experience, but, despite everything, something was wanting. Christmas is a family time, and I missed mine in the company of this large and awesome gathering of the Great and the Small. The Child whose birthday we were celebrating that night seemed far from me. I had neither heard nor joined in singing any Christmas carols, and I retired to bed later with very mixed feelings.

The Air Ministry was as good as its word. Exactly six weeks after my arrival at Bomber Command, I was given a Railway Warrant (free ticket) to Lakenheath station, and was instructed that I had been posted to RAF, Feltwell - wherever that was?

# R.A.F. FELTWELL

RAF Feltwell turned out to be an operational air-field and a peacetime base a few miles from the railway station at Lakenheath, and close to the small village of Feltwell in the Norfolk fens. All that greeted me on my arrival was miles of flat land-scape, drab and colourless as it waited for Spring, when the empty fields would be sown with seed and the pastures would become verdant again. There were some green lanes, as they were called, recog-nised by the few trees and hedgerows that lined them, but, despite their name, they were still brown from winter. These lanes were little more than cart tracks giving access to the fields and pastures, and villages appeared to be few and far between.

Ely, with its beautiful cathedral and ancient houses, was, I found out, the only town sufficiently close to visit on a day off. It was twenty miles away at the end of a very rough potholed road. Due to no pub-lic transportation, we had to synchronize our days out with any RAF transport that happened to be both going that way, and returning again in the evening. By the time we emerged from the back of the lorry at Ely, our clothes and our faces were usu-ally so dusty that we deserved a reprimand for our slovenly appearance.

Once again my work at Feltwell was different from anything I had done before; Duty Operations Offi-cer was the description this time. After only one morning of observing the work I was about to do, I was let loose on my own, with nothing more to help me than a long list of people to be informed with appropriate information when an operation was to be flown, and a log book in which to record it. I learned how to use the telephone switchboard with the help of two WAAF Sergeant watch-keepers, my permanent day staff. Otherwise, I was left to my own devices and was told that I would learn the rest as I went along.

Again, I resumed the three-day cycle: Day One, 1 pm - 8 pm, the following day, 8 am - 1 pm, and 8 pm - 8 am next day; then I had twenty-four hours off. Night duties here were not too wearing, due to this being a daylight bomber station. Night shift duty comprised mostly keeping watch and receiving any kind of offbeat information, plus finishing off anything left over from the day watch. Our two squadrons of Venturas were smallish, fat-bellied aircraft and were far from the latest design, but they were all that the Air Ministry could give us. Their main task was to attack specific coastal or near-coastal targets. The range of the aircraft was limited, as their fuel capacity would not allow them to fly much farther than the enemy coast and back. The general intention was that the attacks would complete two goals, one to put factories, hydro stations, shipping, etc. out of action, and the second to encourage the local people living under Nazi rule to realize that they had not been forgotten, and that sooner or later an invasion of Europe would liberate them. By this type of action, Britain was beginning to show the occupied countries that she was gradually turning round from defending her own Island only, to a more offensive position.

While in the Ops. Room during the first couple of weeks, I spent my spare moments reading the log book that recorded the past activities and operations. In this way, I learned the routine and what emergencies to expect, but there was always the unusual turning up that did not seem to fit into any category. The maxim seemed to be: "If you don't know who to inform - tell Ops!" For example, a few times in the early hours of the morning, I was warned that enemy parachutes had been seen descending nearby. The information was usually false, but so long as I had passed the facts to the appropriate authorities, my responsibility was over. I was glad though, that there was always an armed guard at the entrance to our building, who allowed people to enter only if they gave the right password. This was one of the Duty Ops. easier jobs - to choose the daily password. There were times when we had fun with it, taking the opportunity of a good-humoured dig at one of our department's supervisors.

Our target information was kept in well up-dated dossiers. Air photographs were included, but were not necessarily of the most recent coverage, as factories and other immovable objects seldom changed, unless they had been under attack. After logging the instructions from the 3 Group broadcast one morning for an attack that afternoon, I picked up the brown envelope that had been placed on my desk. It contained an aerial photo of Le Havre. I looked at it and was particularly interested to see the target of the afternoon raid. It was my old friend the whale oil factory ship, OLE WEGER! So, the repairs had been completed at last! I scanned the whole harbour with interest and then noted the date on which the photo had been taken - four days earlier! Fortunately, I was the Duty Officer that morning, for it was a chance in a million that any one else would know the movements of that ship. While I was working at Medmenham during the time of its repair, it was towed regularly from one basin in the port to the other, or to another location within the same basin, almost every day. The reason was to make it more difficult to locate during an air attack. I guessed that was exactly what would happen if the enclosed photograph was used to pinpoint the target. If the aircrews were looking for the ship in one place, while it was moored in another, they would either bomb an empty dock or have to take another run at it. As Venturas flew no higher than 13,000 feet - perfect height for flak - a second attack would make them extremely vulnerable to the now-alerted gun crews below. It was imperative to get a more recent cover than this four-day-old picture. I knew that Le Havre was photographed almost daily.

Full of confidence, I rang the Squadron Leader, Duty Ops. Officer at 3 Group and asked him to put me through on the scrambler phone to C.I.U.(Central Interpretation Unit) at RAF Medmenham. He was shocked at my request. "I can't do that," he said. "Well, will you ring through to Medmenham for me?" I asked. "I have no authority to do that for you either," he replied. "Then, Sir, please will you put me in touch with someone who *does* have the authority", I asked as politely as I could. He muttered to himself and then said, "Hold on a minute. I'll see what I can do."

A few minutes later, a Wing Commander came on the other line. "What's going on? What do you want?" he said a bit perplexed at my request. I said my piece all over again. "I need a connection to CIU Medmenham please, or will you get me the information that I need, Sir!" "I can't do that for you", he replied. "But my information needs updating, and we have to have it for briefing at mid-day," I pleaded. "I'll ring you back," he said and he sounded a bit annoyed.

About five minutes later, the scrambler rang again. I found myself speaking to a Group Captain this time, and a rather irate and irritable one at that. I looked at my one blue ring on my cuff and wished for elevated rank quickly. "What is all this fuss about and what do you want?" he asked and added "Haven't you got the picture of the target that was sent to you?" I gulped, I didn't like the sound of him much, but I knew I had to obtain the information somehow.

Once again I explained my plight, this time to the Group Captain, adding, "I know the history of this ship, Sir. I used to be a photographic interpreter, and I know that it is towed around to a different mooring nearly every day. The port is photographed almost daily. Therefore, there has to be a more recent picture. All I want is confirmation of where it was moored yesterday. Can you help me?" He sounded decidedly peeved and, after pausing, said rather shortly, "I'll ring you back," and slammed down the phone. Time was getting on, and the briefing of air crews was in just over an hour.

Not more than five minutes later, the scrambler buzzed once more. "Well! He's got that information quickly," I thought, as I picked up the receiver. I was even more surprised and dismayed this time. In fact, the small blue stripe on my cuff was fading rapidly into oblivion. At the other end of the phone I was confronted with the voice of the Air Officer Commanding 3 Group! I had reached the top. If *he* failed me, there was nowhere else to go, unless it was a hasty transfer to some desolate post in the Outer Hebrides.

"What is your problem, and what do you want?" he asked, almost kindly. I went through the rigmarole for the fourth time, after which he said, "Tell me exactly what information you need and I'll get it for you". "Thank you very much, Sir," I said and I meant every word this time, and I added quickly "Please can you get it before the briefing at 12 o'clock?"

For the next half hour the scrambler phone next to my right hand was silent. There was no reply and there was nothing I could do but wait. I had gone as high as I could and the A.O.C. was the only person who had taken me seriously. Surely he would instruct someone to follow up my request.

Just after 11:30 am, 3 Group rang again; the grumpy Group Captain was returning the call. He read out the information I had requested and said impatiently and irritably: "Is *that* what you wanted?" "That's exactly what I wanted," I replied "The ship *has* been towed to another position, thank you Sir!" The "Sir" was said with great sarcasm, and I hoped that he had not noticed. He said nothing more and put down the phone with a slam again.

When the squadron arrived over Le Havre that afternoon, the *Ole Weger* was found exactly where yesterday's more recent photo had shown it. The operation was a complete success and all our aircraft returned safely. Inwardly, I felt that I had had a very small hand in the success of the day's events. I hoped that the men who had spent so long repairing the ship had been transferred to the needy causes of another vessel, but such were one's chances in time of war.

Maybe this example of the success of one particular operation may sound very callous to the present generation fifty years later. But it should be remembered that, at the time, Britain was fighting for her life and freedom. Two of our greatest allies were the English Channel and the North Sea. More than a couple of years earlier after the evacuation from Dunkirk, we had little else on our side. With the exception of the people of Italy, who were Germany's reluctant allies, and the neutral countries of Switzerland, Sweden, Spain and Portugal, all of Europe was overrun by the Nazi invaders, from Norway and Denmark in the north, to Poland in the east. In the west, the countries of Holland, Belgium and France had fallen to the tyranny of an enemy that terrorized all in its path. Until our Allies in the U.S. came to our aid, first with arms and then with their fighting men, Britain, together with her volunteers from the Dominions and enemy-occupied countries, was battling alone for freedom from the threat of an

invasion of her shores, the only country left not occupied by Hitler.

Winter was almost over and early signs of spring
were all around us. The sodden fields were drying
up, and the farmers would soon have their tractors
busy on the untilled ground. The weather was dry
and pleasant and soon the race to plough and plant
began. The fen district in which we resided was
given over mostly to growing vegetables and sugar
beet. At a time when cane sugar had to be transported in convoys across the Atlantic, it was, needless to say, on the lowest priority list, if on the list at
all. Therefore, much of the land around us provided
us with the only type of sugar we were likely to see
for a long time. The farmers' work in the fields was
soon completed.

The weather had been good and all that they
wanted now was a good rain to encourage the
growth of the much-needed future harvest. Instead,
the warm sunny weather continued to be more suitable for the holiday-maker. Then, one day, a warm
wind which, during the morning grew stronger and
stronger, ended up by midday a gale force phenomenon. The recently seeded powdery soil was
sucked up into the air until it resembled a desert
sandstorm. It was difficult to see objects at any distance, and everyone and everything was soon covered in a reddish brown dust. We breathed it in our
nostrils and it irritated our ears, eyes and throats. I
left the comparative clean air of the house to ride
my bicycle to the Ops. Room for the 1 pm shift, but
ended up pushing my two-wheeler all the way
against the boisterous wind and the swirling dust.

All the people I passed on the way along had their heads down and were holding on to their hats. As we glanced briefly at each other in passing, I noticed that their faces looked deeply sunburnt, and their bloodshot eyes peered out through sockets surrounded by encrusted brown layers of dust. On arrival, I had to retire to the washroom to remove the layers of soil from my face and hands, and to shake out my clothes. By the next day, the wind had died down, but the fields for miles around were bare and denuded of seed of any kind. The farmers had to start the cycle all over again.

It was around this time that I realized how little I knew about the "Ventura" aircraft. I had not the slightest idea what one looked like inside, yet the Duty Ops. Officer was the first person to receive detailed target information for an operational mission. I decided to ask the C.O. when he next came into the Ops. Room, if he would give me permission to fly occasionally on cross-country exercises. In this way, I hoped to appreciate a little better what the air crews might be confronted with on a real mission. Just knowing where the pilot and navigator sat, the position in the fuselage of the wireless operator, and the isolated position of the rear gunner/ bomb aimer, would help me to understand more, the tasks they were asked to carry out at the briefing. I longed to do some map reading which, with no opportunity of interpreting aerial photos any more, seemed to me to be the most logical way to help to fill in the void. I wanted to see some aerial photographs in reality. My only experiences of flying had been before the war when I travelled to Jersey during my school holidays in the summer, at first in a seven-passenger plane, and later in a more up-to-date fourteen-seater aircraft. There was no airfield there then, and we used to land on the beach in St.Aubin's Bay at low tide. Occasionally, we had to make a few circuits while waiting for the tide to go out, when the sand was not sufficiently dry for us to land on. Arriving by air was always a highlight of the holiday.

The men in our Intelligence section were permitted to fly whenever they wished, and on rare occasions, they were allowed as observers on operational flights, thus giving them the experience of flying on an operational mission. The next day when the C.O. visited the Ops. Room, I took the opportunity to ask his permission to fly. He gave it without demur, and a few days later I climbed into a Ventura for a cross-country flight.

First, I was given a tour of the cockpit, navigator's table, and wireless ops. paraphernalia (of which I understood nothing) and a glimpse of the rear-gunner's isolated and cramped quarters. Confidently, I settled down for take-off as I was to fly with one of the most experienced pilots on the station, a Wing Commander with three tours of operations (ninety sorties) behind him. In 1943, his record was almost unique. He had also collected a D.S.O. and D.F.C. and bar on the way along.

As we rose in the air I looked down and saw Feltwell as on one of our aerial photographs, except that this time it was in colour. We had plenty of pictures of enemy airfields in our files, but this was the first time I had seen the layout around my temporary home. For about three-quarters of an hour, we flew over the flat countryside to an area near Daventry where a high radio tower dominated the scenery. I was quickly to become familiar with the ground beneath me. We circled the beacon while "Sparks" practised his radio skills for another hour. This was all rather dull and disappointing, and not quite up to the standard I had expected. To make things worse, my head was beginning to swim from the continuous circling, and I wished they would turn and go the other way round!

Our pilot was also bored, so the moment he got the O.K. to return to base, he put down the nose of the aircraft and dived steeply with great enthusiasm. He levelled off just before we reached *terra firma*. By that time I had almost passed out. The speed was too much for me; I knew I would never make a pilot! The next thing I remember clearly, was hedge-hopping over the permitted low-flying area - he took hedge-hopping literally. We skimmed over meadows, scattering the cows as they ran for the protection of the hedgerows. We shot up a train, then rose suddenly to clear the tips of the trees in the woodlands ahead, and then dropped again over the open fields. I hoped all the telegraph poles were of uniform size and that he knew the height of them.

We shot across a farmyard full of cows herded together outside the barn ready for milking, and caused pandemonium. The racket of our unheralded arrival brought the farmer from his house. He showed his gratitude to the RAF by shaking his fists as our shadow passed. He must have had a hard time milking those panic-stricken animals that evening. I hoped that nobody could identify our aircraft and so lodge a complaint. That would have been the end of my cross-country flights, which had only just begun. By this time I was thoroughly enjoying the experience, as the crew pointed out places and things of interest as they came upon us in rapid succession; map reading was out of the question! There was no doubt we had a superb pilot, and I realised that it was with some of the skills he was displaying now, that he had survived ninety operational sorties. I hoped that his good luck as well as his ability to handle the aircraft would continue until we landed back at Feltwell. After returning to the WAAF Mess, I was asked how I had enjoyed the afternoon. "Very much," I replied, and kept quiet about the details.

I was reliving this recent experience while sitting at my desk in the Ops. Room one morning, for there was little else to do. The log book was relatively empty and the switchboard in front of me was unusually quiet. To-day was a stand-down for our squadrons. The normal air of activity was missing, as the air crews were given a day of freedom to do exactly what they pleased. The Squadron Leader in charge of Intelligence came into the Operations room. "News is beginning to trickle down from above," he said. "What news?" I asked. "News about the future invasion of Europe", he replied. "I've been informed that I will be joining the British Expeditionary Force once it has a foothold in Europe, and I am permitted to choose the staff I want to go with me. Would you like to come along?" he asked. That was a sudden and unexpected question on an otherwise uneventful day. He continued, "You'd be most useful with your knowledge of photo interpretation. How about it?" I was delighted and accepted without another thought.

For the next ten days, I imagined myself somewhere on the other side of the Channel behind the front line - not too close I hoped - on a re-occupied airfield with plenty of interesting work coming in, and being flooded with aerial photos to interpret. My morale was way up.

Eleven days later, the rug was pulled out from under my feet. The reply came back from the Air Ministry, stating in no uncertain terms that women were not permitted to go! My only consolation to such news was that I had been on the temporary list of the B.E.F. for ten days. I was pleased that I had been asked. At the time it was a real let-down, but looking back fifty years later and fifty years wiser, I am thankful that my wishes were thwarted, and I wonder now how I could have been so enthusiastic. Was it the lack of fear that accompanies the young, or the lack of imagination and common sense, or just loyalty to the country and the cause? Whichever it was, I know now that the powers-that-be made a very wise decision by keeping women away from places and situations where they would have been more trouble than they were worth.

Generally speaking, the work of a WAAF, no matter what her work or rank, was to perform tasks normally carried out by men, thus freeing them for air-crew and front-line duties. I think that is what most women succeeded in doing successfully during

World War II. As for myself, I was never sent far afield. After leaving Bomber Command, I spent my time successively on three completely different types of operational airfields within 3 Group in the area of East Anglia until the end of hostilities.

Some days later, I was sitting bemusing my fate, while eating a leisurely supper, when my eyes wandered to the clock on the wall. It was 7.45 p.m. and I was due on the night watch at 8 o'clock. Hastily, I gulped down the last few mouthfuls of dinner and left my share of dessert to whosoever wanted it. I went upstairs to collect the trivia I wished to take with me and ran out of the house. Pedalling more quickly than usual, I arrived in front of the main door to our building in record time. Having secured my bicycle in the rack, I reached the bottom of the flight of steps on the dot of 8 p.m. Phew! I'd made it! I started to climb the steps to the main door. "Password?" said the armed sentry. In my effort to arrive on time, I had completely forgotten the all-important word. "Oh," I replied, "for the moment, I've forgotten it, let me think," I said playing for time. "Sorry, Ma'am" came the reply. "Can't you let me in?" I asked. "It may sound stupid, but I made up the password myself this morning. Now I can't remember which word I chose. "Sorry," came the reply. "How about asking someone inside to go and fetch the Duty Ops. Officer to come out and identify me," I suggested, "Otherwise, she may be in for a long wait." He looked in quickly through the open door and then said, "There's nobody about in there and I can't leave my post to find anyone. Sorry, Ma'am." This was quite a dilemma. Really, I suppose, only a "storm in a tea cup", but for the moment I was stumped. I had no choice but to stand on the steps, denied permission to walk through the door.

Then suddenly, as easily as I had forgotten the word, in a flash I remembered it. "HEDGEHOG!!" I almost shouted at him. "Pass, Ma'am," said the guard, jumping quickly to attention and giving me a smart salute. I was covered with confusion and embarrassment. "Hedgehog is quite a prickly word, isn't it? Particularly when you can't remember it" I commented lamely. But he was not in a mood for conversation or weak jokes. He just gripped his rifle firmly and waited for me to disappear inside. With what little dignity I could muster, I bade him goodnight, walked rapidly up the steps and dived quickly through the open door.

I was on morning duty a few days later when the C.O. entered the Ops. Room, and holding the door open, stood aside for his guest, a tall and imposing figure, to go ahead. I quickly noted the rank of the officer who, unescorted, strode smartly across the room and up to my desk. I rose from my chair and, as I stood facing him, I could not miss seeing the pilot's wings and rows of medal ribbons on his breast pocket, for they were just at my eye level. While trying to decide whether I should say, "Good morning, Sir" or just keep quiet, I looked up, a little flustered, into the penetrating eyes of Air Chief Marshal Sir Hugh Dowding, G.C.B, G.C.V.O, C.M.G, and the Air Officer Commanding Fighter Command during the Battle of Britain. He solved my dilemma at once, for he had no time to waste. "Are you the Duty Ops. Officer?" he asked briskly.

"Yes, Sir," I replied, his question saving me from having to decide on the right protocol. Without more ado, he gave me an on-the-spot oral exam, asking me questions in rapid succession about my work and how I would handle it under unusual conditions. He grilled me for about five minutes, then, indicating that he was satisfied, turned round and marched out again. It was then that I noticed the C.O. still waiting by the door at the far end of the room. I thought that he looked almost as nervous as I felt at that moment. I was glad that I had not let him down.

The next day, when I asked my colleagues if they had been subjected to similar treatment, neither they, nor my friends or acquaintances, even knew that that powerful personality, Sir Hugh Dowding, had visited Feltwell the day before. I guessed that, by the apparent unease of the C.O., the Air Chief Marshal had dropped in on an unheralded inspection to check up on the organization, administration and general working efficiency of the station, and of its Commanding Officer in particular.

Not long after my name had been deleted from the "B.E.F." list, another unexpected thing happened. The Squadron Leader walked into the Ops. room one morning and explained that he was supposed to attend a three-week course for Senior Intelligence Officers, but he was unable to go, and would like to send me instead! "But I'm not a senior officer and there is no promotion in my job," I answered. "Don't worry," he said, "You can go as my representative. I'll fix up for someone to take your place while you're absent." I felt very honoured.

About a week later, I took the train to London and arrived at Kenwood Towers, a very large house in the expensive area of Highgate in north London. A long wing had been added to the mansion for extra bedroom accommodation, and the beautiful trees and gardens of the stately home of Kenwood House graced the other side of the road. A few hundred yards down the hill there was a barrage balloon site, manned by WAAF. The fat, bloated and ugly silver-coloured balloon protected our area from dive bombers as it hovered at varying heights up to about 3,500 ft. Other balloons were dotted around in the vicinity, flying at different levels. These big blobs in the sky protected us on clear days from low-flying enemy aircraft that might try to make a low-level attack.

On the day I arrived at Highgate, we all gathered in the lounge for sherry before going to dinner. This was an elegant affair in luxurious surroundings, quite unlike the usual assembly in the RAF Mess. There was something to be said for slipping in with the senior ranks! Among the twenty-five to thirty people present, I noted that they were wearing a variety of uniforms - Army, Navy and Air Force, several of which bore the insignia of countries still occupied by the Nazis.

I felt very much at ease, despite being the only girl on the course, and I was treated with equality until the second day. The lecturer of the previous morning was in the classroom continuing where he left off, and was illustrating a mock interrogation, using very colourful language. He gave the impression of being a tough and merciless character, who would stop at nothing to get the answers he wanted. I would not have enjoyed being interviewed by him, and might have fallen to pieces under his interrogation. Suddenly, he noticed me in the group, stopped in mid-sentence, spluttered and said, "Since when did they start sending women on this course?" He appeared very embarrassed, then looked at me and said that he would try to watch his language in future. His resolve did not last long and, from the way he continued, it was obvious that we were not being treated to a watered-down version of his lectures. My presence had not spoilt anything for the other participants. I learned a lot about the organization and enjoyed the freedom from night duties for three weeks.

A naval Captain occupied the desk next to mine during lectures. He was a pleasant and approachable man, senior in both age and rank to the rest of us, and wiser and more mature than any of us. He wore the insignia NORWAY on his shoulder. One day I asked him if he knew Bjerke, the Norwegian architect with whom I had worked at Medmenham. "Oh, yes!" he exclaimed, "I know him very well. We escaped from Norway together in the same small fishing boat, and landed in Scotland a few days later." Now, I understood how Bjerke had been so successful in his escape from his homeland. With good planning, lots of luck, and a four-ring Captain as skipper of the tiny craft, how could he have failed?

The sessions continued to be fascinating and were designed to put us in the general picture of what went on behind the scenes. Under normal circumstances, it would not have been permitted to discuss with others, any of the subjects mentioned on the course, unless they were directly pertaining to one's own work. Here we were given an overall view which helped us to put the jigsaw together. The next lecture began with challenging words: "Try to imagine that your aircraft has crashed and that you have just landed on French soil with your parachute trailing behind you. Assuming that you have not been seen by the enemy, how would you go about trying to find your way home again?" Quiet murmurs circulated in the classroom, but suggestions were not forthcoming. Slowly, the group came to the conclusion that it would be almost impossible without help. That was when the cardboard boxes on the desk were opened one by one, as we inspected the numerous Escape Aids. This was the first time since coming to Highgate that I was sure of what was coming next, for we distributed these souvenirs to our flying personnel. A penknife, designed to hang from a belt, included a pair of pliers, one very strong cutting blade, plus several saw-toothed blades capable of hacking through prison bars. The first blade could be used to cut wood chips for a fire, chop up stolen vegetables from the fields and serve generally as does every Boy Scout knife. The pliers could cut through barbed wire, the saw-tooth blades, small as they were, were very powerful for their size , but everyone hoped to return to base with them still new and shining. ( I still have one of these penknives, which my husband finds very useful when we go on camping trips, and for doing odd jobs around the house.)

We were shown waterproof silk maps the size of a handkerchief, just large enough to give general directions, landmarks, main roads, rivers and railways. Most innocuous of all were the brass uniform buttons, in appearance the same as those worn on all RAF and WAAF jackets. Each button had a minute compass embedded within it. Whereas all regular buttons were moulded in one piece, these were hollow and unscrewed at the neck to retrieve the compass. After a while, the Germans discovered this fact, so the British decided to continue to issue the buttons, but with the thread unscrewing in the opposite direction. It took the Germans another six months to find out that they had been fooled again! Maybe one of them was left-handed!

Emergency rations were squeezed tightly into a small pack, small enough to be stowed in a uniform jacket pocket. The contents comprised many of the things a kid would love - a tube of condensed milk, a chocolate bar, malted milk tablets, pills for purifying water, and Benzedrine tablets to keep one awake for twenty-four hours or more beyond one's normal sleeping hours. Benzedrine was used in an emergency only, as the end result meant one or two days of heavy sleep afterwards to overcome fatigue.

We listened to stories of escapes, most of which were better than fiction. One amusing escape story stands out in my mind. After having to bail out from his fighter aircraft in broad daylight, one of the aircrew of a disabled aircraft floated down to earth, his parachute clearly marking his decent. As he came closer to the earth, he noticed a farmer driving a horse drawn-wagon, piled with hay, along a country road. The pilot drifted nearer to land and the wagon drew closer to the pilot. Suddenly the descending figure made landfall on top of the wagon! Speedily he pulled in the strings of the parachute and drew the now lifeless piece of silk towards him. Rolling it up as small as possible, he burrowed into the hay, clutching his crumpled lump of white cloth, and disappeared from sight.

The farmer continued his journey at a leisurely pace as though nothing had happened until he reached the farmhouse. It was probably one of the few occasions that members of the Underground Movement had no need to obtain absolute proof of the genuine identity of the escapee before helping him. Members of the local Underground always had to be extremely cautious as Stool Pigeons, German informers, were very active in the area, and were responsible for the betrayal of many courageous people.

Our various speakers continued discussing communications, organization, interrogation, sabotage and other related subjects. They illustrated how escapees made their way back home, and gave examples of some of the innovative tricks that made the difference between a successful escape and a long stint in a German prison camp. Our fearsome interrogator gave real life examples of how one could play bat and ball between two prisoners kept in separate cells, each of whom was unaware of the other's capture, but who shared the same knowledge. The interrogator would go back and forth from one cell to the other, displaying whatever new knowledge he had acquired to each prisoner in turn. It gave a false impression that the British knew everything already. This often lowered the resistance of a prisoner in holding back information of which he mistakenly thought his interrogator was already aware. The Germans played the same game with us, but often added physical torture to the mental agony.

One of the most useful and reliable methods of communication with the occupied countries was by wireless transmitters. These were supplied to the agents and underground organizations by the British - but more details later. Another interesting form of communication which was of a non-technical nature, required no spare parts. Neither was there any risk of it being picked up on the enemy's radio homing devices that so often pinpointed some of our best wireless operators and their hideouts. Only a handful of grain kept this "machine" in working order - the carrier pigeon!

Tourists who visit London usually make a trip to Trafalgar Square. There, the National Gallery and Canada House face the fountains in the Square and Lord Nelson high up on his column. Many visitors take home a souvenir photograph of themselves. In it, they are seen feeding the pigeons, perched on their heads and shoulders, and surrounded by many more birds fighting for the fallen grain at their feet. Could there possibly be a more suitable place for these birds to alight than the roof of a top-floor office of the Air Ministry overlooking the Square? There, the homing pigeons would land and await the removal of the messages which had been strapped to them. A few birds, whose colour might vary slightly from the others, would never cause a passer-by to notice anything unusual. This is how these minute flying members of the RAF unknowingly carried vital information for the allies.

Highgate was not far from Hampstead where my grandmother lived, so while I was staying nearby, I decided to go and see her. My visit would be one of those where I just turned up, for she had no telephone and did not want one, but I knew that she would be at home. Now that she was almost blind, she seldom, if ever, went out. My two aunts, who still lived at home, cared for her, one having given up her career at the Air Ministry to do so. It was not going to be a very exciting evening, for nothing ever seemed to happen to them for us to talk about. The conversation usually turned into a monologue given by myself, as they looked forward to my visits and was always anxious to hear the family news.

After dinner one evening, I walked to the cold and windy bus stop and, almost immediately, the bus turned up. I climbed up the stairs of the red double-decker, and sat in the front seat as I began my journey. I tried to think of what we were going to talk about when I arrived, but my mind was blank. I had not seen my family for a while, had no recent news of them, and I was not permitted to talk about my work. That left only the topics of the weather and my aunts' and grandmother's health. The bus rattled along, stopping every few minutes to pick up or to drop off passengers. Soon we neared my stop; I rang the bell and hurried down the stairs. As I alighted from the bus, I was still no nearer a solution. I would just have to hope for inspiration when I arrived.

After a short walk up the hill, I reached my grand-mother's house. I went up the steps, rang the bell, and waited ready to receive the sincere, but polite and restrained, welcome. Good manners were far more important to them than an exuberant greeting. The door opened and my aunts ushered me quickly into the hall, darkened in accordance with the blackout regulations. Then, the door was shut and the lights were put on again.

Both of my aunts were surprisingly cheerful as they took my coat from me. Instead of going straight in to the sitting room to greet my grandmother, I was taken upstairs. They had something to show me, and they could not wait to do so. I wondered why they were so full of life tonight. We went in to my grandmother's bedroom, and above the bed I saw a huge hole in the ceiling, about five or six feet in di-ameter. It was charred and black around the edges, and was a rather disturbing sight. "Well, what do you think of that?" asked my aunt Alice proudly. "It looked just like a beautiful chandelier when it hap-pened," she said adding, "You should have seen the sparks as they blazed upwards." "Was it an incendi-ary?" I enquired. "Yes, and it stuck half-way through the ceiling. We got mother downstairs at once, then ran next door to phone the fire brigade - the fire engine arrived almost immediately. The firemen were wonderful," she said admiringly. "There was another bomb burning the gate beside the house, and two more were flaming away in the back garden," said her sister, Ethel. I was shocked to think how close they had been to losing their home and maybe their lives, but my two aunts were more cheerful than I had ever seen them before. They seemed proud of having experienced some of the dangers of war and survived. Like so many Londoners, they had shown that they could "take it".

"Tell me! What happened?" I asked tentatively, but this question was totally unnecessary. They could not wait to tell me more. The house had been in the path of a line of incendiary bombs dropped during an air raid one night. Only the speedy arrival of the fire engine had saved their home. Aunt Alice, at this stage, added to the story. "Do you know," she said," it was my birthday and we had a wonderful party. When the fires had been put out, we sat round the kitchen table at 2 o'clock in the morning with all the brave firemen and had tea and enjoyed my birthday cake. It was a most exciting beginning to my birthday."

The hole in the roof was quickly repaired, but it was a long time before the ceiling was fixed. I need not have been concerned about the lack of family news during that visit. No time remained to report anything about my family. I left my aunts' home later that night full of admiration for two middle-aged ladies who, so unexpectedly, came up to scratch, and far beyond it, at a time when their courage and strength were so sorely tried.

Three weeks flew by and it was time to report back to our units and stations. The type of work each of us carried out was the only aspect of the course we never discussed, but we left Highgate with a good idea of the duties to which many of us would be returning. It was a sunny day when we departed; the familiar shiny blobs of barrage balloons were flying at varying heights around us. Whether they succeeded in warding off any air attacks, I do not know, but we had been lucky during our stay. Not once did we receive a visit from the German Luftwaffe.

Back at Feltwell when it was my turn for Sunday night duty, I often stopped at the little RAF chapel for Evensong on the way along. It was a bright and cheerful little church with its many windows. The interior light oak was clean and simple against the off-white walls. The colours applicable to the day in the church calendar adorned the altar and, together with the Union Jack and the Air Force flag hanging from the walls, it was a colourful yet peaceful and quiet retreat. Needless to say, it did not enjoy run-of-the-mill popularity. Usually there were no more than nine or ten of us at the Service.

Each time I went, a different group of RAF personnel were there. I remember only one of them who always attended - a young pilot who very seldom missed Evensong. I had not met him in the Ops. Room, nor had I seen him in there at any time. I never spoke to him nor knew his name. One Sunday, however, he was absent from the small group in the chapel. I guessed that he had gone on leave. The following week, he did not turn up either. I hoped that he had finished his thirty operational sorties, and had now been posted elsewhere to a less dangerous job. The next week, I decided to ask the Chaplain what had happened to him. I was concerned as two of our aircraft had not returned to base recently. The answer was what I had feared. His aircraft had been shot down in flames, and he was posted as "Missing, believed Killed". This, one of many similar small incidents, will never reach the pages of the history books, but to his family, his loss was something which changed history for the rest of their lives.

It is memories like this that flood again into our thoughts on Remembrance Day, November 11, when we are reminded of the missing friends we knew well, and some not so well. It was their sacrifice, combined with the anguish of their families that we think of on that day.

## The Royal Observer Corps

I digress, once more, this time to mention a civilian organization that provided valuable information to Intelligence throughout the war - The Royal Observer Corps (ROC). It was formed shortly before the war began, when the possibility of hostilities became a serious probability. The volunteers were given intensive training in aircraft recognition and, therefore, were qualified and ready for service on the day that World War ll was declared.

At Feltwell, a daylight bomber station, we relied on the R.O.C. for visual sightings and other information of approaching enemy aircraft. These trained volunteers were the eyes and ears of our Operations room when our squadrons crossed the English coast on their return from raids over enemy territory. The organization comprised men from all over Britain who were in reserved occupations, such as farmers, fishermen, etc., and men who were not young enough to join the armed services. Many of them

were veterans of the First World War. My uncle,
Frank Earle, had been an Observer in the Royal
Flying Corps (RFC), the predecessor of the RAF.
One of his duties, in World War I, had been to photograph the front line areas of the Somme in northern France, while leaning over the side of an aircraft, tightly clutching a camera in his hands. He
was assigned to take pictures of enemy positions
and, while doing so, had to attempt to avoid the
splashes and streaks of castor oil coming from the
engine of his own aircraft. On returning to base, he
would develop and print the pictures himself. From
the information obtained from these prints, he
would update the front line maps. Many copies of
the revised maps were usually required, and this
caused a problem. He had not been issued with a
printer or duplicator of any kind, and it took too
long to update each map by hand. Being an innovative person, he solved the problem. The small village church and graveyard nearby had been shelled
and bombed beyond recognition. He selected a
grave stone with a high quality grain, which he
found lying in the mud far from its original site. "It
was the closest I could find to a lithographic stone,"
he told me, an enthusiastic lithographer myself. "I
thought that the original owner would not have
minded. In fact, he might even have been pleased to
help!" he added. My uncle drew the maps directly
on to the stone and, from this, he produced as many
copies as he needed.

He succeeded in running a one-man show at his
unit about twenty-five years before our complicated
multi-departmental photo interpretation unit at
Medmenham was in full swing. Whereas he worked

from single photos, we had the added advantage of stereoscopic overlaps which gave a three-dimensional model. His photographic sorties were carried out from a small, slow, one-engined 'plane that flew, sometimes at a few hundred feet, the engine spraying oil over both pilot and observer. Our pictures were taken by sophisticated cameras from a Spitfire flying at 30,000 feet. He completed the whole cycle on his own, from taking the pictures to developing and printing them, then to drawing the new maps on a stone, and reproducing the required numbers of copies. We, on the other hand, had specialized departments for everything. Only after having completed this cycle, was his next step similar to our own. He sent his information by dispatch rider on a motorbike, who had to plough through a sea of mud to reach Headquarters behind the lines. Our information was despatched to the War Office at 8.00 am each morning in a vehicle that travelled along well paved roads to London in time for the daily 10.00 am meeting of the Prime Minister and his aides.

The Observer Corps was an integral part of our defence system during the Second World War, and it was the responsibility of the men of the R.O.C. to recognize all enemy and Allied aircraft coming into their sectors, and report back these sightings immediately to Headquarters. Their observation posts were always situated on the highest land in the area, giving them the best visibility possible in all directions. I visited one of these posts, perched high up on the edge of a cliff face at Fairlight, four miles from Hastings. My uncle, from the day war was declared, took his turn at this post identifying aircraft, both friend and foe. This high, exposed lookout, with near full-circle visibility, put the aircraft spotters in a vulnerable position from the enemy's slap-happy habits with machine-guns. Therefore, they camouflaged their little observation hut and dugout to blend as far as possible with the surroundings.

One of their regular daily visitors was the lone JU 88 bomber of the German Air Force. Its crew would aim short bursts of machine-gun fire at anything moving below that it fancied. The local East Kent busses, painted bright red, were prime targets. The intruder would continue north a few miles inland, then turn south towards Hastings, fly low over the hill behind the town, and swoop down almost to roof level to dive bomb the seaside resort, just as it had done during the early days of the war. With its cannon shells blazing, it would catch unwary shoppers walking along the streets. This entire operation took no more than a few minutes, from the recognition of the enemy aircraft to the release of the bombs; consequently there were many casualties. It always happened so quickly that the air raid warning usually sounded after the raid was over.

Recognising this problem, the responsibility for activating the air raid alarm was shifted from the Hastings Police Headquarters to the little outpost at Fairlight. As soon as the members of the Observer Corps saw the approaching JU 88, they pressed the alarm button to alert Hastings and set off the undulating whine of its sirens. Afterwards, they confirmed their action to the authorities by telephone. It did not stop the bombing, but, with the extra few minutes warning, it reduced the civilian casualties during these attacks. There were still no spare fighters to combat this type of lone raider.

Hastings was a seaside town with no military targets, and its defences comprised mostly gun emplacements and other fortifications designed to ward off an invasion by sea. It was a tourist, not an industrial town, and the single-bomber raids were intended solely to lower morale, and to play on the nerves of the town's inhabitants, mostly hotel-keepers, shopkeepers, fishermen and retired people. Over time, though, these single raiders left behind them a lot of accumulated damage and many related casualties.

During the Battle of Britain, the volunteers of the R.O.C. took over visual identification from the radar, as the enemy approached our coast. The spotters often had to dodge machine-gunning, as they gave a running commentary on the dog-fights taking place above them, and, at the same time, informing headquarters of the numbers and types of aircraft flying in their direction. These civilians deserve great credit for their contribution throughout those difficult years.

# MAY 3, 1943 - A DAY TO REMEMBER

It was a perfect Spring day for early May. The sun shone and the air was fresh and warm, with smells of newly mown grass wafting on the morning breeze. As I made my way to the Ops. Room for the 8 a.m. - 1 p.m. shift, I looked forward to a spin on my bicycle in the countryside during the afternoon. It would be a pleasant outing before returning for the 8 p.m. shift. Some exercise and fresh air in the afternoon always helped me to keep more alert during the early morning hours that followed.

The Ops. Room was a large and dreary place, on ground level, with barred windows and thick opaque glass. One could not see out, and the penetration of light was so weakened, that it made little difference whether the sun shone or not. However, it provided security, particularly during the night hours, when the duty officer was the sole occupant of the whole building, apart from the armed guard outside the front door of the building. I arrived at eight and took over from the night shift. About half-an-hour later, the Squadron Leader in charge of Intelligence dropped in to tell me that I would have to do a twenty-four hour stint today. My relief officer for the 1 p.m. shift had been granted forty-eight hours compassionate leave, and there was nobody else to carry on - so much for the afternoon's outing - I accepted, but made sure to ask for one of his staff to take over for the lunch and supper breaks. Maybe I would be lucky and we would have a stand down, then I could always bring some books to read during the night. It really was not going to be too bad when I thought about it. The scrambler phone rang. It was time to plug in for the daily Group operational broadcast. Duty Ops. officers from all 3 Group stations would hook up and listen in, logging everything that related to their own squadrons.

Feltwell was to carry out a mission today, so under the heading of May 3rd, 1943, I began writing in the log book. After having completed all the pertinent details of the forthcoming raid, right down to the number and type of bombs and their fusing, a counter-order came up. "Hold it!" we were told, "We are changing the target, the Met. men think there may be cloud cover over it." I waited about ten minutes while the Meteorological Office found a more predictable area, and Bomber Command decided where to direct the attack. Half-way through the second broadcast, the same thing happened again - "Cancel the instructions - the weather may deteriorate there also."

By this time, the log book was filling up rapidly, giving the impression of our having had a very active morning, but, so far, no real decisions had been made at all. This type of behaviour at Group was quite out of character, and, to my knowledge, had never happened before. I waited about another five minutes, when a third alternative came up. After I had written down all the given details of the proposed raid, I asked: "Would it be an idea to wait ten minutes before passing on the information, just in case it is scrubbed again?" "No," I was told, "this one holds firm."

The target chosen finally was a power station near Amsterdam, and Feltwell's New Zealand Squadron 487 was to fly on a daylight mission to put the power station out of action. Power of any kind was in desperately short supply in Europe, and any disruption would not only be highly inconvenient to the production of all industrial plants within the area, but would also help to slow down their war effort. I passed the information to the Commanding Officer and to the appropriate sections and departments. Later the participating flying crews were briefed, and it was time for lunch.

Nobody remembered that I was hungry. So after calling the Intelligence Office, the boss came down and took over for my lunch break. He thought that he could easily persuade the cooks at the RAF Officers Mess to give him a late meal, whereas in our small Mess, there would likely have been no food left if I was not on time. So I went first, and after a quick meal, I returned to the Ops. Room. In the early afternoon, 487 Squadron took off. Thirteen Venturas left the airfield, with instructions for No.13, a backup for the squadron, to return to base after reaching the English coast if all was well with the other twelve aircraft. He returned to base as instructed, and the wait began.

This was always a tense time, as we noted the estimated times of crossing the English coast, making landfall over the enemy shoreline, and then the estimated time of arrival over the target. Soon after the aircraft had made their rendezvous over the target, we would begin to relax as the squadron turned for home again. After they had braved and survived the flak in the target area, they also had another unpleasant hurdle to cross, as they passed over the enemy coast on their way out to sea. Fighters and anti-aircraft guns were always a potential danger, until our aircraft were well away from the enemy shore.

As the squadron had to keep radio silence until close to base, we were always kept completely in the dark, until the Observer Corps reported visual sightings of aircraft returning over the English coast. Radar picked them up first, but it was spotters of the Observer Corps who reported the numbers and identity of the aircraft as soon as they came into view. But on that particular day, the Observer Corps did not appear to be up to its usual standard.

The spotters were more than five minutes late in relaying any information of our aircraft crossing the English coast. Maybe, the squadron had been delayed with flak on the other side? I waited, but, when about ten minutes had gone by and the telephone was still silent, I broke the normal routine. As they had not rung me, I rang the Observer Corps instead. "Have you spotted any of our Venturas?" I asked. "No we've seen nothing" came the answer. "Is the visibility good on the coast?" I enquired. "Yes, quite clear, but we have seen nothing." "Will you please call us immediately you sight them, as they are over ten minutes late now?" I asked them.

Very soon, the telephone rang and, with relief, I heard a member of the Observer Corps at the other end of the line. "One damaged Ventura is crossing the coast, heading in your direction," the voice said. "Only one?" I questioned, "There should be eleven more!" "There's nothing approaching us yet" he said, "but we'll keep a sharp look out."

I rang Group Captain Kippenburger, the C.O., "Please sir," I said "Can you come to the Ops.Room? I can't explain on the phone." Within a minute or so, he arrived. News of the one lone aircraft was all that I had to report to him. He called up 3 Group to ask if any stragglers had landed elsewhere. As the answer was negative, he put Group in the picture. A little later, Flying Control came on the line; the Captain of the damaged aircraft had radioed as he neared the airfield and had asked for permission to land. He requested fire engines and ambulances to be at the ready. There were two injured crew on board, and the shot up aircraft had an unserviceable undercarriage. The pilot was preparing to make a belly-landing. Flying Control returned his call saying, "Put your aircraft into George (automatic pilot), set it in the direction of the North Sea and bale out!" The pilot replied, "I can't bale out; the wireless operator and gunner are badly injured and can't jump. Please have everything ready. I'm coming in."

The Group Captain spoke briefly to Flying Control, who confirmed that everything was in readiness for landing and that the pilot had jettisoned his surplus fuel. The C.O. next requested that the Captain of the aircraft come round to the Ops. Room as soon as he landed. I think we both wondered if the pilot would be capable of complying with the C.O.'s wishes; we would know in about five minutes.

I was told later that evening that a small crowd had gathered around the perimeter to watch the unfolding drama. But the iron bars and opaque glass, plus the hanger between us and the landing strip, left us with only a running commentary on the telephone to compound our fears.

"They've landed!" was the next comment from Flying Control, and the voice continued, "The kite more or less disintegrated at touch-down, but, so far, it has not caught fire. The fire hoses have been activated, and the ambulances have almost reached the aircraft. I don't think it will blow up now." The phone went down with a click. They had conveyed their message, and now had more important things to do. Once again the C.O.'s role had been reduced to silent waiting. There was nothing worth saying that would help, so we both kept very quiet. The phone rang again as more news began to trickle through from Flying Control. "The injured men have been placed in ambulances; the Medical Officer thinks that they will be OK; he is just leaving with them for the hospital at Ely," the voice said. The phone died once more.

As soon as he had seen his wireless operator and gunner safely off on their bumpy twenty-mile journey to Ely, the Captain of the only aircraft, up till now, to return to base from a squadron of twelve, left for the Operations room. He walked in looking pale and shaken, yet outwardly composed and completely under control. He came up to my desk where the Group Captain was standing, waiting by the scrambler phone.

"What happened?" the C.O. asked. "It was the fighters. They were everywhere," the pilot replied. "How many fighters were there?" the C.O. enquired. "I don't know, Sir. They were everywhere," the pilot repeated, "They came on us suddenly, and they were all over the place."

"Did you see any of ours go down?" asked the Commanding Officer. "Yes. Two or three, and I saw a few parachutes too. I think some of them managed to break through the fighters and continue on to the target," the pilot replied.

"Where were you?" the C.O. continued. "We were hit early on; just before crossing the Dutch coast. The aircraft was damaged; the wireless operator and gunner were injured. So, our only hope was to jettison the bomb load, and try to make it back to base," he replied.

"Were you followed?" he was asked. "No," the pilot responded. "They were too busy attacking the others, and I think they thought I wouldn't make it back home anyway. My navigator was unhurt, so he kept me on course, in between attending to the injured crew - he did a wonderful job."

The questioning ended for the moment. The C.O. rang Group and repeated every detail of the pilot's account. When he had finished, he said, handing the scrambler phone to the pilot, "They want to hear it all in your own words." The pilot picked up the scrambler and, in a quiet but clear voice, recounted his experience all over again.

The Group Captain had another conversation, this time very brief, with Group Headquarters. Then apologising, he turned to the Captain of the ill-fated aircraft and asked if he would mind telling it once more to the A.O.C (Air Officer Commanding) 3 Group. At this point, I would have given anything to have been able to offer the young pilot a cup of tea and a chair to sit on; but I had neither. He would have to relive the last few hours, for the third time, in a little over half an hour.

There was yet one more discussion with our C.O. and 3 Group, after which he handed back the phone to me. He turned to the pilot and asked," Would you mind waiting a little longer? They may want to ask you some more questions."

"How much more could he stand?" I wondered. I had never seen anyone behave with such courage and control so closely before. After the last request from Group, we just waited, while the C.O. continued to speak calmly to the Captain of the aircraft. The Group Captain's quiet manner and obvious compassion under extreme circumstances showed up our C.O. as a leader worthy of the greatest respect. After about ten minutes, the scrambler rang again. The caller asked to speak to the C.O. I handed him the phone once more, and he had another brief conversation with Group Headquarters.

He turned to the Ventura pilot with a kind and admiring look, and said gently, "You have just been awarded an immediate D.F.C. (Distinguished Flying Cross)." The pilot looked stunned, then, mumbling his thanks, asked, "But what about my navigator?"

"He'll be getting a gong (medal) too," the C.O. assured him.

At last, the newly-decorated airman was free to go. He left alone, and walked through the door without looking back. Group Captain Kippenburger, after speaking to me for a few minutes, left as well. Suddenly, the room was very quiet and the telephones no longer rang. On the large blackboard, on the wall opposite my desk was the only reminder of the day's events. On it was displayed a list of twelve aircraft and, beside each, the name of the pilot who flew it. In the next column the take-off time was chalked-in, and, in the last column, was the time of return of the one damaged Ventura. As for the rest, at this late hour, they would all have run out of fuel. The Observer Corps had seen nothing, and none of our aircraft had been reported as landing elsewhere. I sank down in my chair, with a sudden deep feeling of weariness and helplessness. My eyes focussed on the Sgt. Watchkeeper. I handed her the chalk and watched as she walked silently up to the blackboard which covered most of the opposite wall. In the last column headed "Landed", the time of the returning aircraft, she filled in the empty spaces and wrote eleven times the word "MISSING".

I had not noticed the passage of time, until one of the Intelligence officers entered to give me a dinner break. Was it so late? I had no desire to eat anything, but was glad to get out of the building into the fresh air. Arriving back at the WAAF Mess, I sat down at the dining table, determined to eat something, telling myself that it would be more than another twelve hours before I would have breakfast.

Joining the others at the table, I was immediately bombarded with questions, "Are they true - the rumours that are going around? Have we really lost most of the squadron? What has happened? Surely *you* must know!" I had to confirm that the rumours were correct. "Is there a chance that some might still return?" "No! Not now!" I answered. "However, a few parachutes were seen descending, so we are hoping that some of the crews will make it to safety. It may take weeks before we know who the prisoners-of-war are," I added.

Seldom had anyone been that eager to see me in the WAAF Mess before, and the circumstances hardly made it flattering. None of us had been dating any of the missing airmen so, at least, we were spared personal grief. A navigator, with whom I had recently shared a friendship and a love of music, but, fortunately, not a close relationship, had already swapped his digs at Feltwell for a German prison camp. In those uncertain times I felt it would be very unwise to become involved too seriously in something that might end suddenly. I always enjoyed a date, but tried to keep friendships from becoming too personal. The thought of becoming a war widow was more than I could bear. Maybe this was wise thinking, maybe not; but it was how I saw it at the time. Had I not been fortunate enough to have met my husband after hostilities had ceased, I might have regretted my way of thinking. But I entered into a happy marriage, without having to fear for my husband's life every time he left the house. It is a blessing for which I shall always be deeply grateful.

On that disastrous day, I picked at my food, then collected my belongings for the night, and returned to the Ops. Room to take over the night shift. All the Intelligence Office staff were already there. We became a very close and cohesive group that evening, as we discussed the day's events late into the night. We all put forward many questions, but came up with no answers. None of us knew of any operational sortie in which an entire squadron had been annihilated on its way to the target. Had our top secret information been divulged to the enemy? For some reason, the German fighters were ready and waiting in large numbers for our squadron as it neared the enemy coast. That much we knew, but it was all we had to go on.

We changed the topic to Squadron Leader Len Trent, the leader of the eleven missing aircraft. If he were alive, what would his position be? There seemed to be only two extreme alternatives. If, in some way, he had endangered his squadron by poor judgement or lack of leadership at the critical moment, he was liable to be court-martialled. On the other hand, if, despite the heavy fire from so many unexpected German fighters, he had managed to penetrate the enemy barrage, fly through it, and reach the target, surely he deserved the Victoria Cross for extraordinary courage and leadership. It seemed certain to us that, if he had pressed on to the target, it would have been with the full knowledge that it would be a one-way trip for him. We all hoped fervently that he would get the VC, and live to receive it .A few weeks later, we received news of some of the airmen who had jumped to safety, and who were now in German prison camps. Squadron

Leader Len Trent was one of them, and only a short time after hearing that he was a prisoner-of-war in Germany, we were told that he had been awarded the highest honour of all - the Victoria Cross. He was repatriated after the war, and was one of the few recipients of the VC who lived to receive his medal personally. But we had no knowledge of the outcome of these events when the Intelligence staff returned to their quarters well after midnight. I sank back on to the hard wooden office chair, and dozed fitfully in between intermittent 'phone calls, but not one of them shed any light on the events of the previous day.

Next morning, when it was time to hand over my duties, I was more than ready to leave. Breakfast, bath and bed were high priorities. By the time I had crawled under the blankets and curled up to sleep, the house was quiet. Everybody had left to carry out their various tasks around the station. I closed my eyes, but was soon wide awake and mentally going through the last twenty-four hours again. The more I thought, the more I began to wonder if I could, in some way or other, have been responsible for what had happened. Had I written down anything incorrectly - times, places or whatever else that might have changed the course of events? It had been a most confusing morning yesterday, with so many orders and counter-orders. I knew that I would not sleep well until I had re-read the log book; so I got up, dressed and went for a walk instead.

The responsibilities held by so many junior officers came home to me that day, as I felt the weight of a very heavy burden. There was nobody at the WAAF mess in whom I could confide. The log book alone would give me the answer, and it would be another twenty-four hours before I returned to duty and could read it again.

The following day an official enquiry began into the cause of the disaster. I wondered if I might be called to answer some questions, but nobody said a word to me. The Squadron Leader in charge normally visited the Ops. Room regularly, but he was now too busy with the enquiry. There was also a "stand-down" (no operations) that day, so he had no reason for coming along. In the meantime, I read and re-read the log book, but I could find no discrepancies. There was nothing to do except wait for the results of the enquiry.

The days dragged on. Ten days later, when I could live with the situation no longer, I asked the Squadron Leader how the enquiry was going. "Oh! Didn't anyone tell you? It ended three days ago," he said. "What was the conclusion?" I asked him. He continued, "By pure chance, a squadron of enemy fighters on coastal patrol intercepted our aircraft just as they were approaching the enemy coast. Our Venturas hadn't a hope with their comparatively slow speed and lack of manoeuvrability, plus a full bomb load. It was just a terrible bit of bad luck." There was no way that I could begin to explain what that information meant to me. I said nothing but, from that moment, my life began again.

## Marking Time

A few days after the fateful sortie, Feltwell became a non-operational station. The Venturas were not considered suitable for carrying out strikes in enemy occupied territory any longer, and were later transferred to Coastal Command for less dangerous duties such as coastal patrol work. Only our Radar Squadron continued to operate as it flew sorties close to the enemy coast at night. Its specific activities were kept secret from us, and it worked independently of the Intelligence section of the station.

Within less than a week, we received news from Underground sources that, despite heavy opposition of the enemy fighters, some of our aircraft succeeded in breaking past the German Luftwaffe, and attacked the hydro-electric station with some success. They had done an excellent job, but their one-way trip proved that they were a poor match against the enemy fighters. There was still no news of the aircrews who carried out the strike.

Towards the end of the following week, the gloom, which pervaded us all, lightened, when the King and Queen, King George VI and Queen Elizabeth, later the Queen Mother, visited Feltwell to meet and commiserate with the wives and children of the missing airmen. It was a great event, and one which showed the genuine concern of our Sovereign. At Buckingham Palace in London, where they lived during most of the war, the King and Queen were kept up-to-date with information of any unusual current events, both good and bad. Consequently, they were familiar with the circumstances of the

Feltwell operation, and knew the names of wives and children of the missing crews. They chatted with each of them personally and, when conversation became difficult, the King helped everyone to relax, by joking about the number of times he bumped his head on the roof of the car, as they drove along the twenty miles of pot-holed road from Ely.

It was a very joyful and memorable experience for everyone. Unfortunately, I was on duty and could not join in any of it, although, that evening, it was my turn to sit at the dinner table and ask all the questions. It was exhilarating to hear all the happy and enthusiastic answers.

But the atmosphere at Feltwell changed quickly from a vibrant station, with high morale and a sense of purpose, to one of gloom, waiting for direction. We missed the regular sight and sound of twelve aircraft bursting into life, as they took off from the airfield, one after the other to carry out a mission. Each target destroyed made our country a little stronger, and helped us feel just that bit closer to the end of hostilities and the atrocities that accompanied them in the occupied countries.

Now, the only operational exercises carried out, were by the Special Squadron whose aircraft would come and go individually under the cover of darkness. There was no outward glamour to their activities. They were appreciated by the people who lived in the nearby village for being no more than disturbers of their sleep in the middle of the night. Our C.O. was posted to another operational airfield, and a new Group Captain took his place. The new C.O. was a Regular officer and a specialist in radar and radio communications, but without pilot's wings stitched above his tunic pocket, he was re-garded, at first, with less than the respect he de-served by the flying crews remaining on the Station. At the beginning, his appointment did little to raise morale. He was going to have a hard time proving himself before he was fully accepted. No doubt the members of the radio squadron were the only ones who appreciated his true worth on his arrival. It was a tough assignment for him under the circum-stances, and I wished him well.

The remaining aircrews from Squadrons 21 and 487 were soon transferred to another station for training on Mosquitos - the new fast and light bombers. My boss, the senior Intelligence Officer, a pleasant and capable man, was posted with them, and was replaced by a strange and morose personal-ity. Within a few days I realised that, so far as I was concerned, he was going to be an absolute disaster. I was not at all sure how I was going to cope with the new situation.

During most of my morning duties, the new boss made a habit of entering the Ops. Room. He would wait until I had logged the Group broadcast, and then read the information I had entered. Next, he would tell me bluntly that I was *not* to pass on the instructions. When questioning his order, he would insist that none of them were necessary. Puzzled, I asked if he preferred to contact the people on the list himself. The answer was: "NO!" He appeared mentally unstable. I was concerned and mystified.

Never before had I ignored my superior's orders but he left me no choice. Whenever I picked up the receiver to pass on the information from Group, he promptly removed the telephone from my hand. After a few days, I learned that it was wiser to do nothing until he had left the room. Then, often more than half-an-hour late, I would carry out my specific tasks. I pondered as to whether he could be working for the other side, but dismissed that possibility, for he was not bright enough, and he completely lacked any subtlety. Maybe he was heading for a nervous breakdown, or having his family problems out on me? I was thankful that we were no longer carrying out Ops. or there would surely have been disastrous results.

I asked the other two WAAF Ops. Officers if they were having difficulties with him, they both said that he left them alone. I then considered asking the C.O.'s advice. He was the only person to whom I could impart this knowledge, but, on second thoughts, I rejected the idea. As he had just arrived at the station and knew nothing about me, he would surely come to the conclusion that it was I who was going round the bend, when he heard such strange accusations about the head of my department. I kept quiet and coped as well as I could. I hoped that my new posting would come quickly and so solve the problem, for I was no longer needed at Feltwell. Flying Control could now integrate my present low volume of work with its own. I had no real kindred spirits left in the WAAF mess, and I began to lead a lonely existence. The squadrons had left Feltwell and the Station was marking time, awaiting a new role.

Then, one day, the light shone at the end of the tunnel. I was to be posted to Tempsford, near Bedford. Inquiring from the remaining members of the Intelligence section, I asked if it was in 3 Group, as it was not included in the daily broadcast list. "I guess it is not operational?" I said. One member knew of it, and replied, "Oh yes, it is operational!" to which I answered, "But it does not listen into the daily Ops. broadcast. What does it do?" "You'll see when you get there," he replied, and would say no more. I pressed him further, but his only answer was, "You'll find out when you arrive there." I was just beginning to warm up to the fact that I was moving, when the adjutant rang me and said, "Do you know that you have been given an adverse report?" "A *what*" I exclaimed, "Why?" He sounded sympathetic at the other end of the phone. He knew of no reasons for this report, so I explained that it was probably because I was forced to act against the Squadron Leader's orders, but what else could I do? Had I not done so, people's lives would have been endangered. "Don't worry," he replied, "I'll see what I can find out. I just wanted to make sure that you knew." Next day the adjutant rang again to say "I've made enquiries, and have discovered that you are the fourth consecutive Ops. Officer to have been given an adverse report by this man. I will tell him personally that he will have to sign the report in your presence. I'm sure he won't have the courage to do that; so don't worry!" He was right, and the whole unpleasant business was dropped. Some months later I heard that this particular Intelligence officer had been demoted and sent to India.

At that time of doom and gloom, I had one bright and happy memory to look back on, and it came from a most unexpected source. One morning the new C.O.'s wife introduced herself to me outside the "Waffery". Her house was at the end of the same cul-de-sac, though I had never set eyes on the previous occupant. I was off duty that day, and our conversation ended by my being invited for tea. She was charming and we got on well. Her sister, whose husband was a Group Captain in charge of accounts in the Middle East, was visiting with her two children, a boy of about eight and a girl of six. I met and liked them all, as the invitations were renewed with a pleasant regularity. It was most enjoyable to spend a short time in a relaxed family atmosphere. I doubt if Mrs Crosby knew how much her kindness meant to me at that time.

On the day I was due to leave for Tempsford, I was asked a favour. The children's mother had already left for home, while the kids continued their holiday with their aunt. She asked if I would mind taking the children with me, and putting them on their connecting train for home. We would all change trains at the same station, but each going in opposite directions. They were lovely children, and I was glad to have some small way of saying "Thank You."

Having shared some of the best and worst times in the history of Feltwell, I left, with mixed feelings, in the company of two young children, for a destination about which I knew nothing.

# R.A.F. TEMPSFORD

Late that afternoon, I arrived at the WAAF Officers' Mess at Tempsford. It was an ugly one-story wartime building, easy to erect, and easy to dismantle at the end of hostilities. It definitely spoiled the look of our part of the village, as it had been built close to the Vicarage and the old stone parish church. Our Mess and living quarters were so close in fact, that on one occasion, after an evening dance at the RAF hall next door to us, the WAAF bartender was put on a "charge" (an offence against RAF regulations). She was accused of "getting the Vicar's chickens drunk!" They had wandered in, and had taken a swig or two from the dregs of the slop bucket behind the bar, and the Vicar's wife had complained. The next day at lunch time, the WAAF Admin. Officer told us, in between giggles, of the results of the unlucky bartender's charge. "It was such a ridiculous accusation," she said, " that I had great difficulty trying to keep my face straight. I got all mixed up and accused the offender of getting the 'chickers vickens' drunk. I corrected myself and said, 'the vickens chickers' instead. Then we all exploded into laughter. I admonished the girl, and told her not to let it happen again, and dismissed the case!"

The airfield was one of those built hastily to last for the duration of the war, and one which was returned to pasture immediately afterwards. We lived at the top of a hill, with a road leading down a steep gradient to the airfield, which occupied flat land close to the river. Descending the hill the morning after my arrival, I had a clear view of the runways and layout below, and I looked eagerly for a clue as to the type of aircraft that operated from Tempsford. It was with bewilderment that I saw an odd variety of aircraft of various vintages and sizes. The newest and envied Lancasters were conspicuous by their absence. Sterlings and Halifaxes, probably the most powerful four-engined bombers until the arrival of the Lancaster, were sitting on the tarmac. But whatever were the Hudsons doing there? They were similar in looks and vintage to the Venturas, recently grounded at Feltwell. It was even more surprising when, on rounding a hanger, several small Lysanders came into view, dotted around the perimeter of the airfield. They seemed quite out of place. I recognised them as a reminder of the First World War, more than anything else I had seen since joining the RAF. They were strange, fragile-looking little planes with high wings and sturdy struts holding the wings to the fuselage below. To top it all, they had "spats" covering the wheels, giving them a rather comical and archaic look. Usually, the "Lizzies", as they were affectionately known, functioned mostly doing reconnaissance work at the front line of battle, co-operating with the Army. Whatever were they doing here? What kind of help could this station offer to the war effort, I wondered?

Comprehending nothing, but running wild with imagination, I arrived at the Intelligence section to report for duty. The department comprised a larger group of people than found normally on an operational station. There were about nine of us, which included three WAAF officers, instead of the usual one WAAF officer at similar departments on other stations. The Senior Intelligence Officer introduced me to all the members of the group, and showed me round what appeared to be a very dull Intelligence office. There were plenty of filing cabinets full of "I'm not sure what." The maps pinned on the wall were both few in numbers and uninspiring. They gave no indication as to the reason for the existence of Tempsford. My first impression was that of a mediocre station, full of left-overs, in a forgotten backwater. At breakfast time that morning, the officers in the WAAF mess had been generally vague about the aims of Tempsford, and were genuinely unable to offer me any information at all in answer to my questions. I was given the normal office tour to show me where to find everything and how to get it. Then they produced a cup of something they called coffee. It was one of those drinks that resembled coffee, tea and cocoa all mixed up together but, in those days of rationing, we accepted whatever it was our luck to be given.

"We'll take you to the map room when you've finished," they said casually. The room next door was locked, but they produced a key and, in the company of the Senior Intelligence Officer and a WAAF colleague, I entered the *sanctum*. It was a large room containing a map of Europe, which covered the entire wall opposite the door. On it were hundreds of brightly coloured pins, each holding down a small label with a number and a code name typed on it. "These pinpoints represent the dropping and landing areas for our "Joes" (secret agents) and supplies in occupied Europe. They cover Denmark and Norway, beyond the Arctic Circle, to southern France," I was told. "There are nearly 400 dropping and landing areas in all, and the tags are updated every day." The senior officer continued, "The first landing was made three weeks after the evacuation of Europe from Dunkirk, and the whole organization has grown steadily ever since." No wonder my friend at Feltwell had kept quiet about his knowledge of Tempsford. It would have been a court-martial offence for him to have divulged anything. I read, many years later, that the organization was the brainchild of our Prime Minister, Winston Churchill. The nature of the work carried out on the station was kept so secret, that only those whose job it was to know about it, had any idea of what went on there.

I stared in amazement at the map before me and thought, "If the Germans could set eyes on this wall map, they could surely eliminate the entire Underground Movement in Europe in a week!" To be exposed so unexpectedly and so suddenly to this knowledge was a staggering experience. The Senior Officer went on to explain, "The large four-engined Halifaxes and Stirlings drop both Joes and containers. The Hudsons, two-engined aircraft with roomy fuselages, not only drop agents and containers by parachute, but also make landings in France, ferrying Joes over, and bringing others back to England. The Lysanders are deployed specifically for landing in confined areas, and often take a two-way complement of passengers." He revealed a lot in a short time.

I soon discovered that the airfield at Tempsford was also considered a quiet backwater to the people who lived in the village. Single aircraft would take off in the daytime and return after a cross-country exercise. They saw a variety of shapes and sizes of 'planes - Stirlings, Halifaxes and Hudsons and the little Lysanders that impressed nobody. Those whose aircraft recognition was better than average might have wondered about the small cylindrical appendages fixed underneath the fuselages of the Lizzies. To the local villagers they were familiar silhouettes; therefore the significance of long-range fuel tanks meant nothing.

At night, when Bomber Command was sending larger and larger numbers of aircraft to bomb enemy installations and military targets, our squadrons were silent. Most people in the Midlands and southern England heard the droning of the big Armada, as they lay in their beds at night, and thought of the time when the noise above was coming from the other direction, and with very different results. The tabloids next morning were always full of news about the previous night's attack. Tempsford shared in none of this popularity. Whereas Bomber Command chooses to be active mostly on dark nights, which helped to hide the silhouettes of the aircraft formations, Tempsford, on the other hand, was active during the "moon period" only. At such times, a few aircraft would take off in ones and twos during the night, disturbing the sleep of the locals very little. There was no fanfare of a massed take-off, one after the other, nor for them, the apprehension of waiting and listening for their return. There were no heroic headlines in the newspapers the next morning.

What these people did not see, was the arrival of limousines late at night, or in the early hours. These cars arrived with blinds drawn, so that nobody ever saw the occupants. They ferried the Joes from a large manor house about ten miles away, over their last few miles of English soil, before being flown back to their native lands, to continue the fight for freedom under the noses of the Nazis. The limousines would enter the airfield near the WAAF officers mess at the top of the hill, drive down to the bottom and around the perimeter to the farmhouse, the only original building on the station, and one which outwardly still represented peace and domesticity. It was situated in isolation, far from the normal areas of activity. There, the agents would be delivered to complete their preparations and to get their final briefing, before the journey to their homelands. Could any other farmhouse in Britain have had so many courageous and outstanding people pass through its doors in so short a time?

The Intelligence Section was responsible for briefing the aircrews of the four-engined Sterlings and Halifaxes, and informing them of their particular cargo, but an Army Major from SOE (Special Operations Executive) was the kingpin at the farm, and was responsible for preparing and briefing all the agents. This was going to be an interesting place! But I had to wait for several months before I was taken to the farmhouse to see for myself. Back at the Mess, though, domestic life continued as usual.

During my first week at Tempsford, the "Queen Bee", the senior WAAF Admin. Officer looked hopefully around the breakfast table and smiled at each of us in turn. The others continued eating their toast, avoiding her eyes, but I, being new and gullible, smiled back - it seemed the right thing to do. Putting down her tea cup firmly on the saucer with a loud click, she said "Well! Two people are on leave and we are a bit short of staff. Who would like to volunteer for Dress Parade duty tomorrow? It won't take much of your time." I bit into a large piece of soggy toast and, like the others, looked down at the table cloth and the remnants of the breakfast. It must have been almost a year since I had inspected a dress parade. I was not going to volunteer for this one. "Anyway," I thought trying to find excuses, "whoever won a war on dress parades?" Like the others, I kept silent. "What? Nobody willing to pitch in?" the Flight Officer continued, "I have to do it all the time."

Thankfully, I remembered the day when I had turned down a commission in Admin. I would not have survived in that job at all, I was sure. It was just as well that we all had gifts in different areas. She wasn't giving up. I guess that is what it takes to be a good Admin. Officer. She looked slowly round the table once more, and then hesitated as she glanced at me. She said, "How about you, Doreen? It would be an opportunity for you to see where things are, and how our station is run - you are volunteered!" She said it so pleasantly and having previously welcomed me into the fold, I had no choice but reluctantly to accept; I might need her help one day, and, anyway, I liked what little I had seen of her. "Good," she said. "You are to be at the parade ground for the 8.00 a.m. inspection tomorrow. Look out for the usual things, such as slovenly appearance, hair touching the collar, unpolished buttons, dirty shoes and creased uniforms. You know the sort of thing. The WAAF Sergeant will line the girls up for the morning inspection." she added. "Well! That's a relief," I thought. The rest would be easy. All I had to do was walk down past the lines of girls, accompanied by the Sergeant and, unless anything appeared to be very out of place, tell her to carry on at the end of the inspection.

That day, I made a quick tour of the station on my bicycle, discovering quite a lot about its geography, and, most important of all, finding the parade ground. The following morning, I had breakfast in the dining room alone - more than half an hour earlier than the others. I had the choice of eating before the parade, and going straight to the office early, or cycling up the hill again after the parade was over and eating a hurried meal. I decided on the former and, making sure on this occasion that my own shoes and buttons were a pride to the Air Force, I pedalled down the hill in time to see the girls mustering on the parade ground. On my arrival, the WAAF were quickly brought to attention, and were soon standing smartly in line, shoulder to shoulder, upright and motionless, hardly daring to move, and staring straight ahead into space just as they had been taught to do in their initial training. I gave one look and thought them every bit as smart, if not smarter, than the men I had seen marching on the parade ground yesterday.

I began walking down the first line, looking quickly at each of the blue uniforms as I passed by. All was going well, and then suddenly - there she was -

standing in the middle of the first row just ahead of me. Her face was looking straight ahead like the others, but her eyes were not peering into space. They were turned as far to the left as they could possibly go, and there was a suppressed smile of amusement on her face. "Phyllis! Whatever are you doing here?" I wanted to say but, instead, we just made eye contact as I went by, each pretending that we had never seen each other before.

It was just before the War that we had last met, and each had a vague idea that the other had joined the Air Force. We now no longer had any doubts about it. Phyllis and I were distant relatives, third cousins I think, but we never quite worked that out. All we knew was that our maternal grandmothers were cousins, and the families used to visit each other on a regular basis.

We met a few days later and each of us put on our rather dated pre-war civilian clothes, as we had no coupons to buy new ones, and cycled to a nearby pub for afternoon tea. We wore civvies to beat the rule that officers and other ranks were not to be seen out together in uniform. Phyllis told me that she had been at Tempsford for over a year, and that she was a parachute packer. She must have continued doing that responsible work for at least another year, before she finally discovered who the people were who relied on the work of the packers, not only aircrews, but secret agents and leaders of the French, Norwegian and Danish resistance fighters. During my stay at Tempsford, the parachute section had a perfect safety record and, so far as I know, they maintained it throughout the War.

Some weeks later, having just finished breakfast, we were hurriedly reading the headlines of the daily paper before cycling to work, when one of the girls burst into laughter. "Just look at this," she said with amusement, and pointed to a picture in the paper. We all homed in on the apparently amusing edition of a normally dull paper. We saw a picture of a Group Officer, the highest rank obtainable by a WAAF, and equal to a full Colonel. She was very tall and looked highly intelligent. She had a powerful authoritarian face, topped by dark straight cropped hair, which was cut very much higher than the "one inch above the collar" rule for all WAAF personnel. Finally, she proudly wore a monocle!

Group Officer Conan Doyle, daughter of the famous mystery writer, Sir Arthur Conan Doyle, was inspecting her troops! Just to make sure that nobody missed it, the picture was duly cut out of the paper, pasted, mounted and then stuck on the mirror above the fireplace in the lounge. A few caustic comments underneath the portrait completed the exhibit. After causing a day or two of minor amusement, the picture was forgotten.

About a week later, it was announced at the breakfast table that Group Officer Conan Doyle was visiting Tempsford that day, and that the WAAF officers would be entertaining her for lunch - we had better be on time! We all arrived dutifully a little early, eager to see what this rather austere looking lady was really like. About ten minutes before her arrival someone suddenly called out in alarm, "The Picture! The Picture! We haven't removed it, it's still in the lounge!" In a great flurry, with the aid of a knife, sponge, soap and hot water, we prised the offending photograph from the mirror about five minutes before our guest walked majestically in to our humble Mess. Group Officer Conan Doyle was pleasant, cheerful and tried hard to help us to feel relaxed during lunch. We succeeded in giving her a better meal than our usual fare, but it was with great difficulty that we attempted to keep up a congenial and intelligent conversation. Not one of us was a match for her IQ. Two members of our Mess arrived late, and glanced nervously at the mirror on the wall. Then, with obvious relief, they sat down to join us for an intellectual lunch. But it was not so easy to feel at home in the presence of this rather unusual and awesome lady, who spurned the curls and wavy hair styles of the day for a severe "Eton crop" and, above all, who wore a monocle.

From the day I arrived at Tempsford, the Code & Cypher officer and I hit off a lasting friendship, which led later to her being bridesmaid at my wedding. Barbara Hewer (nee Newton) and I discovered that we had many interests in common, which made life in the new Waffery an unexpectedly happy place in which to live, in sharp contrast to the one I had just left. Barbara often travelled to London on her day off to attend a symphony concert. Now that I too was living so much closer to the city, I began going to an occasional performance with her.

One concert in particular I remember with amused delight. We both looked forward to going, particularly because it was to be held in the Orangery of Hampton Court Palace, built by King Henry Vlll in the 16th century. The palace was a wonderful place to visit at any time, with its many paintings and rich interior furnishings. The formal gardens and copious flowerbeds, plus the famous Maze, all added to the attraction on a warm summer afternoon. A concert in a setting like that could only be perfect.

The Orangery was a huge rectangular conservatory built against one of the outer walls of the palace, and was surrounded on all three sides by lawns and flower gardens. I no longer remember if it lived up to its name by continuing in the 20th century to grow orange trees under its roof. The setting in the late afternoon, however, was tranquil and peaceful by comparison, at that time, to the bombing and consequent destruction in other parts of London. We bought our tickets at the official side-door entrance, and went to our seats about fifteen minutes early. Even hearing the orchestra tuning up was, to us, something that always put us in the right mood.

The first half of the concert went well. Then, after wandering around the gardens during the interval, the audience returned to the Orangery and sat down. The members of the orchestra took their respective places, the concert master followed, and the conductor appeared. He acknowledged the clapping of the audience and took his place at the rostrum. We now awaited the entrance of the soloist, Dennis Brain, the young and internationally famous horn player. He was late in following in the steps of the conductor. The audience waited, the orchestra waited, and the conductor waited. People in the audience began to whisper among themselves; the members of the orchestra began to get a little restless in their seats, and the conductor looked rather embarrassed. He turned to the audience and then looked towards the door that we had entered. By this time, people were clearing their throats and fidgeting, and the conductor appeared uncertain as to what to do next. We all wondered how long it would take for him to announce an alternative programme.

Suddenly, the side door opened noisily, and a very young airman, scruffily dressed in an ill-fitting RAF uniform, hurried past the front rows of people to the far end of the stage, and climbed the steps. He clutched a horn under his arm as he walked quickly across the stage, and up to the bewildered conductor. In a voice audible to us all, he said, "I'm sorry I'm late, but they wouldn't let me in. They didn't believe I was the soloist. I told them the concert wouldn't continue until they allowed me in, but they only laughed." "Then how did you get in?" the conductor asked. By this time, we were enjoying listening in to the chatty dialogue. "I waited a minute or two and then said, "You see - they haven't started playing yet - have they?". After that comment, the doorkeeper must have realized his possible bloomer, for he grudgingly and disbelievingly allowed Dennis Brain to go through the entrance. The doorman continued to watch him, then disappeared quickly, as the young musician walked with confidence on to the rostrum. At the end of the lengthy explanation, we all laughed, and clapped enthusiastically, and the young airman, in his badly-fitting uniform, took the honoured place of the soloist, and thrilled us with a brilliant performance of one of Mozart's horn concertos.

Dennis Brain was a member of a section of the RAF Band, and, as such, was recruited as an ordinary airman, without even the distinction of Corporal's stripes. He still had to earn these! The only concession given to him was permission to be absent from barracks on an occasion such as this. "Joining up" certainly brought every one down to size!

A few years after the War, I read in an English newspaper that Dennis Brain had died tragically in a car crash, thus ending his young life, and an international career of fame.

# A COLD WINTER

The season turned slowly from Summer to Autumn, and the leaves on the trees changed colour and fell. There were cool wet days when the winds blew more briskly, reminding us that worse was to come. For us in England, it would not be so bad, but the people living on the other side of the English Channel must have anticipated a dismal winter, with their chronic need for adequate food, warmth and clothing.

The Winter of 1943-44 proved to be a very cold one, with the mercury falling to much lower temperatures than usual. Our daily cycle down the hill became a bitter experience. We put on extra sweaters, making our greatcoats feel tight and uncomfortable, wound scarves around our uniform hats in non-uniform style, and arrived at the office red-nosed and with hands and feet stiff from the cold. One morning the mercury dropped to 17 degrees Fahrenheit, and a thick mist froze on the trees in the form of a beautiful hoar frost. It was the closest comparison I have seen to the icy beauty of the Canadian countryside, sparkling in winter from the aftermath of freezing rain or fog. Our outer clothing was pathetically inadequate. It was a joy to arrive at the centrally-heated office, after having dressed in cold bedrooms, and eaten breakfast in a dining room with a small one-bar electric fire. By lunch time, there would be a fire in the lounge, but, in cold weather, it was advisable to arrive early for a position close to the flames, if one hoped to thaw out.

During one of these cold winter days, a WAAF colleague and I were chatting to the Head of Intelligence when he said, "You two have not visited the
farmhouse yet, have you?" No! We hadn't. We were
just waiting for an invitation. "I'll take you along
tonight if you like. I think you will find it interesting," he said. So that afternoon, for the second time,
I read over the details of that night's operation. A
Halifax was to fly to Norway with one passenger
and some containers. The assignment was to drop
the agent half-way up a mountainside, just above
the tree line. The reception committee would be
hiding in the shelter of stunted trees until his arrival. When the people on the ground flashed the
correct code letters with a torch (flashlight) at the
sound of the approaching aircraft, the agent and
containers would be dropped. If the code letters
were incorrect, the aircraft would gain height
quickly, get out of the area rapidly, and return to
England with the agent. "Why half-way up a mountain?" I asked, "Are there not easier places to retrieve a parachutist and all the accompanying heavy
equipment?" "That is the way the agent wanted it.
He is very familiar with the area, and feels that pa-
trols would not waste their time on an unoccupied
mountain slope," I was told. As the powers- that- be
could see no objection, they had acceded to his request.

We cycled down the hill that evening in the biting
wind, and duly arrived at our office just before midnight. Our chief picked us up and drove us to the
farmhouse barn beyond the main area of the airfield. We were full of suppressed excitement. On
entering this homey little building, my first impres-

sion was that of arriving backstage at a theatre, with the interior filled with all kinds of unusual and un-recognisable props. Sitting on a bench on our right as we entered, was a "fair, young and handsome" Norwegian receiving attention, and being fussed over by two airmen, as he sat there in a snow-white pair of thickly padded ski-pants. They looked huge on his slim body. The "dressers" paused for a few minutes to introduce us to their compatriot. He, in turn, smiled and seemed to be in a happy frame of mind. It was explained to us the next day that he had been looking forward to returning to his own people to work with them against the Nazi occupation. The thought of all those supplies accompanying him, seemed to give him confidence about the outcome of the operation.

As we watched the dressers going about their work, we noticed that the large ski-pants were covered with "leg bags", zippered pockets that were sewn all over the ski-pants. By the time they had been filled with packages from top to bottom, he was unable to bend or rise from his seat. When he had been zipped up in a matching parka, and a harness and parachute had been strapped over everything, he resembled an enormous snowball. The Army Major in charge of the operation made a weak joke about how lucky our Norwegian friend was to have two lovely girls to see him off. He smiled once more but I felt very embarrassed as I thought of my safe job and compared it with his. After the clothing and equipment he was wearing had been checked and re-checked, he was given a few last minute instructions. Suddenly it was time to depart. The dressers applied a strong arm each side of the Norwegian, and lifted the white festooned figure into a standing position. He walked towards the door and, with a helping hand underneath each arm to steady him, he disappeared into the night.

Shortly afterwards we heard the roar of the four engines of the Halifax coming towards us as it gathered speed for the take-off. We listened as it rose into the air, and turned in an easterly direction towards the North Sea. The sound of the engines diminished slowly until they faded into the distance. The night was silent again, and the room in which we stood felt empty, despite the presence of the Major, the Squadron Leader and the two of us. We looked at each other and said nothing; our silence seemed to say everything.

I was due for a week's leave in a few days. The weather was still cold and miserable but, on the Sussex coast, we usually had more than our share of sunny weather. I hoped for the best. I packed my bag and allowed about half-an-hour for the walk along the lane to Biggleswade station; it was just as well, for no traffic came by to pick me up. I arrived barely in time to catch the train, as it steamed into the station, covering those standing too close to the edge of the platform with a shower of small black smuts.

The journey home was no more than about 100 miles, but it took most of the day to reach my village. After I arrived in London, I took the Underground tube train to Victoria station, from which the Southern Railway's electric trains ran between the City and the South Coast. They departed from

Victoria almost every hour, so, after a short wait, I boarded the train for Hastings. The journey took a very long time, spinning out the normal two-hour trip closer to three, due to snow on the lines. The snow interrupted the electrical current, which slowed up or stopped the train in its tracks many times. With sudden jerks, we were jolted in our seats, and the standing passengers, packed in the corridors, lurched against each other as they tried to keep their balance amid the luggage stacked around their feet. Eventually, I arrived one hour late at my destination.

It was a twenty- minute walk from Hastings station to the local bus stop. Gripping my luggage, and with my gas mask and tin hat bumping against my side, I had to run most of the way to be in time to catch the local bus to Pett, or face the prospect of waiting for more than two hours for the next one. I reached the centre of town, and I saw the clock tower ahead of me. It had been built in the middle of the inter-section where five roads converged, forming the points of an irregular star. It was a timepiece well placed, both to control the traffic passing around it, and for the information it gave to all who were hurrying to the nearby bus terminals. The flower beds that had formerly surrounded the tower had been replaced by the more practical "Dig for Victory" vegetation of root vegetables. The Dig for Victory slogan encouraged everyone with garden space to plant vegetables between the flowers, or to substitute vegetables entirely. The vegetable project was carried out enthusiastically in public parks and gardens where, for example, the purple hue of beet tops provided the contrast of colour against the light green of lettuce leaves.

As I passed the clock tower, I looked up, and then glanced at my watch - it was 5.15 p.m., and the bus was due to leave at 5.20. The clock high above me stared down timeless and faceless - the victim of an earlier bombing attack. I hurried on to catch the bus on the sea front. It was high tide and the waves were pounding against the sea wall, throwing white foam, cascades of water, small pebbles and shingle all over the esplanade, and even on to the road behind it. The bus was wet from the salty spray and, with its engine running to give some warmth to the passengers already on board, was dutifully waiting out the last few minutes until its scheduled departure time. I arrived breathless and, with one minute to spare, ran up the steps in to the bus and collapsed into a seat. I had made it!

I arrived home in the early evening and received a warm welcome. A roaring fire awaited me but the weather was no better than that at Tempsford, and the wind was more blustery. During that week, we had a heavy fall of snow, at first beautiful to look at, but soon dirty and slippery underfoot, as it melted slowly into slushy mud. It reminded me of another time in the early days of the war when I was still living at home.

On that occasion, it had snowed for several consecutive days, and did not melt for over a week. My uncle carried out his regular duties at the Observer Corps post with difficulty, as he made his way to the cliff-top lookout at Fairlight. The roads were impassable, so he had borrowed a fisherman's water-proof outfit to cover his outdoor clothing .With a balaclava over his head and face and a large woollen scarf wrapped tightly around his neck, he walked over three miles, sometimes waist high in snow, a solitary figure, through fields and pastures now bereft of any grazing animals. Crossing only the occasional road on his way, it took hours to reach his spotters' outpost, but he was sure that it was both a shorter distance and safer than the challenge of the long slippery road up the hill to Fairlight Church on foot. "At least," he said, indicating a sense of adventure, "it will be downhill nearly all the way back home."

Bus services were cancelled for the whole week and we, at Pett, were virtually cut off from the rest of the world. After about four or five days, our larders and food cupboards were nearly empty, for we had no such luxuries as refrigerators or freezers to back up our food supply. By the fifth day, my uncle and I devised a plan. We hunted for the small and ancient sleigh, which had been discarded years before, and lay somewhere in a corner of the garage. It was just large enough for two people to sit on. My grandfather had made it for his family to toboggan on Hampstead Heath in London in the early 1900's! When we located it, to our surprise, it was still in reasonable condition, not exactly fit for dashing downhill, but strong enough for our needs. We strapped a large box on top of the sleigh, and attached a heavy rope to it for pulling our load. The two of us then set out for Hastings, six miles away, towing it behind us. The main difficulty was, not the distance, but the gradients we had to encounter, both in and out of the town. We were soon quite exhilarated by the experience of trudging into town through the wintry countryside. Views of the undulating scenery of meadows and woodlands, white with snow and sparkling in the sunlight, were breathtaking as we reached the summit. Then came the easy part, sliding down the steep hill from Ore for over a mile to Hastings, and then pulling our sleigh along the promenade beside the sea. The salt spray had melted the snow on the seafront so, during the last fifteen minutes of our excursion to the shops, we almost forgot the frozen landscape we had left behind.

After eating a hearty snack in the warmth of a local restaurant, we bought our food, piled the box high, and began the return journey. Climbing the hill again out of Hastings was a marathon effort, particularly without brakes on our tiny sleigh. Brakes seemed even more necessary than on our descent earlier in the day. It was hard work pulling the sleigh up, and even more difficult preventing it from sliding backwards. More than two miles from our starting point and about two hours later, we reached the crest of the hill at Ore, after which it was downhill nearly all the way home. The expedition took an entire day to accomplish. But the weather on the South Coast was usually much gentler than that which we suffered during that exceptional winter.

In contrast, I remember the strange and strikingly beautiful phenomenon that was witnessed by everyone who lived in our area. It happened one day in the summer about a year before the war was declared. I was sitting sunning myself in the garden, relaxed and content as I glanced lazily into the distance. At first, I comprehended no more than the sun's rays shining down through a break in a cloud. It was typical of a shaft of sunlight illuminating a patch of land below, on a partly cloudy day. I took little notice of it. Then I was puzzled, for the rays were not coming from the direction of the sun. As I looked more carefully, another ray of white light appeared. This time I watched it change colour to a soft tinge of yellow, as it caught the sun that was beginning to lower in the sky. Each shimmering light began to move slowly, turning and altering in shape and direction.

I called my mother who was in the house, and we watched the display together. "It must be the Aurora Borealis,"she said. But in broad daylight and so far south, it seemed to be out of the question. Within a short time, other misty shafts of light, varying in colour from a bluish white to pale yellow, then to orange and hues of pink, appeared like phantoms crossing the valley and beyond to the distant hill at Fairlight. They moved gently, twisting and turning, sometimes touching the earth and slowly ascending again. We were enthralled by the beauty of it all.

Then my uncle joined us; he too had been looking at the unusual spectacle. "I think we should get a better view of all this," he suggested. "Let's go out in the car and drive around for a while and get a closer look of it all," he said. My aunt, uncle, mother and I, plus the dog, piled into the car and drove off. "This is turning out to be quite an occasion," I thought to myself, for my uncle seldom took out his car without a definite reason for getting from A to B, when no other form of transportation was available. We were all amazed at the brilliance of the Northern Lights in broad daylight. The dog alone appeared quite unimpressed!

That afternoon, we drove back and forth along most of the local lanes, sometimes going through a misty wall of white or pink haze, to emerge suddenly the other side into the clear day light again. We passed more vehicles on the roads than I had ever seen roaming our quiet lanes before. Everyone was doing exactly the same thing as we were, sightseeing along the lanes we all knew so well. Time passed without our noticing it, until we realized how hungry we were - it was time for supper. Reluctantly, we went back home, but only to eat a quick meal and return to see the display that showed no sign of abating.

Dusk fell, and then a mantle of darkness covered the sky. We decided to have a final look at the Aurora Borealis from the highest viewpoint in the area. The North Seat was a large, sturdy wooden viewing platform, built on a high ridge beyond Fairlight on the way to Hastings. From the platform, there was an expansive view along the horizon to the north, and about sixty miles inland. We climbed the stairs to the platform and joined other sightseers, who were reading information from a metal plaque which had been installed on the upper level. It pointed out names and directions of many towns and distant villages. The ever-changing shafts of lights in the sky still danced and twisted in the darkness, as they turned to shades of white and blue normally associated with the Northern Lights. We watched, fascinated for a while and then, very reluctantly, turned our backs on the northern sky. We passed some latecomers on the stairs as we descended from the lookout. I remember going to bed that night full of awe and wonder as I relived the day's experience.

Next morning, the story made headlines in all the daily newspapers. What we had witnessed had been far from a local phenomenon. The Aurora Borealis had been seen in all its magnificence from the north of Scotland, throughout England and Europe, and as far south as Spain and Portugal. Despite the fact that so large an area of Europe had witnessed such an unique experience of the Northern Lights, no meteorological or scientific reasons were, to my knowledge, given for such a rare phenomenon.

# SPRING 1944

Eventually we saw the first signs of the awakening of spring, and I began to think once more of asking permission to fly. The interior of the large aircraft of 138 and 161 Squadrons would surely be full of interesting modifications. Having been designed as heavy bombers, they now dropped people, packages and containers instead of bombs.

This time my request was not going to be so easy to make. The other two WAAF officers in the department were not interested in flying, so had not blazed the trail. I barely knew the Commanding Officer, as he came to our department only occasionally and then usually to confer with the officers of higher rank, unlike the regular visits of the C.O. to the Ops. Room at Feltwell. I had no opportunity of approaching him casually, but would have to make an official appointment to speak to him. The idea left me somewhat in doubt as to my success. Our C.O., apart from being Number One on the station, was also distinguished in other ways. Group Captain Fielden had the honour of being Air Equerry to the King, and Master of the King's Flight and, as such, moved in exalted circles. He had a personal telephone line to Buckingham Palace in his office; after the war, he rose to the rank of Air Chief Marshal. I doubted very much that the he would grant me permission to fly, but I thought, "I won't fly if I don't try, so I have nothing to lose.". My male colleagues encouraged me, and off I went to see him.

Entering his office, I saluted smartly. The C.O. looked up from his work a little puzzled. Why did I need to see him personally? I stated my case such as it was and, without any problem at all, he gave me permission at once much to my surprise and delight. In fact, he seemed very relieved that my problem was such a small one (it was not a "little one!").

The following week, I was invited to join one of the crews on a cross-country flight in a Halifax. This was going to be an exciting adventure. So far, I had been up in Venturas only, two-engined aircraft almost identical to the Hudsons at Tempsford. Now I was to experience a cross-country exercise in a full sized four-engined bomber. During the first hour of the trip, I was left to my own devices, entertaining myself with a map on my lap, pinpointing places of interest on the way along, and at the same time listening to the instructions and comments on the intercom. Later, two of the crew gave me a tour of the aircraft. The cockpit, as usual, meant no more to me than that of the Ventura. There was just a lot more of the same on the panel, as far as I was concerned. They then accompanied me further back in the fuselage and pointed out a large circular hatch in the centre of the floor. "This," said the dispatcher proudly "is the hole from which the Joes jump - we won't remove the hatch to demonstrate this time!" "How do they jump from here?" I asked him. He went on to explain, "When we are close to the dropping area, we remove the hatch, and the agent sits on the edge of the opening with his legs dangling over the side. "But," I asked "the wind velocity must be tremendous at that time?" "Yes," he said, "they have to hang on, but by then we are approaching 500 feet above ground level, which makes quite a difference to the strength of the wind. The Joes wait until they get the OK from the dispatcher, then immediately drop through the hole one after another."

"Do you ever have anyone who freezes and is unable to jump?" I asked. "No," came the reply. "Occasionally, we have been asked to give them a push at the right moment, but nobody has ever returned to base, except when we were unable to complete the mission." He continued to explain, "The dropping height of 500 ft. is extremely low, so a static line is always attached from the aircraft to the parachute, which enables it to open automatically immediately after the jump and the aircraft is safely out of range. The larger containers are strapped in modified bomb racks, and are released in a way similar to a salvo of bombs. They too have parachutes attached to a static line, and are dropped to a reception committee waiting below, when it identifies itself by flashing the right letters with a torch. If the code letters are wrong, we have to bring the agents and containers back and try another day." This turned out to be one of the most interesting and informative cross-country trips on which I had flown so far.

As for the Lysanders, they were reserved strictly for the pilots and their passengers. These small aircraft usually operated from Tangmere on the south coast of Sussex, during the time that the moon shone at its brightest. By beginning their trips closer to the French coast, the pilots were able to broaden the range of their operations. After the moon period, they returned to Tempsford, often to train some of the Joes, whom they had recently brought back from the other side of the Channel. They taught the agents how to set up landing strips and dropping areas, the type of landing facilities our aircraft required, and how to prepare the fields for touchdowns at night. Good camouflage was stressed as a most important part of the whole set-up. For example, a field of grain was grown normally in the type of well-drained soil suitable for a safe landing. Therefore, a grain field on flat terrain would make an excellent landing area for small aircraft during harvest time. Stooks of wheat drying in the fields, would be removed by many willing hands in time for the rendezvous, and replaced immediately after the departure of the Lysander. When the sun rose the following morning, the field would look exactly the same as it had on the previous day, still waiting for the gathering of the harvest. Although I knew the type of landing facilities from which the pilots made their pick-ups, it had not crossed my mind that it was the pilots who took over the training of the Joes during the non-moon periods. At that time, only the Head of our Department knew of these matters.

To explain more fully the story behind the little aircraft with spats over the wheels and a cylinder under the fuselage, I quote from the jacket of a book written about thirty years later by Hugh Verity, one of the pilots:

> "*At the height of World War II, when the Germans were in possession of most of Europe, small aircraft landed in France to pick up agents and fly them to*

*England. The pilots who operated this service fought a highly individualistic war, quite distinct from the set piece operations by the bombers and fighters. They belonged to specialized squadrons flying into Europe from bases in England, North Africa and later Italy and Corsica; often in unarmed Lysanders, always at risk from the large numbers of patrolling enemy fighters, these flights were of the utmost importance to the Allies, creating vital links with clandestine organizations and providing first hand intelligence reports to the British and American planning staffs from agents on the ground.*

*"It was a lonely, difficult and exacting role. Finding small isolated fields in blacked-out hostile territory without sophisticated navigation equipment was a daunting task even for a full crew - yet most 'pick-up' pilots flew alone. They faced too the multiple hazards of uncertain weather, complex enemy air defences and the ever present risk of being caught by German soldiers on the ground or of falling into a carefully laid enemy trap. And there were no reports on the radio or in the press of successes or failures.*

*"It was a type of operational flying that called for individual qualities of cool 'four o'clock in the morning' courage, high intelligence, and professional flying skills of the highest order. By their very nature such operations were conducted in the deepest secrecy and reticence about what they were doing was as essential to the pilots' survival as that of the agents they served. That habit of cautious reticence has persisted even into the long years of peace and it was only with reluctance that Hugh Verity, perhaps the most outstanding pick-up pilot of them all, has been per-*

*suaded to tell his own story of the secret operations that gained him a double DSO and a DFC."* We Landed by Moonlight, Hugh Verity, Ian Allan Ltd, Shepperton, England, 1978

During a week's leave some time before the invasion of Europe, I encountered, as usual, the unusual side of life. The Germans made our village quite a lively little place in which to spend one's leave. It was there that I learned to see the war from a different perspective. The better the weather, the greater was our need to keep alert to the possibility of unwanted intruders from above. We could never tell when we would have to make a sudden dive for the camouflage of a clump of trees or to accept the scratches from the roadside bramble hedges. The JU-88 dive bombers no longer kept to their daily 11.00 am visit, but came now with unscheduled low-level surprise attacks.

My uncle's telescope was kept permanently mounted on a tripod under the roofed verandah of his home. From that point, high up on the hill, we would survey the vast expanse of sea, observing the silhouettes of lone ships or convoys passing by. Sometimes our attention was drawn to ships under attack, although their distance from the land was too great for us to hear the gunfire, but we did not need a telescope to see the small puffs of black smoke that hovered above the horizon. As they spread out into grey smudges, more black puffs would take their place in the sky. The enemy would dive on the targets below them, while the ships retaliated with their guns in self-defence. All too often, one or two of the ships would receive direct hits from the dive-bombers. From the safety of the land, we would watch the tragic sight of these vessels, often with a couple of them ablaze, as they continued courageously, trying to keep up with the rest of the convoy. Then, the cliff on the far side of our valley would obscure them from our view.

We were scanning the horizon, one day, for anything of interest when my uncle passed the telescope to me and said, "What do you make of that?" I looked for a long time then replied, "I haven't the faintest idea." *Jane's Fighting Ships* and *Jane's Merchant Ships* manuals had never shown anything even remotely like this! What looked like gigantic square blocks, were being towed along, line astern. We watched them with fascination and disbelief, until they disappeared in a westerly direction behind the cliffs at Cliff End. We agreed that they did not even look floatable. After some discussion, we decided that we should adhere to the advice of one of the many "*Zip-Your-Lips*" posters that adorned the billboards in those days. We guessed that these great floating blocks came within that category. Without comprehending, we had watched some of the "Mulberry Harbour" units being towed on their way to one of the south-west ports of England, in readiness for the future invasion of Europe. These floatable concrete sections, when put together, would complete two artificial harbours, vital for the landing of tanks, transports and materials during the early days of the invasion, until an enemy-occupied port was captured, but more about this subject later on.

# D-DAY

Spring was turning into early summer; it promised to be another fine day. The crops covered the fields with varying shades of green and yellow, and the wild flowers bloomed by the hedges, just waiting to be picked. There was no shortage of wild blossoms, and the law about "observing and smelling them only" did not need to exist then. When I was a child, one of my greatest pleasures was to arrive home after a walk in the meadows, with an armful of flowers and leaves to present to my mother. She always accepted them enthusiastically, even if she had nowhere to put them, because of the ones she had been given the day before. It is sad to think that our children today have never known that pleasure.

Because of the good weather, the squadrons at Tempsford were making many parachute drops in France. Liaison with the freedom fighters was expanding successfully, in preparation for the impending invasion of Europe. Our department was becoming a much busier place. After arriving for duty one morning, I went first into the map room, and updated the positions of the landing strips and dropping grounds on the map of Europe which was spread across the wall. I then returned to the office. Our boss had arrived early and, very shortly, we were all present. He looked cautiously around the Intelligence office, just to make sure that no casual visitors were present; then he asked us to gather round. He had an unusual look on his face, a mixture of anticipation, awe, pride and "I don't know what," all rolled into one. I was not at all sure what to expect.

"The envelope. It's here. It's in the Group Captain's office," he said" I've been told to stand by to wait for the C.O.'s command." "THE envelope?" we enquired, hardly believing our ears. We knew that somewhere in a safe at Tempsford was a TOP SECRET envelope. It contained specific information for our squadrons, giving details for the mission Tempsford was to carry out when the invasion of Europe began. It was to be opened the day before the invasion started. "The C.O. is breaking the seal this morning," he told us. "So does that mean that the invasion begins tomorrow?" we all asked. We could come to only one conclusion - Yes! It would be on June 6, 1944. Shortly after imparting this knowledge to us, the head of our department received the expected summons, and went promptly to report to the C.O. We, the more junior staff, were left to carry on business as usual, except that nobody could concentrate on anything. I was glad that I had already updated the map next door. I no longer felt that I possessed the greatest powers of concentration. We waited. Eventually our chief returned and said, "Yes! D-Day is on! The invasion force arrives at the enemy coast at dawn."

We then read the instructions for 161 and 138 Squadrons, and their contribution to what might be the most remembered day in the history of World War ll. Our Halifaxes and Stirlings were to fly to the Pas-de-Calais area during the night, to carry out a spoof attack, dropping dummy parachutists and firecrackers, which simulated the noise of gunfire. It was hoped that this attack would confuse the enemy into sending troops, tanks and transports into the Calais area, thereby weakening the strength of the enemy onslaught at the real beachheads. It would also be a means of obstructing the roads, with transports going in both directions, when the enemy realized its mistake. For some months, we had been making wild guesses, giving even wilder reasons, as to where the invasion might begin. It had been to no avail - we had arrived at no convictions or conclusions. Now we knew one area where it was *not* going to take place, but we were still as much in the dark about the real spearhead - or was there to be more than one?

In our daily work, we normally handled a lot of Top-Secret information, and we accepted it as part of the job. But this! It made us all feel nervous about going to the mess for lunch or dinner, just in case, by our looks or some accidental reference, we dropped a hint. By lunchtime, however, we had more or less recovered from the shock, but what a day it was going to be somewhere on the south coast of England!

As I ate lunch, my thoughts were not on the meal. We discussed the weather and the quality of the food, which was not too complimentary. I assured the other WAAF officers that we always put a greater effort into providing a good dinner, and that I thought that they would find it passable, even palatable. Not so long before, I had complained rather bitterly about the dull, unimaginative food, so I was promptly voted in as Messing Officer. I deserved it, and found that I quite enjoyed the challenge. To cheer up the new menu, I introduced the cook to a few of my mother's simpler wartime recipes. The girl was pleased with them, and soon proved that she had quite a gift in the culinary arts. When given encouragement, her experiments were usually a success. I hoped that would be the case tonight.

After a long and busy afternoon at the office, I returned only just in time for the evening meal. It was well-timed really, as I was spared being asked how things went today. The other two girls from our section were either on leave or on a day off, as they were both absent that day. Sitting there, I felt suddenly, the terrible responsibility of being the only person present who knew what was about to happen. Attempting to block these imminent events from my mind, I tried to behave in a relaxed and normal manner. Never before had I felt that I needed such ultra care in my general behaviour.

During the evening meal, everyone carried on as usual, nobody complained about the food, and later, as people retired to bed one by one, I followed suit, though I knew it was not to sleep. During the night I dozed fitfully. I was wondering what kind of reception our boys were getting in the well-fortified area of the Pas-de-Calais, and whether they would return safely. The Senior Officer and two of his male assistants were responsible for the debriefing, so I would have to wait till morning to hear the results.

I lay in my bed, picturing the gigantic Armada of thousands of ships carrying many more thousands of men across the Channel to goodness knows where. Had anything even remotely like this ever happened before? I rather doubted it, but history was not my strong subject. In my ignorance, I had not realized that there was another WAAF officer sitting at the dinner table that night, also feigning innocence, and who was probably having a sleepless night as well. When we all met again for breakfast next day, I turned on the radio, making sure that we heard the BBC news at 8 a.m. It was then that I found out that Barbara, the Code & Cypher officer, had been the custodian of the now famous envelope. She had kept it hidden behind the combination lock in the safe in her office. On receiving a coded message the morning before, it was she who released "The Envelope" and took it to the Group Captain. It was amusing to recount our wariness of one another during the previous evening.

The BBC morning broadcast was full of news about the invasion of Europe and, before long, the whole world knew about it. Our two squadrons and other participating aircraft were very successful in their spoof attacks and, when leaving the target area, saw lights on the roads from transports driving towards the parachutes and the dummy men that they had just left floating to earth. Later we heard officially, that the attack helped to cause a major diversion, and added to a significant snarl-up of enemy transports and tanks, attempting to drive in both directions at the same time. All our aircraft returned safely.

The weather on D-Day was not good for crossing the Channel, but to delay would have meant waiting another month for favourable tides. The winds were strong and the sea was very rough. Vast numbers of personnel afloat suffered sea-sickness, despite having been given special pills to steady their stomachs. In that unhappy state, these men had to wade ashore, weighed down with firearms and with heavy kit on their shoulders, to face the onslaught of the opposing gunfire. Our Prime Minister, Winston Churchill, gave the following message that morning to members in the House of Commons: *"An immense Armada of upward of four thousand ships, together with several thousand smaller craft, crossed the English Channel..."* Further, according to *An Illustrated History of the RAF* by Roy Conyers Nesbit (CLB Colour Library Books Ltd., Godalming, Surrey) ... no fewer than 171 squadrons provided air cover for the Navy and the gliders bearing troops, supplies and reinforcements. At the end of the first day, the Allies were fighting hard to secure a foothold on the beaches, and the rest is history.

# A NOISY NIGHT

Just over a week after D-Day, Barbara invited me to go with her to one of the "Prom" concerts at the Albert Hall in London. It sounded a wonderful idea. As the concert would not finish in time for us to return to Tempsford the same night, she invited me to stay with her at her parents' home in Bromley, just south of London. By catching the 6 a.m. train from Bromley South station the following morning, we could be back on duty well before 9 a.m.

Having synchronised our days off, we packed our pyjamas and toothbrushes in the satchels that held our gas masks. With rumours that Hitler's secret weapons might soon be coming our way, we were now more willing to carry the cumbersome appendages than we had been previously. We hung our tin hats over the shoulder straps, and began the walk along the lane to Biggleswade Station in a relaxed and happy frame of mind. It was a beautiful day, the birds were singing, the sheep and cattle were feeding lazily in the green fields, and the sun shone. In these idyllic surroundings, it was difficult to imagine that our country was at war. Our only reminders were our uniforms, which were far too hot for comfort, and our gas masks and tin hats that jolted on our hips as we walked to the station. RAF Regulations required that we be dressed "correctly" at all times. For us, this meant nearly suffocating in a tailor made jacket and skirt, shirt, tie, hat, thick lisle stockings and heavy black lace-up walking shoes.

On arriving in London, it was even hotter, and we envied the American WAACs whom we saw walking around the city in their trim uniforms, flesh-coloured nylon stocking and dainty footwear. By mid-afternoon after a late lunch, it was time to make our way to the Albert Hall, to line up early for the privilege of standing in the now seatless area of the Orchestra Stalls, the seats having been moved for these performances. This, for the young and enthusiastic, was the only way to attend a Prom concert. It meant that the early-comers, all of whom rushed to get the best place as soon as the doors opened, were able to finish up in front, and just below the level of the conductor and soloist on the platform. Whether we really heard the best balance of music, I am somewhat in doubt, but we could almost see the pupils of the eyes of the soloists, and hear the distracting grunts of one or two of the famous conductors of the day. Even the perfume used by the soloist wafted in our direction, when Eileen Joyce performed at the piano. To us, this *was* the Proms!

While standing in line outside this unusual circular building named after Queen Victoria's husband, Prince Albert, there was always an amusing and rather agonizing entertainment we were forced to listen to. A street musician in his down-at-heel shoes and ragged jacket would appear without fail, when the queue was long enough to warrant his presence. With the aid of his violin, he bowed squeaky off-key classical excerpts which were just about recognizable. This entertainment relieved the monotony of waiting in the days before portable ghetto-blasters, as he played for the long line-up of eager music lovers. What greater service could he render to those whose lot it was to stand for about three hours without entertainment until they were, at last, admitted through the doors to hear their long-awaited programme? Needless to say, whether in pity, amusement, or just to get him to move to another location, his hat, when passed along the line, always filled beyond our expectations. Going by his regular appearances, it must have satisfied his own expectations as well.

The doors opened! After the free-for-all rush of the quickest and the strongest, we secured our territory for the next two or three hours. In the crowd, standing close to us, we met a friend of Barbara's, another WAAF Intelligence Officer, who worked at the Air Ministry. After they had passed the pleasantries since last meeting, my new acquaintance confided to us something that had happened a night or two before, about a week after D-Day. During the early hours of the morning, a rather unusual incident had happened. About four strange missiles, each in the shape of a bomb with wings and a tail attached, plus a noisy motor, had hurtled over parts of southeast England. When each missile had reached the limit of its range, the motor cut out and the bomb fell immediately at a steep angle on whatever or whoever was beneath it. She explained, as a way of comfort, that so long as one could hear the motor, one was safe. When the engine cut out, that was the time to run for it! It was thought that this was a try-out of one of Hitler's secret weapons, for we were led to believe that there were more than one.

The concert began and we forgot the problems of the world. At the end of the performance, as we all went our separate ways, Barbara and I discussed this interesting snippet of news. It seemed to us as if the Germans were trying out the range for London; poor old London always seemed to get it! We caught the train at Victoria Station and fifteen minutes later we arrived at Bromley and, within five minutes, knocked on the front door of her parents' house. The door was opened just wide enough for us to squeeze inside quickly. In the dark, we felt our way into the hall. Regulations were very strict with regard to the blackout, so it was only after I had been introduced to Barbara's parents that the curtains were rechecked, and the lights switched on again.

I was welcomed and we chatted politely about this and that. As the kitchen window blackout was thick and secure, we sat around the breakfast table having a hot drink before retiring to bed. Then the inevitable question came up. I guess it was difficult for me to think of anything else to say to strangers whom I had just met in the dark. "Do you have many air raids at Bromley, or do the bombers usually pass over you on their way to the City?" I asked. "We get our share but most of the time it is not too bad" her mother said. I was then taken upstairs and shown my room. We were all tired so we said, "Good Night". They went to their rooms, and I walked down the passage to the "loo", as I did not wish to grope my way along the corridor in unfamiliar territory after the lights had been put out. No sooner had I shut the door than I heard the sound of a distant express train. It got louder and louder as it speeded and rattled closer and closer. Quickly, it became a deafening roar, as whatever it was, passed immediately overhead then faded into the distance. "A flying bomb" I thought, "exactly how it was described by Barbara's friend." I ran out of the loo as quickly as I could. I realized, suddenly, that I feared not only being found dead in my hair curlers, but also being found extinct in such an undignified place.

All four of us met on the landing at the top of the stairs. It was a rather unusual initiation into what transpired later, to be a close friendship with the family. While we were talking, another missile passed overhead with the same deafening and clattering noise, and continued on its path of destruction in the direction of London. Barbara then thought it time to convey our scant knowledge of what came to be known as the "flying bomb". After a sketchy description, which was all she had, she assured them, as another missile followed along the same path, "Don't worry - as long as you can hear the motor, you are quite safe, but, if it cuts out, you dive for shelter," Barbara emphasized. Yet another roared overhead to prove that these were not just isolated incidents. This four-way discussion on the landing came to an abrupt end as the motor of the next flying bomb cut out directly above us. A change in tune from the sound of a rattling express train above to the acceleration of a missile hurtling to earth, prompted us all to run down the stairs as fast as possible. We arrived in the hall just in time to hear the "crump", as it made contact with British soil, a little too close to home for comfort.

Barbara, her mother and I decided to do what all British people do when in a state of uncertainty: we went once more to the kitchen and made a cup of tea! Barbara's father, a retired Colonel from the Royal Engineers, decided that being upstairs or downstairs would make little difference if we sustained a direct hit. So, as far as he was concerned, he would prefer to spend the night in his bed, rather than sit up throughout the raid on a hard chair in the kitchen. We, on the other hand, decided to sit it out downstairs with another cup of tea to keep us going.

For over an hour, the missiles continued on their all-too-predictable course. One or two of them cut out overhead, but the most dangerous ones, we quickly learned, were those whose power cut just before they reached us. It was a toss-up then as to where they would fall, some were unpleasantly close. We came to the conclusion that the bombardment was going to continue all night. So we decided, long after the contents of the tea-pot had been finished, that maybe it would be wiser to get some rest, instead of sitting up till morning. Reluctantly, we walked upstairs again and, after setting the alarm clock for just after 5.00 a.m., wishing that we could accelerate the time, we disappeared into our respective rooms to rest until daylight. The racket continued all night and I, for one, had no sleep at all. At the welcome sound of the alarm clock, Barbara and I rose, dressed, looked at our pale and sleepless faces in the mirror, and decided that even a dab of powder or lipstick was not going to improve our image much. We tried our best, but without success. Then wishing her parents the best of luck, and thankful to be on our way to the unmolested skies of Tempsford, we ventured out into the street.

Having walked for no more than a minute or two, another of the now familiar missiles rattled noisily in our direction. The sun had risen so, at last, we could see the shape of what looked like a small old-fashioned monoplane, displaying a large bomb where the fuselage should be and, a trail of flame gushing behind it as it sped in our direction. The engine cut out just before reaching us, and it ploughed down at a steep angle into the next street. Fortunately, we were sheltered by a high brick wall; in fact, it was the only garden on that part of the street that had one. No doubt, this wall, designed to keep out prying eyes, saved us from cuts and bruises and possible concussion. We were smothered with small branches and leaves from the trees, combined with showers of brick-dust. Our previous efforts to disguise the wan appearance of our washed-out looks faded, as we inspected each other's begrimed faces. We began to laugh as we tried to brush off the clouds of red dust from our clothes, and to wipe it out of our eyes. It was then that we took our hitherto unused, heavy and, up till now, unpopular tin hats that, along with our gas masks , hung from our shoulders, and placed the metal chapeaus very firmly on our heads.

It was only a few more minutes walk to the main road, which was close to the railway station. We arrived safely at the intersection, but our means of crossing the road was blocked by the arrival of the first lorries of an army convoy, which had just drawn abreast of us. The drivers and soldiers in these transports gave one look at the two dishevelled WAAF in tin hats, waiting to cross the road at 5.30 in the morning. They pointed at us and guffawed with great amusement. "I'm not taking off my tin hat for anybody, are you?" asked Barbara. I concurred wholeheartedly.

The convoy had just arrived from the south, and it was obvious that nobody in it had yet realized that it was running into an air raid in progress. Their trucks and armoured cars made so much noise that they were oblivious to the racket that was going on above. By pointing our fingers in the direction of the sky, we attempted to alert them to look up, but our actions only caused more mirth. We gave up trying to help and guessed that, sooner or later, they would get a rude but, we hoped, not too close an awakening. The train was almost due as we waited for the endless stream of transports to pass, but we need not have worried. Because of "circumstances beyond its control", the train came into Bromley South station very late. Thankfully, we found seats when it arrived and, as I sat half-dozing in a corner of our compartment on the way up to Victoria Station, the significance of the night's experience of flying bombs suddenly triggered my memory.

These surely were the missiles we searched for so diligently when I was a photographic interpreter at Medmenham two years earlier. So, it was these flying bombs that were launched from the many sites which we had studied around the coast of northern France. At that time, although the enemy had been unable to camouflage the launching areas, they had very cleverly hidden the real evidence, the bombs.

Babs (Constance Babbington-Smith), who was in charge of aircraft recognition, had searched in vain for the missiles she was sure were present. Even when co-operating with her senior officers, no one had come up with any definite proof. Later, I heard that she had been awarded a medal for having discovered the flying bomb in time to alert the Allies of its existence. There had, until then, been no proof that the missiles existed and no photographs to back up the Intelligence reports of them. Then, one day, as she looked at a long sortie of overlapping photos taken in Eastern Europe, she saw on the last half of the final photograph of the day, the elusive object for which she was searching - the photographic evidence of the flying bomb. Being the very last photograph taken that day, there was no stereoscopic cover. Had the picture been taken a fraction of a second earlier, or had there been an inch less film, the story would have been quite different. As it was, Britain was warned of the existence and probable performance of the flying bomb several months before the haphazard bombing of London began. The enemy did not home on specific military targets with these missiles, but tried to break the morale and courage of the civilian population with indiscriminate destruction. Flying bombs were incapable of pinpointing particular targets so fell indiscriminately within a broad area.

Previously on March 2-3, 1944, one of Tempsford's Lysanders brought back a secret agent from France, who carried with him details of large ammunition dumps hidden in quarries near Creil. In them were over 2,000 V.1 rockets (flying bombs) ready to be deployed for the destruction of London. Early in the month of July, 1944, the dumps were attacked successfully by Bomber Command. Had this not happened, I wonder how many more flying bombs we might have received on that sleepless night at Bromley? As it was, the V.1's continued to harass our country for quite a long time. Later information showed that more than 200 of the missiles crossed the English coast on their way to London within the first twenty-four hours, and over 3,000 followed in the next five weeks. These flew at varying heights of between 3,000 to 4,000 feet and at very high speed, as they were fitted with jet engines.

After arriving late, but without incident, at Victoria station, we continued our journey by "Tube", as the Underground subway system in London is called. The platform of the Underground was crowded when we alighted at the bottom of the escalator. The mass of people comprised mostly mothers and small children, who were waking up slowly, one by one, as the early morning commuters arrived to disturb their all-too-short night's sleep. The only place that one was free to walk was the narrow strip near the edge of the platform. The remaining space was strewn with blankets, sleeping bags and pillows. In between them were picnic baskets, children's' teddy bears, and other precious possessions of the little ones. During the war, the Underground stations were used as air raid shelters late at night for those who wished to take advantage of the facility. During times of probable and unpredictable air attacks, the station platforms were always packed by about 11.00 p.m... For the guarantee of safety, people cheerfully put up with little more than five hours of peace between the departure of the last train at night, and the resumption of the regular - every few minutes - service the following morning.

We picked our way about half-way down the platform. As I passed a mother sitting on a blanket, a sleeping child each side of her, she nodded and smiled at me, as, unhurriedly, she removed her hair curlers, and put them in the small sponge bag on her lap. One of her children turned over, put her thumb in her mouth and fell asleep again. A woman nearby was concentrating on giving her small boy a mug of warm milk which she had just poured from a thermos flask, before gathering her belongings together to return to her home before the morning rush escalated into the usual mad, crushing bustle of humanity.

Lights appeared in the darkness of the tunnel, brakes screeched, and with a rush of air, the train appeared and quickly came to a stop at the station. The doors opened and a few people alighted. We got in and sat down in a nearly empty carriage, leaving behind us on the platform the families, now more intently packing up their overnight things in readiness for their return home. A conversation soon started up between us and the people sitting opposite. By comparing notes, we were amazed to discover that they had experienced a quiet night, and knew nothing about the flying-bomb attacks. In fact, they had no idea what we were talking about.

Well behind schedule, we reached the railway station for the North, and left on the next available steam train for Biggleswade. By then, it was inevitable that I would be reporting for duty nearly three hours late. So, on arrival at Tempsford, despite my disreputable appearance, I went directly to the Intelligence Office, forgoing the luxury of returning to my quarters for a change of clothing.

When I entered the Intelligence office, everyone gave one look at me, then, with much amusement, bombarded me with a shower of derogatory remarks and caustic comments, which beat the gestures of the members of the Army convoy earlier in the morning. "Wow! You look as though you've had a good night on the tiles. Who was the lucky boy? Ever seen a dream walking? Let's hear more about your goings on in the big city?" They all enjoyed the situation at my expense. There was no doubt that I looked as though I had been through a hedge backwards, but I was fortunate that there had been a wall protecting me instead of a hedge, when the bomb exploded. The staff, otherwise, might have been denied the fun of teasing me. When the mirth died down, I explained the reason for my dishevelled looks. "That's a good one!" came the reply. "Bombs that fly! What a joke! Can't you think of a more convincing story than that?" By then, I thought it time for them to let up on the ribbing. "Don't any of you ever read the morning papers or listen to the BBC news?" I retorted. Yes! They had done both, but insisted that there was no mention of a raid of any kind last night. I did not believe them. I thought they were still having me on, but it turned out to be true. For reasons of security, the Doodle-bug raids - the friendly name later given to these missiles - had not been reported. Only after the enemy had rectified its error, and succeeded in homing the flying bombs on to Central London the following night, was their arrival on British soil made known officially to the public.

At lunch time, I pedalled wearily up the hill. There was nothing I wanted more than a meal, followed by a bath and change of clothing. It had been a long time since yesterday afternoon's lunch, before joining the queue outside the Albert Hall. Food was a higher priority than hygiene for me now. The rest of the girls would have to put up with me as I was. Arriving back at the WAAF Mess, I received the greatest welcome. It felt good to have been missed and to be met at the door with such warmth and enthusiasm, even if it was only by a black, curly haired spaniel.

A few months previously, Dorothy, a member of our Mess, became engaged to an officer at another RAF Station in 3 Group. To keep her from loneliness between their visits, he had given her his most prized possession - his little black spaniel - for company. The dog was so gentle and affectionate, that she became known as "Soppy Poppy" within a few days of her arrival. For her food, she was given the scraps left over from our previous meals. After consuming everything put before her, she would then go around the dinner table, systematically sitting beside each of us in turn and looking with appealing eyes, portraying that lean and hungry look, despite the shape of her gradually broadening girth.

It was during one of the regular Saturday night dances at the hall next to our Mess that Soppy Poppy decided to look in too. She entertained herself by picking up titbits of food when they were dropped on the floor. As we danced our way into the latter part of the evening, the band took a rest and we all sat around the sides of the hall chatting and relaxing. Any attempt to decorate this hastily-built hut was completely lacking. The chairs were hard and uncomfortable, the walls were unpainted and the dance floor was now empty. The bar was a makeshift affair comprising a couple of trestle tables and, as we all wore uniform, there was little of colour, beauty or interest to attract our attention. It was a dull and dreary place, unless the band was playing.

Suddenly, a little black spaniel ventured out on to the empty dance floor. Emerging from behind the bar, with slow and hesitating steps, she made her way to the centre. With a great effort of will, she succeeded that far, but this was where she gave up. Her two front paws slipped outwards, until her head was resting between them on the shiny surface of the floor. Her rear was still firmly in the upright position and quite unable to bend or accommodate itself to the level of her front half. There she stopped, stuck in this uncomfortable position. Dorothy came to her aid and placed her little pet's feet firmly together again. With a pitiful look, Soppy Poppy collapsed again except that, this time, her back half slumped to join her front half as she rolled over on to one side. She remained there lying in a semi-stupor on the floor.

The crowd laughed at the unexpected entertainment. Somebody called out, "That dog's a bit tiddly!" Another corrected the unidentified voice by saying, "No, it's not - it's plain drunk!" Sure enough, she was completely squiffy. She had followed the same pattern as in the unholy episode of the "Vicar's chickens". Thirst had drawn her to the slop bucket filled with dregs of beer, discarded from used glasses. Once again, Dorothy ran over to her little animal, scooped her up in her arms and staggered out of the hall with the warm black bundle. She put the pathetic little dog to bed in the basket in her bedroom. Dorothy returned, saying that she might as well be at the party as Soppy Poppy was asleep and snoring already, and the bedroom now reeked with the smell of stale beer, anyway.

Next morning being Sunday, we were given our once-a-week treat of egg and bacon for breakfast. For the first time on record, our little friend was not there to receive the bacon rinds, nor was she around at lunch time. Eventually, while we were waiting to go to dinner, a very shaky little dog tottered into the lounge, looked around to make sure that we were all there, then curled up on the hearth rug and fell asleep. There she remained until Dorothy once again gathered her up in her arms, and placed her in her basket, from which, we were told, she emitted snoring noises on and off during the night. The following day when we had assembled for breakfast, a very cheerful and extremely hungry little dog, with no signs of shame or remorse, trotted briskly into the dining room and, carrying on where she had left off, began cadging on her rounds of the breakfast table, as though nothing had ever gone amiss.

# THE END IN SIGHT

Our cover was blown! The *Evening Standard*, one of Britain's most popular tabloids, published an article about Tempsford's clandestine operations with a surprising amount of accuracy. Now it was out in the open for anyone to read at the minute cost of a penny or two. We were shocked! Until this moment we would have been court martialled for saying considerably less than the *Evening Standard* disclosed. The Squadron Leader in charge of our department immediately made enquiries about the apparent leakage of TOP SECRET information. The answer was surprising: "Yes! It was authentic". With the war this far advanced, and with Germany now having a fairly good idea of what was going on, generalities were allowed to be published.

Our typing pool went to work and, many carbon copies later, all the personnel at Tempsford knew about the organization for which they had been working in ignorance for so long. The new information, when passed around, raised the morale of the non-flying members of the Station beyond one's imagination. The version from the tabloid is as follows:

### EVENING STANDARD JUNE 1944
*Secret Flyers Beat Gestapo In Night Game*
*from James Stuart:*
*Tempsford, Beds., Thursday.*
*Tempsford is just a hamlet in rural Bedfordshire. Its inhabitants mostly work on the land. And none of*

*them knew it, but Tempsford held one of the big secrets of the war.*

*They knew that down a little side road marked, "This road is closed to the public", there was an R.A.F. Station. In the Anchor and the Wheatsheaf they saw the R.A.F. men. But that was all. They had no idea of the job they were engaged on.*

*Names of the pilots and crews who did that job cannot yet be revealed except for one, the late Group Captain P.C. Pickard., D.S.O. and two bars, D.F.C., - the famous "Target for To-night" pilot.*

*When he left Bomber Command, Pickard commanded one of the two "Special Mission" squadrons which the R.A.F. created as <u>a link with the underground movement in all occupied countries.</u> He was an expert in "Pick-up" flights.*

*<u>All Sorts</u>*

*The R.A.F. began this branch of its work immediately after the collapse of France - with one flight of a Bomber Squadron of No.3 Group. By March 1942, Tempsford was in operation, and finally two special squadrons were being employed.*

*From Tempsford they delivered arms, ammunition, radio sets, food, and other supplies to all the underground fighters from the Arctic Circle of Northern Norway to the Mediterranean shores of southern France.*

*From big bombers - Whitleys first and then Stirlings and Halifaxes dropped their parachute containers. Every kind of supply went down, from skis and sleighs for the Norwegians, to bicycle tires - made in England, but carefully camouflaged with French names - to the resisters in Western Europe. For three years the airfield, built over what had been a large area of marsh, was the air centre of the Resistance movements all over Europe. Night after night, the villagers saw airplanes go off and probably heard them droning back in the small hours. But they never saw the people, men and women in civilian clothes, who were driven down the prohibited road from the airfield, the men and women who had been brought to England from Occupied France, under the very noses of the Wehrmacht and Gestapo.*

### No Secret Devices

*There were no secret devices to help this passenger service to operate. The R.A.F. airplanes simply landed in France, picked up their passengers and flew off again to Tempsford.*

*On other trips they dropped Czech, Polish and Dutch agents in their own countries.*

*About 700 resistance leaders made the trip. Sometimes the R.A.F. brought back documents, maps and messages.*

*Not all the story can be told even now. There is still need for secrecy about how the great organization was built up.*

*The romantic - and hazardous - side of the job was flying the old unarmed Lysanders and bigger Hudsons to the secret landing grounds in France, guided only by the dim lights from torches held by patriots.*

*All the pick-ups were made in France.*

*One of the airmen who took part in the adventure said today: "We had to have decent fields, so we brought back men of the resistance movement to teach them the sort of places to select and what to do to help us to land. Then we took them back again.*

*"Others we brought back were trained in England as saboteurs and dropped again in France."*

*"One French agent was caught by the Gestapo, who broke his feet in torturing him. He managed to escape from them and we picked him up and brought him back to England. He could not, of course, make a parachute jump again, but he insisted on returning to carry on his work in France, so we took him over. He was a brave man."*

### Map on Knee

*Usually when a Lysander - only a three-seater airplane at one time used for Army Co-operation work -went out to pick up passengers, the pilot flew unaided, with a map on his knees, doing his own navigation, looking in the dark for a small field somewhere in France. There was no room for a navigator when passengers had to be brought back.*

*Often the Gestapo arrived just as an airplane lifted its wheels off the ground. "There were many hairbreadth escapes like that" I was told. A pilot was just about to land one night, when he saw that behind each torch holder stood a German with a revolver. The pilot realised what was happening, revved his engine and flew off. He was wounded in the neck, but flew back safely.*

*"When one of our Hudsons got bogged down in landing, the pilot rounded up 200 people, 12 oxen and 6 horses and worked for two and a half hours before the aircraft could leave - with a number of important political passengers on board."*

*How secret it all was may be judged by this - said to me by another of the pilots: "Even when high-ranking officers who were not in the know, asked us about the work we were doing, we had to lie like old Harry. It was court martial for anyone who breathed a word about the job. Not even the mechanics knew about the passenger flights."* Evening Standard

With reference to the Hudson that "got bogged down in landing". It was a great surprise when the Hudson finally returned to Tempsford several hours late. It had already been chalked up as missing. By deduction, the aircraft would have been out of fuel long before it actually arrived back at base. Who would have thought of it being "grounded" in France and, at the same time, having been able to evade the enemy?

Another Top Secret subject was now becoming common knowledge; the existence of the "Mulberry Harbours", which were used during the invasion for the disembarkation of men and materials until a port had been captured. But before enlarging on the subject, I would like to take another aside and give a short background of the uncle and aunt with whom I so often spent the night during the war years, when passing through London or attending a course.

My uncle, George Couper, was one of three children born to the wife of a Scotsman, who was the stationmaster at a small railway junction in a remote area of the Yorkshire moors, some miles from the city of York. Later, he and his family were moved to Garforth, a suburban district about seven miles from Leeds. As was all too common in those days, his father was an intelligent man, who had not been privileged with a good education, but was determined to give his children the chance he was denied. So, Uncle George travelled daily by local train to one of the Leeds Grammar Schools, where he distinguished himself in his last school year with the highest marks ever recorded - 100% in everything! His children, Donald and Jean, were taken there one day at their own request to see the "Achievements Board" on which his success was clearly displayed. He was brilliant at Math., and began his studies in Engineering at Leeds University. During these studies, he returned to York to carry out some of the practical work on his degree, apprenticing at the Railway Engineering Works. He graduated just before the First World War with an M.Sc. in Engineering, specializing in pre-stressed concrete. From the north of England, he was sent south to Poole in Dorset for the duration of the First World War, to experiment on the design of concrete boats and lighters. I believe they were not too successful.

It was during this period that he accompanied his parents on a summer holiday to Jersey in the Channel Islands. As they were lining up to leave the boat on their arrival at the port of St. Helier, he is reported to have said, as he glanced along the line of disembarking passengers, "That is the young lady I would like to marry!" She disembarked and so did George and his family. The young lady was met by my mother (her older sister) to spend a holiday with her and my father - they had recently opened their summer tea garden on the seafront at West Park, St. Helier. George and his family, on the other hand went into town to find their allotted guest house.

Some days later the Couper family arrived by chance at my mother's place for afternoon tea. George at once recognised the girl he had seen getting off the boat. From that day on, a relationship began between a short, stocky dark haired Yorkshire man and a slim young girl from London, several inches taller than himself. They married, the war ended and my uncle joined a firm where he was challenged with designing the roof of the White City stadium in London. When it was completed, it boasted the widest roof span of pre-stressed concrete of any other building in England. It was given great publicity and praise. But that was a time of recession in England, and his firm decided to cut down on expenses. My uncle being the highest paid employee was told that he was no longer needed - he got the sack, but his boss was rewarded with a knighthood for a design my uncle created!

For two years, without work and with the responsibility of a wife and baby son, life was hard for the family. Then he took a position as Chief Engineer, specializing in pre-stressed concrete with the London "Gas, Light and Coke Company", where he stayed until his retirement in 1950. It is amusing to note that his full initials spell "G.A.S. COuper" - he was often ribbed for it.

For over twenty years, he could be seen going to the office, impeccably dressed in the accepted fashion of the day, wearing a dark suit, hand-tied bow tie, a bowler hat on his head and an umbrella hooked over his arm. Underneath the dark suit and bowler hat, there was, however, a man of great wit and a dry sense of humour. He was blessed with an excellent bass voice which, at the appropriate times, he used to sing solos in the church choir, or to delight us with his humorous musical skits at Christmas time. As youngsters, we were often convulsed with laughter over the duets which my uncle and my aunt - a good soprano and pianist - adapted to their particular talents for the ridiculous.

When the London Blitz began, my uncle announced that he was changing his attire from now on, and would wear a sports jacket and grey flannels. He said it would be so much easier to hitch-hike into the City on a lorry when the busses and trains were not running, and that he would feel so much more comfortable when doing his stint as Fire Warden on the office roof.

Every evening a few employees would stay on the job and spend the night at the office in Horseferry Road. At the sound of the air raid siren, they would go up to the flat roof of the building to keep watch for any incendiary bombs that might land on it. From this look-out, my uncle often spent the dark hours watching London "light up", having exchanged his bowler for a tin hat, and his drawing board for a large shovel. He was surrounded by an array of buckets of sand and water, plus a stirrup pump (like a large bicycle pump) for spraying water over the fire bombs.

Had it not been for my aunt Doddy noticing a short article in the daily paper some years after the war, my uncle George would have been given no more credit for his wartime contributions than that of his efforts with the "bucket and spade". Doddy looked up from the paper one morning and, pointing to the newsprint, said," George, come and look at this article. I think it will interest you." He glanced over her shoulder and read a headline about the Mulberry Harbours. "Oh, yes", he said "I know all about them. I designed them". He had not told anyone about this aspect of his wartime activities; he was a modest man!

I wrote to my cousin and asked if he had anything to add to my account about his father. I quote the following excerpt from his reply: *"The Mulberry incident is of great interest of course. Dad used to work for the Gas Company by day and do consulting work at home in the evenings. Among his clients were such household names in the construction business as McAlpine and Wimpey. One of the firms he did consulting for, was awarded the contract for Mulberry, and so I have no doubt that the intricate drawings for its construction were made on our dining table at Edgwarebury Lane!"* He continued, *"This last paragraph, by the way, is really just an aside for your interest and should not warrant, I think, inclusion in your account."* I have included it anyway!

My cousin's comments also bear out that, uncomprehending, I must have seen one of the Mulberry Harbour designs in the making on the night that he taught me to use the slide-rule with greater confidence. "A kind of wall," was the explanation my uncle gave me in reply to my question about the blueprints on the table. "What kind of wall?" I asked. "A sea wall,' he said. I could make nothing of the design and, as my uncle had passed it off as being dull and of no importance, I accepted his explanation. We then delved into the intricacies of the slide-rule for the next half-hour.

George Couper, an enthusiastic snooker player, used his dining table as a drawing board, the heavy mahogany leaves covering the full- size games table beneath. I cannot imagine a less likely place than the dining room of a suburban home of a man in his sixties, to go looking for top secret information!

The Mulberry Harbours were essential elements of the Allied invasion plans, and I quote from letters and memos of Prime Minister, Winston Churchill:

## Prime Minister to Marshal Stalin

June 7, 44

"*...Most especially secret. We are planning to construct very quickly two large synthetic harbours on the beaches of this wide, sandy bay of the Seine estuary. Nothing like this has ever been seen before. Great ocean liners will be able to discharge and run by numerous piers supplies to the fighting troops. This must be quite unexpected by the enemy, and will enable the build-up to proceed with very great independence of weather conditions. We hope to get Cherbourg at an early point in the operations.*" The Second World War: Triumph and Tragedy, Houghton Miffin Co.,Boston, Mass. 1953 p.8

## "*To the President of the US*

June 14

*... I had a jolly day on the beaches and inland. There is a great mass of shipping extended more than 50 miles along the coast. It is being increasingly protected against weather by the artificial harbours, nearly every element of which has been a suc-*

*cess and will soon have effective shelter against bad weather..."Idem p.15*

*"By June 19, the two 'Mulberry' Harbours, one at Arromanches, the other 10 miles farther west, in the American sector, were making progress. 'Pluto' the submarine pipeline was also well advanced. Then a four-day gale began which almost entirely prevented the landing of men and material, and did great damage to the newly sunk breakwaters. Many floating bombardons which were not designed for such conditions broke from their moorings and crashed into other breakwaters and the anchored shipping. The harbour in the American sector was ruined, and its serviceable parts were used to repair Arromanche. This gale, the like of which had not been known in June for forty years was a severe misfortune..."* Idem p.20

"(On August 7)... *The damage done to Cherbourg had been enormous, and it was certain that when the Brittany ports were captured they would take a long time to repair. The fertility of the 'Mulberry' at Arromanche, the sheltered anchorages, and the unforseen development of smaller harbours on the Normandy coast had lessened the urgency of capturing the Brittany ports, which had been so prominent in our early plans..."* Idem p.32

"(On September 4)...*The number of divisions that could be sustained and the speed and range of their advance depended however entirely on harbours, transport, and supplies. Relatively little ammunition was being used, but food and above all petrol governed every movement. Cherbourg and 'Mulberry' harbour at Arromanche were the only ports we had, and these were daily being left farther behind. The front line was still sustained from Normandy and each day about 20.000 tons of supplies had to be carried over ever-increasing distances, together with much material for mending roads and bridges and building air fields..."* Idem p.1

# SUMMER AND AUTUMN 1944

As the invasion of Europe continued and the front line moved deeper into France, so the pins marking our landing strips and dropping zones began to disappear from the map. Gradually, these areas were freed by the Allies and, therefore, many of the secret landing grounds were no longer required for clandestine operations. The Nazis were being pushed back towards Germany. We, in our section, noticed the difference in the pressure of work and the general atmosphere; life became a little more relaxed. The aircrews would come in for information as before, but would stay longer, just chatting. Our large four-engined aircraft, the Halifaxes and Stirlings, continued to drop agents and supplies in Norway and Denmark, still under enemy occupation, but in the rest of Europe there were fewer landings and we began to see that the end was in sight. There were times when I discarded my bicycle - my only means of transport - for a drive into the town in a snazzy little sports car, or an old jalopy, for a visit to the "flicks" (movies) or a meal out. Life became much more enjoyable socially.

That summer I became more familiar with the pub by the river. It had always been the exclusive hang-out for the RAF officers, but now more mixed parties took place there. The pub was surrounded by a pleasant garden with a lawn leading down to the river. We could relax and enjoy a beer or shandy with our friends, while sitting on the grass on a warm evening; thus being spared the embarrassment of a serenade of the all too familiar song of

"Good Night Ladies" by those propping up the bar. This was usually belted out by the slightly inebriated, as closing time grew nearer. They were pleasant days to remember, though regretfully, by the end of the war, not all our little group of friends survived the dangers that they faced every time they flew on operations.

On other occasions, Barbara and I, neither of us having a car, often cycled the nine miles into Bedford where we attended a broadcast of the Promenade Concerts given by the BBC Symphony Orchestra. It had been evacuated first from London to Bristol, then, later on, for greater safety to Bedford. Due to the flying bomb attacks, the orchestra no longer performed in London. It was forbidden then for a group larger than about twenty people to gather together in one place in the London area. We no longer had to travel to the Albert Hall for the Proms - the Proms came to us!

Sir Adrian Boult, the permanent conductor, was a friend of Barbara's family, so we were fortunate in being able to obtain complimentary tickets to attend rehearsals and special studio broadcasts. Usually, there were seldom more than five or six of us in the audience. Often, they were members of the family of the soloist, the guest conductor or, occasionally, of the composer. I look back with happy memories on having been able to attend these memorable performances with a privileged few.

Most of the concerts were broadcast from Bedford School - the well known boys' "public" school (it would be called a "private" school in Canada).

However, difficulties arose when a public broadcast was put on the air from the Bedford Corn Exchange. It had a very large hall which was filled to capacity for every programme. All went well in the double forte parts but, in the more delicate pianissimo passages, slight apprehension and anticipated amusement always gripped the audience. The problem arose because of one of the common walls of the hall was shared with the pub next door. As the second half of the programme progressed, the thirsty patrons of the pub were usually gulping down their last drinks before closing time. The ensuing result was often loud and vocal, as raucous ditties were sung enthusiastically, penetrating through the wall to mingle with Mozart and Brahms. Whether the noisy chorus from the pub reached the ears of the music lovers tuned into the BBC, I have no idea, but it was usually rather a shock for the unsuspecting soloist of the evening.

The orchestra remained at Bedford until Britain was once more at peace. It was there that Barbara and I met Joyce Pearson, one of the viola players, and we soon became good friends. On returning to civilian life, the three of us shared an apartment in London, until the time that our marriages changed the course of our lives. It was a very happy interlude and, for me personally, the one good thing that came out of the flying bomb raids.

During the summer of 1944, the Halifaxes and Stirlings from Tempsford continued their dropping operations in Norway and Denmark, and a more limited number of agents and containers were parachuted and landed in the areas of France still awaiting freedom.

Once again, I was due for another week's leave. The prospect pleased me, for not only was I going home, but it also happened to be summer time. This fact had both its good and its bad side, according to the way you looked at it. The countryside in which we lived was in one of the most beautiful areas of Sussex. As much of it belonged to the National Trust, it has stayed that way to the present day. To walk along the grassy footpaths through meadows and woodlands was a joy in such beautiful surroundings. The bad aspect of it was that the German Luftwaffe, only about thirty miles south of us on the other side of the English Channel, continued to make the most of the fine summer weather to give us surprise visits. I wondered what would be new this time? My mother never mentioned any of the enemy activity that occurred around the village when she wrote to me. I always had to wait for a blow-by-blow description when I went home. She said that she did not want to worry me with things I could do nothing about.

I left for home on a warm day with a cloudless sky above. In Bedfordshire one always felt hundreds of miles from any enemy activity, and people were happily unconcerned about attacks from the air. With this feeling of security, I walked to the railway station. I was sure that I would soon see, in sharp contrast, the events that were taking place along the south coast.

As we sat around the dining table during the first evening of my leave, I learned that the roof of our home had just been repaired. It had been pierced with two holes from cannon shells fired by a Spitfire. The fighter had been attempting to shoot down a flying bomb, missed it, and hit our roof instead. My mother was quite matter-of-fact about it, and seemed somewhat amused about the whole incident. She said how lucky she was that nothing had penetrated through the ceiling! It brought the fact home to me that a bungalow gave little protection against such events. She promised me quite an exciting week as far as the flying bombs were concerned. "They rattle over us quite regularly," my mother commented casually, and went on to say, "It did not affect us too much at first, when they were on their way to London. Now," she said, proudly waving her arms in the direction of the cliff on the other side of the valley, "we have masses of anti-aircraft guns on the top of the hill. When a doodle-bug is sighted, all hell breaks loose as they try to shoot it down - we stay indoors to avoid the shrapnel - sometimes they are lucky, sometimes not." She paused for breath and then continued, "We have Spitfires around as well. It seems that they try to shoot down the buzz-bombs over the sea, but often they intercept them over the land. That's how my roof got shot up." "But you just wait until one of the doodlebugs only gets damaged," she emphasized, "It's quite a sight to see it going round and round in circles after its compass has been put out of action."

She went on to tell me about the excitement which took place a few days before I arrived, "A doodlebug came hurtling above our valley on its way inland, when a Spitfire appeared from nowhere. It approached the buzz-bomb at an angle, and intercepted it by touching the tip of the wing with its own wing-tip. I thought they would both crash," she said, "but instead, the flying bomb immediately changed course, turned in a wobbly half-circle, trundled out to sea again, and went down in a spray of water and disappeared! The Spitfire, having done what it set out to do, just banked and disappeared over the hill." I soon discovered what my mother was trying to tell me.

The next day was a lively one for flying bombs. Several rattled overhead at a fantastic speed. Then a Spitfire hit one just before it reached the coast. Only the magnetic compass of the flying bomb was put out of action as it came straight at us; then it began turning gently to the right. It flew overhead as my mother, uncle, aunt and I watched fascinated. There was no time to go to the bomb shelter, so we just looked and chanted out loudly together, "Not now! Not now! Not now!" I got the impression that they had reiterated this phrase many times before. Then, with relief, we watched it continue on its path, flying in a wide circle as it made its way out to sea again. "I hope it blows up now," said my uncle, but no, it continued circling, returning to land a little lower in altitude and in an ever-decreasing circle. It came inland once more but, on the third pass, it just cleared the cliff on its outward journey, and miraculously escaped the gunfire. The ugly missile, still circling, headed towards the wide expanse of sea. We all watched intently, hoping that it would not turn in our direction for a fourth time. Suddenly, its nose pointed downwards, and it hit the surface of the water and blew up in a cloud of flame and spray. Within little more than a minute, we were looking once again at the calm sea glistening in the sunlight, with only the sound of thrushes and blackbirds breaking the silence. After my week's leave, I returned to Tempsford with greater understanding of the war that was still being fought on my own doorstep.

Long after the war was over, I read that, during the latter part of July 1944, our defences were redeployed to bring down the flying bomb. A strip of coastline between Beachy Head in West Sussex and St Margaret's Bay, close to Dover in east Kent, was allotted for the use of anti-aircraft guns. It comprised a narrow strip no more than 5,000 yards wide. The guns fired at the flying bombs as far as 10,000 yards out to sea. Beyond that line, the Spitfires patrolled, taking on the task of shooting the missiles down into the sea. This tactical defence was backed up by another ribbon of airborne fighters further inland, and it was intended that the barrage balloons around London would bring down the ones that managed to get through the cordon.

About 8,000 flying bombs were launched in the direction of London and about 2,400 got through. The civilian casualties were just over 6,000 killed and more than 18,000 seriously injured. On September 8, 1944, when the main onslaught of the V-1's had ceased, London received yet another surprise. The first V-2 rockets were launched. The initial one landed at Chiswick, not far from the centre of London, followed less than a minute later by the second that hit Epping in the Thames Estuary. For the next seven months, about 1,300 of them were fired against England - about 500 hitting different areas of London. This "silent" bombardment - for one heard nothing until the rocket exploded - only ceased after The Hague in Holland was liberated by the Allies. The most important V-2 rocket sites were situated in this area. Nearly 3,000 people in England were killed by these rockets and over 6,000 seriously injured.

Despite these hazards, we continued to visit London. I was sitting, one day, with a soggy towel around my neck, and a water-resistant cape covering my clothes in the hair-dressing salon in Selfridges' department store in London's Oxford Street. My hair was exuding the usual acrid smell associated with a perm, as I waited with my head covered in rollers. These had been firmly attached to my hair, and were connected with electrical cords to the hood above my head, the know-how that heated the rollers in the 1940's. At that stage of the game, there was no running away from the octopus-like contraption above me. I was anchored to it and had no choice but to wait immobile and helpless, until my hair had received its full treatment. As I sat in the salon in that vulnerable state, there was a sudden, heavy crump, which vibrated through the floor and the chair on which I was sitting. "There goes another one!" said one of the hair-dressing assistants. "That's the second V-2 today," she remarked with resignation. "But it must be a mile or two away," said the consoling voice of one of the customers. There were no more comments, and the hairdressers continued to beautify the patrons in their various stages of treatment. "We get used to it," another girl said to her not-too-confident customer, "it's all in a day's work!" With that exhortation, the salon assistants carried on the normal daily routine. Nobody took any notice of me, for I still had about ten minutes to wait before being detached from the "octopus". So, I just sat quietly and hoped for the best, counting the minutes until I was free to go.

That was the first time that I had experienced the unwelcome arrival of a V-2. On several occasions afterwards, I heard these deadly missiles exploding in the distance when visiting the capital, but I was fortunate enough never to be close to one. The philosophy of the Londoners was, "If you hear it, you are alive; so why worry? If you don't hear it, you are dead; so you can't worry!" The V-2's were silent and gave no warning until they hit the ground. But the attitude towards the flying bombs, V-1's, was quite different. The reaction was automatic - when you heard the engine cut, you ran for it and dived for shelter. For people like myself who visited the city only occasionally, the strain was not too hard to endure, but I felt very sorry for those who had to stay in London permanently. The strain under which they had to live must have been very wearing.

Some time later that Autumn, Tempsford had to carry out a very unusual operation. Our four-engined aircraft were to drop agents by parachute over Norway to sabotage a "Heavy Water" plant. Our dossiers always provided sufficient general information about the chosen target, but, with this one, we all drew a blank. What was Heavy Water? We had no idea. The instructions were only that it was vital to stop the Nazis from transporting this "water" to Germany. At the time, very few people knew of the preparations for atomic warfare, or that the Germans were making advances in this field. The operation was carried out but, at that time, we understood that it was not a success. In retrospect, it is possible that this operation was a preliminary to the main attack.

A few months later, the plant was attacked again. It was bombarded by a daring combined air and sea operation, and was a complete success. Had Germany's atomic scientists been ahead of the US , I wonder if the first atomic bomb would have been dropped on London? But there is no definitive answer to this.

### Once in a Lifetime

We were asked to a party - by the word "we", I mean all the members of the Intelligence Section. It was going to be one of those once in a lifetime affairs, like something out of a story-book. The Joes were giving a party for all the non-flying officers at Tempsford, whose work was, in some way, connected with helping them in their comings and goings in their clandestine operations over the past years. We were deeply touched by their very generous "Thank You" gesture, and we waited impatiently for the day. As there was a shortage of girls at the Joes' residence, they extended the invitation to the officers from the WAAF Mess as well.

A few days later, we brushed up our uniforms, some members of our Mess even polished their buttons, and we waited in anticipation for the cars from the "Big House" to pick us up. The Joes were quite definite about providing us with their own transportation. It was thoughtful of them, but I guess that the real purpose was to make it difficult for us to find the whereabouts of the House again. They were still carrying out clandestine operations in France, and this house was their base, while waiting to return on our aircraft to their homelands; they still had to be cautious. Although the house was only about ten miles from Tempsford, I never discovered its actual location.

It was a very dark night when we arrived at our hosts' mansion, for the agents were transported to their homelands only during the moon periods. We were ushered into a large hall and were introduced to the Joes. We, wearing our formal regulation Air Force uniforms, shook hands with a colourful bunch of people in fancy dress costumes. They were a cheerful, welcoming and warm-hearted group. Most of them spoke with French accents, and all were introduced by their code names. I find it disappointing now, when looking back on that evening that I gleaned so little information about the group, for it included both a man and a woman who were quite famous for the large underground organizations they ran in France. Regretfully, I shall never know their true identities.

The woman was a striking personality, tall, slim and attractive, and had a slight French accent. She was dressed in a flowing Eastern-style gown, and was heavily made-up, with lots of mascara on her long artificial eye-lashes. It would have been impossible to recognize her without the make-up and, I guess, that was probably the idea behind it. The man was, I believe, a great organizer of the Underground Movement both in London and in France, and was the only one of our hosts wearing his official uniform. He came to the party dressed in what he actually was - a Major in the British Army. We were introduced to him only as "The Major". He spoke with an educated English accent, but I will never know his name.

The party began and we danced to the popular tunes of the day, which blared out from a well used gramophone in the corner of the room. My first dancing partner, a man disguised as an Arab, wore a huge black beard which covered most of his face. His eyes were bright and twinkled; and, apart from his nose, were the only real parts of his face that I could see. It was impossible to imagine what he really looked like without that menacing beard: there is no way that I could have identified him in a police line-up. A "farmer" was also having a very good time on the dance floor. Maybe, he was just being himself, or was he wearing the fancy-dress disguise he used on the job in France - who knows? For all of us, I guess, this was the first and last time that our dancing partners would be genuine secret agents. They were wonderful hosts, humourous, light-hearted and relaxed. They were obviously enjoying the party as much as we were, in the safety of a friendly land. When the time came for us to leave, we were lined up and inconspicuously counted, making sure that all who came were safely returned. We climbed into the limousines waiting for us in the driveway and, on this occasion, without blinds drawn, we returned back to the Mess and reality, after an evening of non-fictional fantasy.

In October, I received my marching orders. I was given two days notice to leave for Waterbeach, near Cambridge. We no longer worked overtime at Tempsford, so, I suppose, the last person to come was the first to go. After fifteen months in the same place, it was quite a wrench to leave the work and my friends and acquaintances. My emotions were very mixed as I departed from Tempsford. I thought of the aircrews still operating who, hopefully, would survive the war, and of those who were in prison camps, and of those who would never return.

I remembered the sad and all too typical story of one aircrew, who had gone on a parachute dropping mission over Norway a week or two before. They had twenty-seven operational sorties to their credit. Three more successful sorties and they would be released from operations for at least six months to train new recruits, or to do something similar. Sortie Number 28 came up. They arrived over the reception area to be flashed the wrong code letters from the ground. There appeared to be some unexplained activity going on down below, so they returned to base with their containers. Sortie Number 29 materialized about four days later. They were to repeat the operation. It was imperative that the supplies be dropped to the organization as soon as possible. They set out for the same area that night. Early next morning, we realized that they would not be returning - they would have been out of fuel by then.

Some days later, a coded message was received from Norway to say that the containers had been dropped and retrieved safely. No information was given about the aircraft having been attacked or of its crashing in Norway. Were they attacked, but managed to limp part way across the North Sea, or were they struck by lightning - a very rare but possible hazard? The crew sent no radio transmissions. They were posted as Missing and, after three months, officially posted as: Missing, believed Killed. Nothing was heard of any of them again. So close to the end of hostilities and with one operational sortie left to complete their tour, it seemed particularly sad.

At the end of their four year existence, the special duty *"Moon Squadrons"* completed 2,562 sorties comprising 995 agents, 29,000 large containers, 10,000 smaller packages. They suffered a total loss of 70 aircraft. (Source: *We Landed by Moonlight* by Hugh Verity)

# R.A.F. WATERBEACH

The airfield at Waterbeach was situated about four miles north-east of Cambridge on the road to Ely, the beautiful little cathedral town built on a solitary hill, or "hummock", in the middle of nowhere, surrounded by the fens. The fenlands of East Anglia were once undrained peat marshes, and were first reclaimed by the Romans and later, in the 17th century, by the Dutch. The Cathedral at Ely dominates the landscape for miles around, with its beautiful octagonal lantern tower above the transept. This was built by Alan of Walsingham in A.D.1322. Sir Christopher Wren is thought to have been influenced by its design, when he planned St. Paul's Cathedral in London.

The River Cam, from which Cambridge derives its name, flows along the "Backs" behind the ancient and historical University Colleges. But, as it passes by the village of Waterbeach, it loses much of its beauty and is just another undistinguished little river that meanders through the flat and almost hedgeless fields of the one-time marshes. There it flows quietly past the garden of the pub, a popular haunt of the RAF, where we often went for afternoon tea, and gathered in the evenings for social events. Sometime later, after VE-Day when peace in Europe had been declared, the pub on the river briefly gained even greater popularity, when the RAF put on a water sports event to celebrate the end of the war in Europe. A high diving board had been erected by the pub's waterside gardens and, from there, some of the aircrew participated in an excellent diving display. Their latent talents were discovered and appreciated only now that there was more time to relax, and to look forward to things, other than hoping for a safe return from the next bombing mission.

However, Waterbeach was still very much a wartime station when I arrived in the late Autumn of 1944. The dispersal areas around the airfield perimeter were dotted with powerful four-engined Lancaster bombers. There was no sign of operational missions waning at this RAF station as they had begun to do at Tempsford. Bomber Command was still carrying out heavy night raids to destroy, among other things, military targets, weapon stores and ball-bearing factories - the Nazis were particularly short of ball-bearings for their trains and other transportation. The main attacks were now concentrated over Germany, with the hope of bringing the war to an end as quickly as possible. By now, most of the French ports and military targets had already been freed by the Allies. It was going to be quite a new experience for me to work on a night bomber station.

The WAAF Officers' Mess and sleeping quarters were in a house in the village, but they were already overcrowded, so I joined the company of three other WAAF officers who also worked shift duties. We shared a four-bedroom sleeping hut, the rest of the huts in our quiet cul-de-sac being occupied by aircrews. I enjoyed the freedom and quietness away from kitchen noises during my daytime sleeping hours, and no one ever invaded our privacy. We ate all our meals in the main Officers' Mess, so never went hungry when working irregular hours.

On the first morning in my new surroundings, I walked to the Intelligence Section and was greeted by a cheerful group of people. After the usual cup of tea to make me feel at home, I was introduced to the duties I was to undertake. Everything seemed very straightforward until it came to the subject of "Interrogation". It was then that the Squadron Leader in charge, a plump, balding and cheerful middle-aged man, nicknamed "Tubby" for obvious reasons, tried to explain a recent change in policy. "The C.O. has decided that WAAF officers are no longer to be allowed to interrogate the crews after their missions," he said. "As far as I am concerned, it would be no problem. Your predecessor did it all the time," he added. I was not at all sure what to think about that last remark. Why had the C.O. made his mind up about me before even seeing me? Realizing that he had not put it at all tactfully, my new Department Head cleared his throat and said, "Well! You see, she was a smashing blonde." By this remark, I was even more embarrassed than he was. The comment made me feel that I must look distinctly mousy, despite the fact that I had fair hair in those days. He hurried on, "She was a bit too smashing, you see. As a matter of fact, she put off the aircrews, both with her looks and her way of interrogating. I'm sorry, but the C.O. insists that no more women are to do the job." I began to wonder why I had been sent here at all. However, when one by one more details came out, we were able to laugh about the situation, and my future colleagues turned out to be a genuine, helpful and friendly group of people. I only regret that I never had the opportunity of setting eyes on the offending blonde.

A few days later, the Squadron flew on a night operation to Germany. I attended the briefing for the crews in the afternoon. It was held in a large wooden hut, built for the purpose, and was filled with nearly a hundred participating crew members and staff when I arrived. Most of the crews, having already assembled, were sitting in rows on hard chairs with their note pads on their knees. I grabbed a seat near the back of the room. At the Intelligence Office, we always received the target information during the morning, but it was not until the briefing that the aircrews would learn the name of the target for the night. There was an atmosphere of restlessness in the room before the briefing began. By 4.00 pm, all the members of the contributing departments had arrived. In turn, each member stood at the front facing the crews, a large blackboard on the wall behind him, and gave his specialized knowledge such as target, route, height, bomb load, enemy flak, weather at home and over Europe, rendezvous time and position when joining the main bomber force. This information was backed up, where necessary, with appropriate maps and charts which were pinned to the blackboard. I concentrated hard as I watched the complete picture unfolding. The briefings, I was to learn, always ended up with a wise and encouraging word from the Squadron Commander, and a warm "Good Luck!" from the C.O.

After being asked at dinner time that night to be in the office before the return of the bomber force, I arrived early, but without knowing what duties I was expected to fulfil. The girls in our typing pool worked only in the daytime, one of their less glamorous chores being to make tea for everyone. I could at least do that, I thought. So I prepared tea in the urn for the returning crews who, I hoped, would be able to face drinking the brew with its accompanying spoonfuls of Nestlé's milk. The Air Commodore (Air Officer Commanding the station) arrived well before the aircraft had landed, to greet the men on their return. That was one of the many nights he had decided to look in. I gave him the first mug of tea, for which he thanked me quite graciously. A few minutes later, I was asked "You did give the A.O.C. his tea in the bone china cup and saucer, didn't you?" "No," I replied, "I gave him a mug like the rest of us." "But we keep special china for him," I was told. "Well," I replied "at least I made sure that it was clean and uncracked. I'll know better next time," and I wished I had made a better start.

Soon we heard the drone of heavy engines in the distance and, shortly, the Lancs. were circling the airfield. We listened intently for any irregularity in the sound of the engines, but everything sounded normal that night. The runway lights were activated and, in record time, the circling aircraft landed one after the other. When the last Lanc. had reached the end of the runway safely, the lights on the airfield were extinguished to leave Waterbeach and the surrounding countryside in pitch darkness once more. Within about twenty minutes of hearing the aircraft overhead, the first arrivals began crowding into the room, as the airmen clumped across the bare floor in their heavy flying boots. Looking tired but thankful to be back, they took their places around the trestle tables for interrogation. They loosened their sheepskin jackets to display a variety of white sweaters and fancy scarves underneath. About fifteen minutes later, the room was full and the crews were lining up for interrogation. Hurriedly, I was handed a pad and the necessary forms and was told to "Get on with the job - we can't keep them waiting unnecessarily." "But," I said, "I'm not supposed..." "Forget the orders, we've got to get them off to breakfast and bed as quickly as possible," was the reply.

After my little pep talk, I was uncertain about the reception I might receive from the aircrews, but I was more than glad that I had attended the briefing the afternoon before. I walked over to an empty table, sat down, laid out the forms in front of me and just waited. If they wanted to get the formalities over quickly, they had the choice. One crew, waiting in turn, decided to take the quick way out to the breakfast table, and asked me rather diffidently if I was interrogating also. I replied in the affirmative, and they sat down and soon provided the required information. The C.O. wandered in my direction and hovered behind my chair for a few minutes. I think I must have felt more nervous at that moment than the crew facing me had been, when flying over the target a few hours earlier. The Group Captain said nothing, and then walked over to a nearby table where another group was going through the same process. That night turned out to be the first of many busy ones for me. The original pep talk was never referred to again!

As the last crew left and retired to the Mess, the room became silent, except for the sound of shuffling papers. Our Department Head summed up the twelve reports, then phoned the Duty Officer at 3 Group to give him a verbal description of the raid, and the observations of our squadron before forwarding all of this by teleprinter. It had been a successful operation as far as we were concerned. When the office work had been completed and filed, and the appropriate documents locked in the safe, we switched off the lights, locked the door and walked out into the chill air. The sky was still very dark as we made our way to the Mess. When we arrived, the far end of the dining hall, closest to the kitchens, was filled with aircrews finishing their breakfast. A wonderful smell of fried bacon greeted us as we sat down, famished. We had qualified for the "Egg Line" breakfast having gone no farther than from the office to the Mess. Eggs and bacon were scarce commodities during the war, so a rule was instituted to qualify for such a treat. If a squadron on an operational mission crossed the enemy coast, whether or not it reached the target, the flying crews were entitled to an egg and bacon breakfast on their return. Should they, for some reason, be recalled before flying that far, they missed out on the deal and were given one of the less popular breakfasts instead. The rule was waived for our own small team, not so much, I suspect, for the sake of good PR, but because it would otherwise cause unnecessary work for the kitchen staff.

Our breakfast was soon ready, and we began to eat heartily in the reflected glory of the men in white sweaters and flying boots who were, one by one, leaving the table to retire to bed. When all of them had disappeared, the Intelligence staffs, four of us in all, were the sole occupants left sitting at one end of a long refectory table in a very large empty dining room. It was a relaxed and social meal as we discussed the night's events, particularly as all had gone according to plan. When the kitchen staff began making extra loud clattering noises as they cleared the dirty plates, we took the hint that they too wished to go to bed, for they had already prepared neatly laid tables in readiness for the early breakfast rush. Those whose night's sleep was about to come to an end, would soon carry on where we left off.

We got up from our seats and walked out of the dining room. I picked up my newly-acquired bicycle from the front entrance just as dawn was breaking, and began pedalling towards my sleeping quarters. A cold and cheerless morning greeted me. As I rode along the lane, a faint orange glow appeared on the distant horizon. Within minutes, the first bright rays of the sun burst upon the bedewed and sleeping countryside. The sun rose, transforming itself quickly from a tip of orange in the distance, to a half circle and then to a full ball of fire. The hedgerows, flowers and wayside grasses suddenly glistened like shining stars. Newly spun spider webs, delicate as lace, yet heavy with droplets of dew, sparkled like clusters of diamonds. The small grey clouds that scurried across the sky, lit up in colours of red and orange as they hurried along, seemingly without purpose, on their way towards the Eastern sun. Songs of the early birds broke the silence. As the musical trills of the skylarks, thrushes and blackbirds filled the air, the caw-caws of the crows were the only jarring notes, as they competed with their more musical feathered friends. The catch phrase, "All the difference between night and day," seemed to take on a new meaning. The dawn awakening of the song birds contrasted dramatically with the silence, which was broken only a couple of hours earlier, when the four-engined Lancasters arrived in pitch darkness to circle the airfield and wake the sleeping village, as they came in to land one after the other and for the crews to live in safety for yet another day. But the birds took off and landed for the sheer joy of it, knowing nothing of life and death.

The morning papers would soon be carrying the headlines announcing the success of last night's attack. Life at that time was full of contrasts. I turned my thoughts from the night and, in a fresh light, I saw anew the hitherto uninteresting flat fields of vegetables and sugar beet, as my eye wandered to the wide and far away horizon. To witness the dawning of a new day in circumstances like these was an uplifting and joyful experience. I went to my room, slipped under the blankets - and slept.

One afternoon later in the week, I asked my new boss about a picture of an aircraft that was pinned to the notice board in our office, "Why does this large photo of a Lanc. have such pride of place here? Is there something special about it?" I enquired. He replied at once and said with emphasis, "The pilot of the aircraft got a 'gong'. It happened just before you arrived." All the staff reacted with pride and enthusiasm to my questions, each wanting to tell his version of the story.

"It had been a rough night over the other side, the flak was heavy and the enemy fighters were all over the place. This particular aircraft was hit by flak near the target, putting one of the engines out of action," the chief explained. "But," added one of the members of our department," the crew continued on their course for home. Then, as they crossed the enemy coast, another engine was hit, and it was not long before that too went *kaput.*." By now, the staff were all adding their little bits to the story. "The aircraft was loosing both height and speed as the crew continued across the North Sea. Then, when they had nearly reached the English coast, a third engine went US (unserviceable)," said another member of the staff. "No! They didn't bail out when they crossed the coast. They stayed put," added the third member of our team admiringly, and continued, "Somehow they managed to stay just above stalling speed, keeping enough height to reach the airfield." All the staff added their own few words to the last part of the saga - the pilot pulled off the impossible. He landed the aircraft and the crew safely. I looked again at the photo on the board. Apart from the shot-up engines, which barely showed up in the photo, the Lanc?. appeared to be intact. Though severely damaged, the aircraft and the crew, not only survived the landing, but, after a thorough repair job, the Lanc. would be airborne once again. This story, which I received second hand, may not be completely accurate in all its details but is, I think, one that deserves mention.

For the next six months, throughout the autumn and winter until the spring of 1945, Squadron 514 carried out regular operational missions. As time went on, these attacks became more and more hazardous. The Allied forces in France were slowly advancing, freeing the French ports, cities and towns from four years of enemy occupation. This meant that we now concentrated on targets in Germany, the distances being far greater than those to France. German cities were heavily fortified and their fighters were always in readiness to protect them, now that their position had turned round from the offensive to the defensive.

Towards Spring, the US Ninth Army and the British Second Army in Europe brought freedom to the Allied P.O.W.'s and to the prisoners in the notorious concentration camps of Belsen, Buchenwald as well as many other camps. The Auschwitz camp in Poland was liberated by the Red Army. It was only when they set the prisoners free that the Allies discovered the whole truth. (Only the code breakers at Bletchley knew of the atrocities taking place in Nazi occupied Europe but nothing could be done about it or their vital secret would have been blown) These concentration camps were extermination centres, chiefly for the Jewish people and for a few other "undesirables", such as Gypsies and political and religious leaders - including men, women and children of all ages. Millions had died before the Allies' arrival, and those still alive to greet them looked like living skeletons. Only their stomachs, distended through starvation, protruded under their blue and white-striped prison uniforms, which hung loosely from their bony shoulders. It was in the light of this discovery that our eyes were opened fully to the character of our enemy, and to "The New Order of

Nazi Germany" and "The Final Solution to the Jewish Question."

Throughout that winter, I used to marvel at the quiet courage of our aircrews, whose morale remained high through the many tests of endurance to which they were exposed. These men in blue uniforms, with wings sewn above their jacket pockets, lived a life of extremes. One day they would enjoy the freedom of the quiet and peaceful countryside, where, far from the threat of German air raids, most of our 3 Group airfields were located. They would relax in the local pub, rubbing shoulders with shopkeepers, businessmen, and the farmers whose day had been spent ploughing fields and milking cows. The next night these apparently carefree young men might have to adjust to being in the thick of battle, dodging searchlights, flak and enemy fighters. As they flew in formation with hundreds of other bombers, the worst and most critical time came when it was their turn to make a straight bombing run over the target. The fear of being caught in a searchlight, attacked by fighters or hit by flak at that moment must have been terrifying, knowing that they must not take evasive action until their bombs had been released. The war against Hitler unfortunately necessitated this terrible destruction in an effort to force as quick a surrender as possible by the enemy. But it must have made the missions of the bomber crews something very hard to bear. Despite everything, they remained cheerful and usually kept their feelings private.

Small incidents at times, though, brought home to us the strain and sensitivity the airmen normally kept to themselves. One afternoon after a briefing for Berlin, one of the pilots came into the office. He approached me with a letter in his hand. "Would you mind keeping this for me?" he asked. "If I don't return, please send it to the address on the envelope." He made no mention of the forthcoming raid on Germany's capital city, but probably indicated the feelings of many of those taking part. Incidents like this happened sometimes, making our staff feel both humble and honoured to work for them. There was much I would have liked to have said to the young airman, but all I could say was, "I'll lock it in the safe and give it back to you as soon as you return in the morning." When he left the room, it seemed that a burden had been lifted from him. Thankfully, I was able to give him back his letter after he had landed safely in the darkness of the early hours of the next day.

# VE-DAY AND AFTER

On April 28th, 1945, Germany's ally and Italy's dictator, Benito Mussolini and his mistress were assassinated by the Italian people. In the early hours of the morning of April 30th, Hitler, when his empire was crumbling around him, unexpectedly married his mistress, Eva Braun. Both committed suicide on this their wedding day. At the age of 56, he had been in power for just over twelve years. Admiral Donitz succeeded him and, on the day he took command, the German forces in Italy surrendered. On May 3rd, Donitz sought terms of surrender from the Allies.

On May 7th, a week after Adolph Hitler took his life, people everywhere in England heard, via the BBC or by word of mouth that the Prime Minister, Winston Churchill, would be broadcasting to the nation that evening. After the many staggering events of the past week, we all guessed what the message would be, but dared not allow our thoughts to run away with us until we heard the words from his own lips.

The BBC announcer introduced the Prime Minister. We all waited by our wireless sets, tense, impatient and excited, anticipating his pronouncement. Simply, without embellishment and, as always, to the point, he said, *"Hostilities will end officially at one minute after midnight tonight,"* and continued *"... but, in the interest of saving lives, the first cease-fire began yesterday and was sounded along all the fronts. The German War is, therefore, at an end. We may allow ourselves a brief period of fore, at an end. We may allow ourselves a brief period of rejoicing."*

Later, he wrote, *"The unconditional surrender of our enemies was a signal for the greatest outburst of joy in the history of mankind. The Second World War had indeed been fought to the bitter end in Europe. The vanquished as well as the victors felt inexpressible relief. But for us in Britain and the British Empire, who had alone been in the struggle from the first day to the last and staked our existence on the result, there was a meaning beyond what even our most powerful and most valiant Allies could feel. Weary and worn, impoverished but undaunted and now triumphant, we had a moment that was sublime. We gave thanks to God for the noblest of all His blessings, the sense that we had done our duty."* Source: *The Valiant Years*, LeVien, Jack and Lord, John, Corgi Books, Transworld Publishers, London p. 27.

By the time the war had ended, Squadron 514 had carried out over 300 operations comprising 3,800 sorties. It had attacked forty-seven different targets, of which many operations were in the heavily fortified Ruhr. Sixteen times the Squadron was part of the main force that bombed Berlin. On D-Day it attacked Oustreham and carried out three operations over Caen around that time. On January 1, 1943, 514 Squadron flew its first operation from Waterbeach to Dusseldorf and its last to Bad Oldesloe on April 24, 1945. During this period of less than two and a half years, seventy-three of our aircraft did not return. These statistics were compiled by our Intelligence Office just after VE-Day, and were as accurate as could be ascertained at the time.

On VE-Day, following the Prime Minister's announcement of the night before, I walked into the lounge of the Mess after breakfast to read the news of the events of the previous day. Everyone else had the same idea - there was not a paper left. The room was scattered with aircrews relaxing in comfortable armchairs and not so comfortable chairs, devouring the newspapers' headlines on the first day of Peace for more than five and a half years. With nothing else to do but wait my turn for the printed word, I sat down and glanced around, ready to pounce on the next discarded morning's edition.

For the first time since joining the Air Force, I looked at the group of young officers and was able to see them as men no longer living from day to day. Now they could look forward to the prospect of marrying and having children and grandchildren, and to living a full span of life. So many I had known had lost the chance of such a future. It was a strange feeling, having adjusted to living in unpredictable times, and now being able to think about the years to come. Soon we would be demobbed and would become civilians with no rank, and most of us had no marketable skills or qualifications for peacetime careers.

On that day of rejoicing, thankful as we were, we also felt unneeded, redundant and obsolete. For the members of aircrew, it was particularly difficult for, overnight, they had become superfluous. Some of the WAAF officers' duties would continue to have meaning and purpose, particularly those in Admin., the Assistant Adjutants and Equipment Officers, but even their work would continue only for a limited time. For those of us who worked in Intelligence and Code & Cipher, we could only wonder what our next role would be.

For us who were unmarried were left with a feeling of uncertainty. We felt that our lack of knowledge and experience of civilian life would not help us. We would be returning to a world very different from the one we had left, in the majority of cases, more than five years before. Most Air Force personnel had joined up either as teenagers or in their early twenties, when they had few, if any, ongoing responsibilities. Now, even our surviving civilian clothes no longer fitted - they were out of date and looked ridiculously young on us. We hoped that we would soon receive civilian clothing coupons to help to replenish our almost non-existent wardrobes. The girls, in particular, felt this acutely as, for several years; there had been no reason or opportunity to join the trends of fashion. When we went out on a date, only our hairstyles varied, and they were always cut short. The type of make-up we wore, or lack of it, was the only difference that distinguished us from one another. Even our stockings were of grey lisle and our shoes were black and heavy. Maybe character was a more discerning factor then, and played a greater part than we realized in finding the type of friends we made.

During this interim period before being demobbed, I assumed that those who were already married would find it easier than we would to settle down to a normal life. They could take up their lives where they had left off. The men's' wives would, at last, be able to stop worrying about the personal safety of their husbands. Yes! they definitely had an advantage over us.

Later I had a chance conversation with one of the pilots; we began to discuss our return to the market place. He then told me of his fears on returning to "Civvy Street". "I have a wife and two year old son," he said, "but I don't know what is going to happen to my life. Finding a job is the least of my worries. My wife and child were asleep one night when our house was bombed. They were rescued from the rubble and escaped with no more than scratches and bruises." He reflected for a moment and added more quietly and, it seemed, with difficulty, "Our little boy is now being looked after by my parents, because my wife suffered severe shock. She has been in a mental hospital now for well over a year. She remembers very little of what happened, and is disoriented and in a constant state of fear. There are times when I wonder if she even recognises me during my visits." He was silent for a minute, as he tried to control himself before continuing to speak, then he said sadly," I don't know if she will ever recover."

There were many stories of this kind among the unrecorded casualties of World War II on both sides of the English Channel, but one only hears of them from chance conversations such as the one above.

Shortly after VE Day, Waterbeach returned to a state of purpose and activity. Our Lancs. were ordered to fly to India on a regular basis to take supplies to the Far East. The war was still being fought bitterly in that part of the world, and casualty lists were phenomenal. Any available additional help to bring the war to a quicker conclusion was being used to the utmost. Our aircrews were once more happy and enthusiastic in their work, particularly as there was little or no danger involved in their long flights to India. They would return home proudly showing off their souvenirs, in most cases, very attractive hand-made Indian rugs. Such things were as precious and as rare as gold in England. Few rugs of this kind or quality were to be seen in our country for some time after the war. Further, they could be bought only with special coupons issued to newly-weds to help them start a home.

To my delight, one of the crew members said casually in a conversation one day, "Would you like me to bring a rug back for you on my next trip?" In a very few minutes, I had described the colour and size - a 6 x 9 rug, cream coloured, with a touch of green in the design of the corners. I paid the ridiculous sum of ten pounds sterling, and waited impatiently for the first acquisition for my future home. About ten days later, I received the new rug, which soon graced my very dull barrack-style bedroom. The pilot had brought exactly what I wanted. Only later did he tell me that flying home that day turned out to be a rather a tricky business. Fog had begun to cover the Cambridge area as he was returning to base, and he was advised to land at another airfield. "But I couldn't do that!" he said. "There is a Customs set-up at that station, and it would have cost quite a lot of money to clear the rug through them. I chanced it and headed for Waterbeach. The fog was just beginning to close in as I landed."

## Preparing for Civvy Street

The British Government brought out a policy in early summer soon after VE-Day, which advised anyone who had previous experience of a particular kind to consider returning to a similar type of work or study after being demobilized. Our immediate and rather sceptical reaction was: "What's new about that?" After the incredible brains that had helped to bring us through the war, it seemed that a dismal echo of their talents was going to ease us into the peace. The problem was that most young men and women in their early to late twenties, no longer wished to do the same type of work they had done before joining up. They had all seen more of the world now, and what it had to offer. They looked forward now to something more interesting and challenging, but what? Those whose university studies had been interrupted began to wonder if they could ever settle down again in one place to burn the midnight oil, as they read one textbook after another. Late hours in the pub were far more enticing and much less demanding. The way we felt, however, was, in retrospect, only the initial shock of knowing that we would have to adjust to a new way of life in the near future.

As for myself, after some thought, I approached the Education Officer, whose duty it was to listen to our questions and to try to solve our problems. I asked if he could arrange for me to attend the Cambridge School of Art one day a week. He was quite re-lieved at my modest request. A recent query, he told me, had come from a Canadian who wanted to learn embalming! It was unheard of in England at that time, and the Education Officer was not getting any helpful advice from the "undertakers", as funeral home directors are known in England. He told the young man that he thought that his future customers could wait till he got back to Canada! He soon arranged for me to attend classes on my day off, and I signed up for the most challenging subject, namely, Life Drawing.

The following week, with trepidation, I entered the Life class and claimed an easel. The room was full of teenagers, all of whom stared at me in disbelief, as I entered their class in WAAF officers' uniform. The model walked up to the dais and took the required pose. The outline of her feet was marked with chalk, to help her to take up the same pose after her rest period, and we settled down to draw. I was surprised to find that my first reaction was that of embarrassment. The fact that I was sketching a nude model while wearing His Majesty's uniform seemed slightly immoral! Had I been dressed casually in civvies like the rest of the students, I doubt if the thought would have ever entered my head. But it could have been of the way the youngsters looked at me. Their glances made me feel very old and very out of place. The students would probably have studied Antique drawing from Greek and Roman plaster casts for up to a year before upgrading to the Life class. As far as they were concerned, I had just "walked in" without any prerequisites. I guess it did not seem fair to them. I wanted to tell them that I had studied Antique drawing and Anatomy a few years before at the Hastings School of Art. But an explanation seemed unnecessary and futile. Why should I have to explain, anyway? What was wrong with me for letting a few young people unnerve me? With a great effort of will, I closed my mind to the group around me. I felt that we had nothing in common, but that was to be expected. I then tried to concentrate even harder on the work ahead of me. It was not until the "Rest" period, as I wandered around the room observing the efforts of the class in general, that I knew that we had at least one thing in common: none of us had the slightest idea of how to put the beauty of the human figure on to paper! "This weekly class will dictate whether or not I ever return to Art School," I told myself glumly. It was a depressing thought.

The following week, as I was walking out of the front door of the School of Art, from the afternoon session, I was surprised to see a slim figure in RAF uniform waiting by the entrance. It was the navigator I had known at Feltwell. "Hello! I have come to take you out to tea," he said cheerfully. He had been a P.O.W. in Germany for over two years, and was about to be demobbed early. The Government had decided that there was little point in retraining aircrew now that the war was over. He had just been accepted as a student at one of the colleges at Cambridge and, during the next few weeks, until he left the Air Force officially, was entitled to wear his uniform before eventually settling down to his future as an undergraduate.

Having discovered that I was stationed at Waterbeach, he had looked me up, as we had been out together a few times before. But this was a most embarrassing moment, for I already had a date! "I thought this was your day at the Art School," he said, priding himself of his good memory. I was covered with confusion. Under other circumstances, it would have been an enjoyable interlude, but how was I to tell him that I was meeting someone else at 4.30? The previous Wednesday I had returned to camp and nobody had noticed whether I was there or not - just my luck! "I would love to come out," I said," but unfortunately I am already doing something else. How about next Wednesday instead?" Mike was not settling for that one. "I might be tied up with lectures by then," he said, anyway, who's your friend?" "I didn't say it was a friend, did I?" I replied unconvincingly. "No. But it is, isn't it?" he retorted. I resented being interrogated, that was my job, not his. But I could see that there was no way of getting out of it, so I just said," Yes.," weakly and offered no explanation. "Sorry, Mike, maybe another day, but I'll have to go now," I added. He was not giving up. "Where are you meeting him?" he asked. "In the centre of town," I said vaguely. "Whereabouts?" he insisted," I'll take you there." "Outside Heiffers' bookstore at 4.30," I answered hopelessly. Now I knew I had cooked my goose with both of them. We started walking to the centre of town together, trying to talk lightly about this and that when suddenly he said, "What's his name and what does he do?" "Well, he does the same thing as you - he's another navigator," I replied, feeling the noose around my neck growing tighter.

We arrived at the bookstore on time. Alex was already there and seemed surprised and perplexed to see me turn up with someone else, and it was not even an officer he knew in the Squadron. I introduced them to each other, and we chatted politely for a few minutes while they gave each other time to sum up the situation, and me in particular. Nothing like this had ever happened to me before, and I was completely out of my depth. I was angry with myself for showing my embarrassment. After what seemed like an endless five minutes, the party broke up, Mike in the direction of his college, and Alex and I for a meal at the popular teashop nearby. Then on to the "flicks" (movies). I cannot recall the film, except that it was a good one, and saved us from an evening of conversation. He drove me back to Waterbeach in his little sports car, and we parted good friends. I never received an invitation from either of them again! I hope Mike adjusted happily to his newly-found freedom and to life at Cambridge, after existing for so long in a Nazi prison camp.

## "Bombs Away!"

They came bursting in to our office, three or four of them, some of the crew of "C for Charlie". They looked a sickly bunch with yellow jaundiced faces. Their appearance did not hinder their zest for life as they popped in to hear the latest "gen" (news). The war in Europe had been over for a couple of months, and they were all flying to India regularly. Daily doses of Mepacrine were mandatory for the aircrews' protection from malaria. The medication dyed the skin a dirty yellowish colour, which gave everyone who took it, an appearance of belonging to some race unknown on our globe. In the office, we no longer suffered from any great pressure of work. We now did some things of considerable importance and more of lesser importance, so we shelved our work and brought out the tea. During the tea and buns break, conversations inevitably came round to flying.

I was asked a question out of the blue, "How would you like to come and watch us drop some bombs tomorrow? I bet you have always wondered what 'Bombs Away!' really looked like?" "That sounds interesting," I replied. "And what specific target have you in mind?" I said, with slight scepticism. "The middle of the North Sea," piped up one of them cheerfully, "The fish won't mind." After this apparent teasing, they presented the facts. "We have had instructions to dispose of all our remaining incendiary bombs, and have been ordered to drop them far out in the middle of the North Sea," he explained. Today, it would seem a strange way to dispose of one's battle inventory, but the words "Pollution and the Environment" were unknown catchphrases then. The seas were teeming with fish of all kinds, and we often substituted the "Catch of the Ocean" for breakfast and dinner to eke out our meagre meat ration. Seafood, sold in our fish shops, was always fresh, plentiful, cheap and unrationed.

Within a few minutes of our conversation, I had been granted my weekly day off for the following day - the Art School could wait until next week. The following morning, wearing my battle dress for comfort and my greatcoat for extra warmth, I climbed up the ladder and into the aircraft. It was a cool, bright and sunny day as we took off, circled the airfield, and headed towards the East coast in the direction of the North Sea. I was soon comfortably settled in my seat in the fuselage, while all the crew were working at their stations. It always thrilled me to see the patchwork of fields below, dotted with villages and hamlets here and there. My gaze followed a railway line as it made a wide curve in a southerly direction. This, I thought, glancing at the map on my knee, is where I can pinpoint our position.

Seconds later, to my horror, I was looking through the window at the under wing of a Spitfire, then the underside of its belly, followed by the other wing. It could not have been more than twenty to thirty feet from us, as it made a steep U-turn to avoid us only just in time to prevent a mid-air collision. It was a split-second experience. In his exuberance, the Spitfire pilot must have decided to practice attacking us from above, and had misjudged his distance badly. Our crew had not been warned of any air activity in the area, and the Spitfire should not have been there at all. I had come on this trip, partly to try to understand something about the work and problems of a Lancaster bomber crew. Instead, I learned what it must have been like to have taken part in the Battle of Britain. I was not enamoured with the experience at all. One of the aircrew came back to see if I was OK. They too were badly shaken, and had radioed back to Flying Control to tell them to report the "Blitherin' Idiot", and have him recalled to base immediately. A mid-air collision, with our load of incendiaries, would have been quite a spectacular way to say good-bye. After that unpleasant diversion, everyone settled down to the task in hand and, passing north of Norwich, we crossed the coast and began our flight across the North Sea.

After some time, I was taken to the nose of the air-craft to observe the imminent operation through the bomb aimer's bubble. I stretched out on the floor with my eyes glued to the sea below. At any minute, the bomb doors would open and the incendiaries would be released. I waited in anticipation, but the crew were slow in jettisoning their load. The bomb aimer then returned to me and said brightly, "Well. Did you see them go?" With embarrassment, I had to admit, "No. I didn't. I'm sorry, but, somehow, I missed them. I didn't see a thing," "That's not pos-sible," came the firm reply. "But I saw nothing hap-pen," I repeated. He changed his tone, "Then, they can't have gone," he said, "We'll have a look." I fol-lowed him back along the fuselage where he knelt down and opened a small hatch in the floor and looked down. "You're right," he said, "They're still hanging there. Have a look. We'll have another go."

I returned to the Perspex window and stared down again. Suddenly, three incendiaries came hurtling into view, at first wobbling out of control, then set-ting a firm course and rapidly diminishing in size, as they streamed down towards the grey sea below. The bomb aimer returned again to me, "Did you see 'em this time?" he enquired with confidence. "Well," I answered, "I saw three of them going down, but no more." He looked very concerned. "Are you sure?" he asked. He went back to the hatch to have another look through the hole in the floor. Then he came back to me and said, "You had better return to your seat and hang on. We'll have another go at dislodging the load by diving. That'll do it!" Obediently, I returned to my seat, prepared to hang on. Now that the war in Europe was over, I was getting a belated on-the-spot experience, dis-covering a few of the problems our crews had so often experienced behind the scenes. Apart from the expected and inescapable tragedies and near-tragedies of their daily lives in the past, I saw more fully now, that they were also vulnerable to many kinds of emergencies that continued even into the time of peace.

We began a steep dive, gathering momentum with an increasing roar of the engines. Without warning, we rose sharply towards the sky again. Two more incendiaries were dislodged. We repeated the exer-cise, but to no avail. This time, after some discussion in the cockpit, the bomb aimer returned to where I was sitting. "We're going to have one more go," he said, "but we'll have to jerk a bit harder this time to free the load." After dive number three and with no success, the pilot decided to abort the sortie alto-gether, and return to base. "So this is what evasive action must have felt like," I thought. The Lancaster had proved to me that it was as sturdy an aircraft as it had been cracked up to be. Somehow, I was still hanging on to my seat - I don't remember having a seat belt!

We turned towards the west, our load of bombs hanging precariously beneath our feet. I hoped very much that we would make a smooth landing. We flew over the grey-blue sea, now brightening a little in colour towards mid-day, then crossed the coast of East Anglia on our way to base. Flying Control had already been alerted to our predica-ment, and the fire engines and ambulances had been ordered to stand-by. As we neared the airfield,

I was given instructions to sit tight, and then make my way, after landing, as quickly as possible to the exit door. "As soon as the door opens, get down the ladder and well away from the aircraft as fast as you can. We'll be following right after you," I was told.

There had been other times when I had been involved in near emergencies but, on those occasions, things had happened so quickly that there had been little or no time for the situation to sink into my mind, and there was no point in worrying after the event. By then, one was just thankful that nothing worse had occurred. But now, I had plenty of time to consider whether or not I would be eating dinner at the Mess tonight. Quickly, I pushed the thought from my mind, and concentrated on the present situation. Somehow, I must not panic, but how could I be sure of this? It took only moments to realize that there was only one answer: "Sit tight in your seat, don't move, don't talk, don't think, and don't do anything. Then you will have everything under control," I told myself. I felt much better when I had worked out the simple strategy that I must remain immobile until I ran for the exit after landing. I concentrated so hard on stifling my imagination that I even forgot to invoke the Almighty!

After cruising above the peaceful landscape, we arrived over Waterbeach. The pilot made a circuit of the airfield, to make quite sure that everything was ready for our arrival. When I looked down, I got the impression that Royalty was expected. Red fire engines and white ambulances were parked on the grass close to the runway. It certainly looked like a

Royal reception. The pilot lined up the aircraft, and we descended to the runway, making a very bumpy landing. For the next few seconds, I listened for the sound of explosions and for the smell of smoke, but everything appeared to be normal. We had made it! I would be able to eat my dinner in the Mess to-night as usual. The fire engines and the ambulances followed beside us at a safe distance, until we came to a stop near the end of the runway. I was already at the door when it was opened. Scurrying down the ladder, I ran over to the transport lorry, which was waiting a short distance away to pick us up. It was only then that I remembered to offer a fervent "Thank You" for a safe landing. Very quickly the crew joined me and we waited for a short while to see if anything would happen, but the aircraft just sat on the runway looking forlorn in its isolation, as if it were wondering why it had not been taxied to the dispersal area as usual. We left it surrounded by fire engines; it was up to them now. After a reason-able interval, when the incendiaries were considered safe, the boys from the Armoury would be called to empty the bomb bays of their precariously balanced load. There was great amusement in the office next day, when I told my colleagues how I had been en-tertained on my day off. "Chalk it all up to experi-ence!" they said, and then told me to sit down and gave me a cup of tea.

### "Lost Him!"

There was quite a commotion going on at the Flight Office as I was about to pass by it a few weeks after the incendiary episode over the North Sea. One of the aircrew came running out of the door, crossing the path ahead of me. He was bending down, flapping a newspaper in front of him, furiously. He then saw me, stopped, and looked rather self-conscious. "Whatever's the matter?" I enquired, for there was no way I could pretend that I had not seen this odd demonstration. "Lost him!" he said with conviction. "Lost whom?" I replied. "The mouse," he answered, "it's been running round and upsetting everyone in the office all the morning - we can't get down to work. I tried to shoo it out, but it was too quick for me," he admitted. "Then why not try cornering it instead and catch it in your hands - with gloves on," I suggested. "I couldn't touch one of THEM," he said with disgust and, after hesitating for a moment, added "I don't think the others could either." "I'll catch it for you if you like," I volunteered, "but I'd like to borrow some gloves from you first, preferably bite-proof ones."

I felt full of confidence as I had captured the occasional mouse at home. As our garden fence separated us from a field of sheep, it was easy for a field mouse to lose its way and finish up in our kitchen. I suppose it was our own fault really, for leaving the side door open most of the time. Anyway, it was the type of incident with which I had some familiarity.

The pilot ushered me into the office, where about four aircrew were standing, glancing around nervously, ready to jump out of the way at the appropriate moment. One of them produced a pair of thick leather gloves, and we began searching systematically in each corner of the room. We soon found the unwelcome little guest hiding in a gloomy area between the wall and a large map chest, his little beady eyes shining with fear at his discovery. For some reason, everyone had already assumed that it was a "he". I moved up to him too quickly, made a grab and missed, as he jumped sideways and disappeared. After resuming the hunt, we found him next time in a dark, dusty corner behind a table. Why were these brave men so afraid of such a helpless little creature that was frightened out of its wits, I wondered? Perhaps none of them had ever lived in the country.

I crawled under the table, glad that I was wearing battle-dress that day. This time I used a more cautious approach. He was sitting squashed into the corner under the table, alert and ready to spring again. I edged up to him, crawling on my stomach, and, when he was a few inches away from me, I made a quick grab with both hands. The thick leather proved to be quite impervious to bites, as I held a warm and wriggly little piece of fur in my gloves. Backing away from the wall on my knees and elbows, I held him cupped in my hands. As I squeezed out from under the table, the already-open door was opened even wider for me to pass through it to the outside with the tiny offending creature. I straightened up slowly to avoid losing my prize, and walked out of the door to the grassy area at the edge of the path, bent down and opened my hands. The little mouse was dazed for a moment, and just sat there looking at me. Then, with a lightening turn of his body and a whisk of his tail, he leapt into the air, landed on the gravel, scurried into the greenery by the side of the path, and disappeared.

## The First Jet

Our office was no longer the nerve centre it used to be; in fact, life was quite dull at times. Then, one morning, news went round the Station that a "jet" aircraft was going to visit Waterbeach in the afternoon. None of us had ever seen one before, so our Department Head soon arranged our work so that we could be out on the airfield to watch it land, while he manned the telephones. We arrived at our vantage point near Flying Control later in the day, where a crowd of flying types, mechanics and other personnel, were already waiting impatiently on the tarmac. As the ETA of the jet drew near, we kept looking in the direction of its expected approach. Suddenly, out of the clear blue sky, a small black speck showed up in the distance. It grew rapidly in size as it began to descend at a steep angle and, with incredible speed, it appeared to fly almost straight at us. Then it touched down, streaking past the waiting crowd with a tremendous roar. Finally it came to a halt at the far end of the runway, barely long enough to accommodate a jet, though more than adequate for a four-engined propeller aircraft.

Any Lancaster attempting to land at that speed would have finished up a heap of flame and twisted metal in the middle of the landing strip. It brought to my mind the jet aircraft I had seen on the factory airfield in the stereo photos at Medmenham over three years before. "Why," I wondered, "had the Air Ministry of the German Reich been so tardy in not giving top priority to such a brilliant and incredibly powerful invention during the war?" Thankfully for us, it had not. German jet aircraft were not operational on any scale until Europe was once again at peace.

That day's demonstration of a totally new concept of the aircraft of the future came as quite a shock to us all. Our gallant Lancs, it seemed, had become redundant, maybe obsolete, and overnight. Had anyone told me then, that not so many years later, I would be able to travel anywhere in the world by jet, I would, I think, have considered the idea as realistic as flying on a magic carpet. That was the only jet aircraft I ever saw during the entire time I was in the Air Force. Now, fifty years later, I still marvel at these enormous and powerful flying giants that take us so easily all over the globe. I also remember well the next time an aircraft other than a Lancaster visited our Station.

Joanne Woodward, known as Jo to us, was the girl who occupied the bedroom next to mine. Like me, she loved flying. Until now, we had not been on a cross-country flight together but, on this particular day, we both had an unexpected invitation to take a trip in a B-22 American Liberator of Coastal Command. For some reason the aircraft had touched down at Waterbeach and was remaining for a few days. We each quickly claimed our day off and arrived at the Flight Office the next morning well in time. After having been driven out to the air-craft on the perimeter of the airfield in a Jeep, we were given a tour of the cockpit and the fuselage. We then returned to the fuselage of the 'plane to sit down for take-off. It was a large, spacious and cumbersome aircraft compared with our Lancs, but then the "Lib." was used for very different purposes.

After take-off, and having been in the air for about twenty minutes, one of the crew invited us to go to the nose of the 'plane, where we could either stand or lie flat on our stomachs to look through the clear plastic bubble at everything passing beneath us. The view was superb, with nothing but Perspex between us and the patchwork landscape of fields of grain, vegetable and pasture lands and small villages below. I felt like a bird on the wing! After a while we got up from our prone position and stood upright, leaning against the nose-wheel behind us, which was retracted and locked into position after take-off. We still had a good view of everything below us.

As we continued to absorb the fantastic view, the same member of the crew returned. He seemed rather subdued this time, as he asked us quietly and politely if we would mind going back to sit in our landing positions as there was trouble with one of the engines. He apologised for so short a flight, and then quickly disappeared. It was a little disappointing because, after our anticipating a long cross-country flight, we had been in the air not more than three-quarters of an hour; but we both agreed that to have the experience of even that short trip was well worth it. So far as we were concerned, that was the end of the affair. We had landed safely despite the engine trouble and we thought no more about it.

That evening Jo and I were eating our dinner at the Mess, when we overheard a conversation among some of the RAF types sitting opposite us. "Hey!" said one of them, "Did you hear what happened this morning to old Bill? He took a couple of

WAAF up in his Lib. and one of the engines went US. When he was preparing to land and was about to let down the nose wheel, his navigator yelled 'Don't let that bloody thing down! There are two WAAF sitting on it!' They almost jettisoned the girls!" Roars of laughter came from his friends! We pretended not to have heard their conversation and, with difficulty, smothered our surprise until we had finished dinner and had left the table. But I think this was the closest I ever came to a sudden, unexpected and untimely end.

Despite the experience and our near annihilation, Joanne requested and received permission to leave the WAAF soon after the War ended, as she had been offered a job with BEA (British European Airways) now BA (British Airways). She became the first British air hostess ever, so far as I know.

Soon after that incident, two Admin. courses came up. I think the higher authorities considered that our department was now under-worked and over-staffed. Our team kept going, as new and different duties took the place of the old and, although the time of winding down was probably good for us all, we did not appreciate it then. We would have preferred to have been more challenged, but the fact remained that, to some extent, we were now coasting. I was sent first to RAF Thetford in Suffolk, not very far from Waterbeach. This was a three-week course which was soon followed by another at Stratford-on-Avon.

Looking back now, I can recall very little of either course, although I remember, quite clearly, incidents relating to my stay in each place. It was at Thetford that I become friendly with Honor, a very pleasant girl and a fellow art student. We got on well and discussed, among other things, our return to civilian life. The decision that she had made for the future was far more practical than mine. She, wisely, I think, considered that a long training in Art would probably leave her qualified in a badly paid and precarious profession. She was sure that she would have to work for the rest of her life, in which case she needed more security. Therefore, she had made up her mind that she would become an occupational therapist. It was then that she explained that her fiancé, a pilot on the station, had been killed on a raid over Germany towards the end of the war. It was still a far too recent and deeply personal experience for her to be able to imagine that she might marry one day, and be able to choose to practice Art professionally, or to do it just for pleasure. I admired her bravery as she made a great effort to be sociable and cheerful at a time that, for her, must have been one of almost meaningless existence. I hope that her life eventually took a turn in a happier direction.

Another thing I recall brings back memories of quite a different nature. When I went walking on the heath land surrounding the airfield in the early evenings, I was often surprised at the sight of some of the most exotic and beautiful moths I have ever seen. There were large and small ones of colours, sizes and shapes that I had never noticed before. Why they were in that area or what species they were continues to puzzle me, but they conjure up one of the pleasurable memories while on the Admin. course. Had my studies been in the natural sciences, I might have returned to Waterbeach with better results.

Almost as soon as I returned to camp, I was notified that I was to be sent on yet another Admin. course - this time to Stratford-on-Avon. The RAF officers in my section were quite amused at the way the RAF was keeping me busy for they, for some unfathomable reason, were not inconvenienced with any extra curricular courses at all. Their life in the office had become passive and fairly predictable. Well," I thought, if I have to go away again, I'll see that I enjoy the three-week stay at Stratford as much as possible." I had no doubt about it being an interesting place to visit, and I hoped that I would be given sufficient free time while there, to take advantage of doing some of the things and seeing some of the attractions that Stratford had to offer.

On the day I arrived, my hopes rose beyond my wildest dreams. With the address and precise directions of the new billet in my hand, I found the place quickly and easily. It was not one of many Nissen huts like the ones provided at Thetford. My temporary home turned out to be "The Falcon", a charming 16th century half-timbered Elizabethan hotel, in the centre of town that had been requisitioned by the RAF. With a light heart, I stepped inside, reported my arrival to the WAAF clerk sitting at the desk in the lobby, and then went upstairs to find my room. It was a spacious room with a low ceiling, criss-crossed with large unevenly cut oak beams, roughly hewn by hand and black with age, giving authenticity to their antiquity. The small leaded windows were placed well below the ceiling, allowing shorter people of an earlier century to look out of them. We, on the other hand, had to bend down to see out. The bare floor was polished and shiny, enhancing the beauty of the oak boards made from huge pieces of wood, now also blackened with time and cut in irregular widths by the original carpenters.

The only jarring note was the presence of three Army issue beds, side tables and dressing tables. One bed had been claimed already, and a pile of clothing and other personal belongings were strewn all over it. It was just as well that officers had no kit inspections. I was left the choice of one of the other two beds, so I took the one near the window.

Soon the third occupant of the room arrived, and by the time we had both unpacked our belongings, the owner of the untidy corner joined us. Almost at once we began asking each other questions about the upcoming course. The first occupant, the "Untidy One" as she was soon named, for she continued that way to the end, gave us a little information that she had gleaned from a friend who had recently completed the course. "I'm told it's not so bad," she said, the Senior Officer usually makes sure that we have a free evening when her brother takes the leading part at the Shakespeare Theatre. We were to discover that our lecturer was Squadron Officer Scofield, and that Paul Scofield, one of the most famous Shakespearean actors at that time, was her brother. As predicted, we were free to attend several performances at the Shakespeare Memorial Theatre, beside the River Avon during our time there.

After completing the first few days of the lectures, about which I remember almost nothing, our instructor asked for volunteers for the choir at the local parish church on Sunday. About eight of us raised our hands, although I doubt if any of us had ever been in a church choir for, in those days, choirs were almost exclusively made up of men and boys. That evening, we arrived at the church for a practice. We tried out a few hymns from the hymnal, and all went passably well until we were told that we were going to learn the Sevenfold Amen for Sunday morning. "Do any of you know it?" Sqdn. Off. Scofield asked hopefully. One by one we muttered, almost inaudibly under our breath, a kind of "No. I'm afraid I don't." "Well, never mind. It won't take long to learn," she said encouragingly. But that was as far as it went. We had to practice and memorize it quickly, and the choir of eight young WAAF officers came up to pitch, but not to scratch.

We were nervous and a little in awe of our choir director, obviously a highly intelligent woman of many talents, music being just one of them. None of us had used our voices in a choir for a very long time, if ever, and - to say the least - we were rusty. I, for one, had the confidence to sing only if the music was in front of me. But, being just after the war, printed music was almost impossible to obtain. We had no organ accompaniment to help us, and there was only one copy of the Sevenfold Amen. The choir director had that, and we badly needed eight more. After attempting an obviously hopeless task, we switched to a simpler rendering of an Amen, which probably pleased God, but not our choir director! As for the rest of our repertoire, we kept our eyes glued to the only accessible music, which was in the hymnals, and hoped that somehow we would make a joyful noise on Sunday, for our choir was the only one available. Whether the congregation enjoyed it, I do not know, but both we and the Sunday worshippers came loyally to the church for the three weeks we were there. Hopefully, after our departure a more talented group arrived to take our place.

On our free days, we became typical tourists, visiting Shakespeare's birthplace, an old 16th century half-timbered house in Henley Street. But, as the old market town of Stratford had not yet reverted to tourism, the house was not open to the public. We had better luck when visiting the church where Shakespeare was buried and, also, Anne Hathaway's cottage, both of which were open to visitors. The front garden of the picturesque thatched cottage was ablaze with flowers, all of which were varieties that were grown in Shakespeare's time. We went up to the door, paid our entrance fee and waited until there were enough people for the guide to take us around the cottage. He was a grey-haired man, thin, elderly and very zealous. He had obviously learned his history well, so we ventured to ask a few extra questions. But that was a great mistake, and we soon stopped asking him extra details. After each interruption, our guide would start his story all over again. Having learnt his spiel, parrot-fashion, he proved himself incapable of continuing from where he left off. It was one of our more amusing afternoons. On returning to Waterbeach this time, I arrived somewhat more knowledgeable about the plays of Shakespeare and their background, and I still hoped that I would never be called on to do administrative duties

## Surprise Sortie

During the next few weeks as most of us continued to carry out an increasingly dull routine, our daily lives suddenly brightened. All non-flying members of the station were to be given the opportunity to fly over Germany. I understand that other RAF stations offered the same opportunity to their personnel.

Our Commanding Officer had recently announced this, and thanked everyone for their loyalty, hard work and cooperation during the dark days. He emphasized that, without the willing help of all ranks performing their many skills and tasks well and cheerfully, our record as a bomber station would not have been so outstanding. His next words surprised everyone. He told us that a flight over Germany had been authorized for all non-flying personnel on the Station who would like to go. We were to be able to see for ourselves the results of some of the dangerous attacks that had been carried out by our aircrews. He hoped that we would understand better what they had faced to ensure our final success in the battle for freedom

Today was my turn. I was to travel with men and women, most of whom, despite their RAF uniforms, had never been up in any type of aircraft before. Our little group represented various categories of trades and professional skills. Some of the passengers were quite apprehensive prior to take-off. Others were so thrilled that they could not wait to get started. It took only a few reassuring words from the Captain of the aircraft to point out the fact that we would be flying in a Lanc, and not taking a voyage on a cross-Channel ferry. Therefore, we could forget worrying about our stomachs. This last remark seemed to relax the group, and we climbed up the ladder into the aircraft, and made ourselves as comfortable as possible. As far as I remember, there were very few seats, and no seat-belts to keep us in place!

We began our flight that morning by crossing the English Channel. We then followed the borders of France and Belgium, as we made our way to the south of Germany. From there we circuited and headed back in a northerly direction, to follow the course of the Rhine, flying not more than about three thousand feet above the river. It gave the appearance of being a small meandering stream, rather than a mighty and powerful river, on which much of the war weapon industry of Germany had depended so heavily.

I concentrated intently, not wanting to miss anything. My eyes darted from one place to another as I stared down, pausing momentarily, to study the origin of a glint of some object that was caught in the rays of the morning sun. Following the bends in the Rhine, I noted the green fields on either side of its banks, and the higher lands and forests, with small towns and villages spread at intervals across the landscape. Everything looked so peaceful below. Then, as we changed direction, the sun lit up the water, accentuating the silhouette of a bridge spanning the river, followed closely by another bridge - or more accurately - what was left of both of them.

Continuing our flight, the two damaged bridges were soon far behind us. As we approached Cologne, the great twin-spired cathedral towered above the surrounding badly bombed city, and was the only edifice in the vicinity with a roof remaining to protect it from the elements. The cathedral was almost undamaged. As we flew further north, we approached the industrial centre of the Ruhr, flying over Dusseldorf, Wuppertal, Duisberg and the enormous Krupps plant at Essen. In these highly industrial areas, we saw the remains of factories, warehouses and rows of adjacent dwellings that had been reduced to tumbled walls and piles of rubble. The walls that remained seemed to be standing in defiance, as they appeared to be guarding, hopelessly, the charred and blackened shells they enclosed. Not a roof was to be seen anywhere close to the river. The general effect was that of a checkerboard of tiny black squares, outlined by the lighter coloured walls that were in various stages of disrepair. The intense heat from earlier bombing and the fires that followed had left the blackened remains in a state of utter devastation and desolation.

Britain and her Allies had sent some of their highest concentrations of aircraft to this crucially important area of Germany, for here a very large proportion of her weapons of war were manufactured. The picture that we saw beneath us was a grim reminder of what the people in London had suffered in 1940 and 1941, when the city's East End and the dockside areas of the Thames were bombed mercilessly for months on end. The damage and the casualties then were beyond belief. But it was another three or more years before the Allies were powerful enough to retaliate with a strong offensive. Tragic as the results must have been to the German civilians living in the area, the Allied aerial attacks comprised a vital all-out effort in preparation for the forthcoming invasion of Europe. We too suffered many casualties among our aircrews, the Ruhr being one of the most heavily protected areas in Germany.

I thought of the people I had known, who had been fortunate enough to return home at the end of the war after long terms in prison camps, and of those who never came back at all. Then there were those who, like our present flying crew, had survived the ordeal. They had braved the searchlights, flak and enemy fighters on so many occasions right over the very area over which we were flying at that moment. The Allies had attacked regularly to eliminate the manufacturing capabilities of the Nazis, while the enemy fought back with their guns and fighters, determined to protect their productive capacity. Now that peace had come, the Allied Forces stationed in Germany were on a very different mission. They were giving emergency aid to feed and house the most needy and, together with the German people, were helping to rebuild their country.

The war still continued bitterly in the Far East, and it looked as though it was going to be a long drawn-out, bloody affair on land, sea and in the air. Losses of men were very high on both sides. Suddenly, without warning, the war came to an abrupt end. In the middle of August, 1945, the Allies' most secret weapon, the atomic bomb, was dropped on Japan, and hostilities ended within a few days. However, many Japanese soldiers would not believe that their Emperor Hirohito had surrendered. Severe fighting continued in Burma and elsewhere for many weeks after the formal Japanese surrender, and, indeed, it was some fifteen years later that the last Japanese soldier gave himself up out of the jungles in the Philippines.

# LEAVING THE RAF

It came as quite a shock. It should not have been a surprise at all. But as I opened and read the letter, suddenly my whole life was put into perspective, and the reality of the future flashed vividly before me. The time was October 1945, five months after VE-Day, and I was informed that, towards the end of next month, I was to become a civilian again - in other words, my demob papers had arrived. It was foolish to react with such a feeling of uncertainty and insecurity, for we all knew that this would happen in the near future. So far, however, only one of our WAAF officers at Waterbeach had left, but then Jo had requested to do so, having her air hostess position to go to. A couple of others had "stayed on" by signing up for another six months. Thus, we had felt little of the effects of general demobilization in our ranks.

It was not so much leaving the Air Force that disturbed me, as the fact that I was to depart at the end of November. What a dreary time to face the unknown, with months of winter ahead of me before I would see the dawn of a new Spring. It would be a depressing month to look for a job, and the timing would be even more difficult for someone wanting to sign up for further education.

I pondered over the alternatives. Having recently completed two Admin. courses, I was qualified to sign up for a minimum of one more year in the RAF, to serve in Germany with the occupying forces, but it would have to be in an administrative capacity. The idea was something definitely worth considering, but I did not wish to be occupied with work in which I had little interest, in return for having the chance of learning another language. The opportunity to study German was a strong motive, but I doubted if I would advance much in the language while living and working with English-speaking people. The uncertainty of what to do was brief, but real. Then I made up my mind to keep resolutely to my original decision. It took only a few days to decide that I still wanted to complete my studies at a School of Art, but the next academic year would not begin until the following September, nearly ten months later. Having sorted out those problems to the best of my ability, I applied the next day to stay in the RAF for another six months. The month of May, I reasoned, would be a much more appropriate and cheerful time to be thrust into the changed world of post-war life.

Barbara, my friend from Tempsford, and I were to be demobbed within two weeks from each other. We decided to take a vacation in the Lake District before settling down to our studies. She had already done some research on the Westmorland/Cumberland area, and that was good enough for me. Together we would try our luck, combine our ignorance, and hike over mountain tops, clambering along ridges, and discovering the valleys of the area after we left the RAF.

Well before the appointed time, we each bought ourselves knapsacks, very simple affairs made of "semi" water-repellent canvas - as we discovered later - with back straps of webbing for the shoulder harness. That was the extent of our equipment. We realized the necessity of taking sufficient warm clothing for unpredictable weather, and enough food and water for the day. With that amount of marginal knowledge, we considered ourselves adequately qualified explorers of the wilderness. We would look at our acquisitions with pride and anticipation, picturing ourselves striding out in the beauty of a part of England unknown to either of us, and by a way of travelling completely new to both of us.

As the time grew closer, the prospect became more and more exciting, for holiday travel during the past six years had been, to say the least, restricted. The upcoming vacation also helped to soften the thought of the approaching day, when life would change suddenly. We would walk out into a world we did not know, without a map for guidance, as we tried to set our feet firmly on the ground and in the right direction. What could be better than a map of the Lake District, to help us to take our first footsteps in one of the most breathtaking and beautiful regions of England? But things seldom go as planned.

Less than a week before being demobilized, I wound up with a badly infected finger, similar to the one I had suffered at Ormskirk, except that this one threatened to be worse. With that experience behind me, I used more powerful disinfectants and ointments, and poulticed the finger at every opportunity. Try as I would, it became more inflamed. While I was visiting the WAAF Officers' Mess in the village one afternoon before going on night duty, the problem came to a head. My finger was badly swollen by now, and the poison had still not come to the surface. The throbbing and the shooting pains I remembered so well, told me that I must seek advice right away. After finding a colleague to take my place for the night shift, I was free to phone the Sick Bay on the Station for an appointment. "You probably won't get an appointment," my friends said, "They will come and pick you up instead." "What do you mean? I can cycle there!" I protested. "Not after the shot they'll give you when they get here," they said not unkindly, "Our Doc takes no chances." I rang the M.O.'s Office, got a prompt reply and, within about fifteen minutes, an ambulance arrived at the door. Two medical orderlies jumped out of the vehicle and came into the house. They took off the bandage and examined my finger, while the WAAF officers present stood round and watched. Then one of the orderlies gave me a jab. Within a few minutes, while I was putting my belongings together, I felt so unbalanced, distant and woozy, that I had to be helped into the ambulance.

On arrival at the M.O.'s surgery, I waited a very short time before the Medical Officer came in. He took one look at my finger and said exactly the same thing as the doctor at Ormskirk had done nearly five years earlier. "I'm sorry, but I will have to lance this without a local as I am alone tonight - my helper has gone to the hospital at Ely," he told me kindly, but firmly. There were no gas rings here; the scalpel was taken from a professional sterilizer, and the Doc got to work. In my half-awake state, I put all the strength I could muster into squeezing my finger as tightly as possible and, as I had done before, I turned my head in the opposite direction to avoid jumping when he operated. The Doc completed the task in seconds, leaving me sitting there weak and shaky, but the throbbing and the shooting pains had almost disappeared. I was not allowed to return to my quarters, but was sent upstairs to a bed in the Sick Bay.

Next morning, I was given breakfast in bed! It was brought up by a medical orderly, not more than about 21 years of age. He sat at the bottom of the bed and talked as I ate. He asked me to let him know of anything I wanted or needed, as he had been told to look after me. "You see." he said, "I have lots of time. You are the only patient here at the moment." By the second day, I was still an in-patient. After the doctor had visited me again, the orderly returned and told me that he had wanted very much to try some new brand of medicine on me, but the Doc had said "NO!". It was in very short supply, and must be saved for something much more serious. He continued, "If only he would let me try it, I think it would cure your finger in a couple of days - I'm longing to see how it works." "What is this marvellous medicine?" I enquired with interest. "It is something quite new, called Penicillin - it comes from some kind of mould," he replied.

I wondered why this enthusiastic young man in a medical orderly's white coat was here. "He does not fit in," I thought. He appeared to be a typical flying type. "Have you been working in Sick Bay for long?" I ventured to ask. "Only a month" was the reply, "and I'm loving it. I'm really a pilot," he said, "but now that we can remuster, I applied for this job. I'm hoping to go to Medical School when I'm demobbed, and this is an excellent way of getting started."

A few days later I was discharged and allowed to return to my quarters. The finger was still bothering me, but the M.O. said it would heal soon. The holiday had to be postponed, for there was still the clearing up at the office, and the packing to be done. After the rounds of farewells and a few "Good Luck" sessions in the bar after dinner, I left Waterbeach for the last time, hauling two large suitcases and an Indian rug with me.

I returned home to leave my possessions and to spend a few days with my family at Pett. Our village was, once more, a peaceful place to live in again. We no longer had to keep a watchful eye for the sudden appearance of the low flying marauders of the German Luftwaffe. I looked from my front door at the bright green fields, with cows browsing in the marshland in the valley below, and at the sheep grazing quietly in the meadow beyond our garden fence. The lambs were growing fast and were no longer gambolling around, but were trying hard to follow their mothers' example by learning, half-heartedly, to chew the grass. Now and again, they would forget their continuous need to eat to live, and would suddenly gather in a group, and go bounding together over the large hummocks and anthills down the slope from one end of the field to the other - just for the fun of it.

I had not realized until now how much I had missed that side of life. Woodlands straddled the undulating landscape, the dark green of the deciduous trees, contrasting with the meadows and fields of young grain. I looked towards the distant view of Fairlight Church, with its square tower a tiny silhouette against the setting sun. Almost nothing had changed in the last five years. I scanned the panorama from west to east, where the sparkling sea was calm and blue. Soon the mines, tank traps and barbed wire would be removed from the sea shore and, once more, we would be able to walk on the beach and watch the rising and the ebbing of the tide.

At the end of the week, I stuffed my haversack full with my needs for the two-week vacation in the Lake District, and, with a light heart, I took the Southern Railway electric train from Hastings to London. There I met Barbara, and together we boarded a steam train to Windermere. Not far away from there, we spent our first night at a Youth Hostel - the latest thing for outdoor types and nature lovers. It was a pleasant house that recently had been converted to the simple needs of the hiker. The lounge was warm and cheerful, with a fire blazing in the hearth, for the evenings were still quite cold in the north of England.

Two Army officers in uniform were standing close to the fire warming themselves, when we walked into the lounge. I think we four were the only people staying there that night for we saw nobody else. During casual conversation, we discovered that they, like ourselves, had just been demobilized and had two more days of their vacation left. "Where are you planning to go on this trip?" they asked us. We explained that with our lack of knowledge of the mountainous terrain, we thought we would begin in the valleys and then work our way up. It was easy to see that we had gone down in their estimation badly. They could not believe that we would waste our time doing that. "But we have no experience of mountains, and I doubt if anyone would come to our aid should we need it," I said making excuses. "We are going to do Helvellyn and Striding Edge tomorrow," one of them volunteered. "How about coming along with us? It's a steep climb up, but Striding Edge is more or less downhill all the way once you reach the top .Can you take heights?" he asked as an afterthought.

Helvellyn was definitely on our list, but we had planned doing it towards the end of the holiday, for we considered it to be the most challenging. However, with two strong experienced guides, what were we waiting for? The *AA Illustrated Guide to Britain*, published many years later (1971) by Drive Publications Ltd, London, describes the mountain as follows:

> "... *Helvellyn, 3118 ft, is the third highest peak in the Lake district. It can be tackled by any fully equipped and hardened hiker, but a head for heights is needed along the one mile long Striding Edge...*"
> (page 401)

Fortunately, that description was not available at the time. We gladly accepted the offer and, after an early breakfast the next morning, the four of us left for Thirlmere to climb to the summit of Helvellyn from its west side. From its base, it looked like a solid perpendicular wall of scrub and rocks, giving us no idea of its real height, for we could see only as far as the crest above. There was no way that we would have tackled it alone. Trying to look cheerful to hide our apprehension, we began, with the aid of a few helpful hints from our friends, to climb up the very steep slope. It did not take long to discover that our shoes were anything but adequate, as we kept slipping on the stony ground, finding little purchase with the soles of our shoes. As a few well equipped hikers passed us on the way up, we noticed their thick studded soles and the ankle supports on their hiking boots, and saw that their haversacks were on frames that fitted snugly to their backs. We had nothing like that, and had no idea whether, or where, one could buy anything of the sort. We concluded that they were using pre-war equipment, and that we would have to make do with what we had got. We continued scrambling from one clump of greenery and bilberry patch to the next, and from rock to rock, navigating rough gravel slopes in between. After climbing for about an hour, we began to hope that the next crest would bring us to the summit. The view to the west was tremendous, and was our only guide in judging how high we had climbed. We continued scrambling up, but, as one crest of the hill after another came into view, we gave up guessing as to when we would reach the summit. Our knapsacks, fortunately, were fairly light, as we were returning to the same hostel that evening, but they were beginning to be bothersome. The wind was strengthening as we went higher, and the awkward shapes of the containers of food, water and extra clothing in our knapsacks, were beginning to swing from side to side across our backs. It was becoming increasingly difficult to secure firm footholds.

More than two hours after beginning the climb, we scrambled over the last crest, to find ourselves surveying the most breath-taking scenery. The day was clear and cool, but the wind blew at us mercilessly, as we paused for breath after the strenuous climb. We looked around us with awe, as we viewed the panorama of the fells and valleys in the Lake District, as well as the Pennine mountain range in the far distance in the east. Even the hills on the Scottish border were visible in a slight haze to the northwest, more than sixty miles away. We stopped for a quick snack from our backpacks, then, with one of our Army guides taking the lead and the other following in the rear, we began the one-mile walk along Striding Edge in single file. The extremely narrow path was rough and stony, as we snaked our way along the sharp knife-edged track, which dropped away at an acute angle on either side of us. The bare rock appeared fearsome and dangerous. On our left, we looked down on Red Tarn, a small isolated lake below, in the hollow of the mountain. On our right side, the slope was almost sheer, as it continued down to the valley. As we made our way between the stones and boulders, our knapsacks seemed to grow heavier and more cumbersome, and felt like rounded lumps of rock on our shoulders. Without a frame, they did not adhere to the shape of our backs at all. We had tried to pack correctly, but the wind blew our awkward bundles mercilessly swinging them from side to side with every step we took. After hiking along the footpath for over an hour, stopping now and again to survey the panorama, we began our descent to Ullswater in the green valley below.

We had the company of our military friends for one more day but, first thing the next morning, we paid an early visit to the local cobbler, and had the soles of our Air Force shoes covered with metal studs. After that, we felt competent to challenge almost anything, even without our friendly guides.

For nearly two weeks, we hiked along countless footpaths, on ridges and over and around pikes and fells. When the paths petered out, which they usually did, we followed the cairns made of roughly piled mounds of stones, which were distanced strategically for our guidance. We slipped and scrambled on our way past streams and waterfalls, with mountain peaks rising majestically above us and fertile valleys and peaceful lakes glistening in the sunlight below. We were surrounded by some of the loveliest countryside in England.

By the end of the first week, we barely noticed the badly designed and ungainly packs on our backs, each of us now carrying a full load, for we seldom retraced our steps back to the same lodging for the night. Throughout the trip, the weather was unusually good. There was little haze, for the temperature was cool and the rain was minimal, with one exception. We were caught in a deluge and were completely soaked, while passing through Seathwaite in the Borrowdale valley. But what could you expect? The village is notorious for being officially described as the wettest place in England! Another of our ambitions was to tackle Great Gable - the pyramid-shaped mountain, almost 3,000 feet high. But it was going to be a long hike to complete in a day. So, we booked in at the Youth Hostel, near the top of a steep hill on Honister Pass. It was a long way from any habitation, but it was the closest lodging to Great Gable. When staying at these convenient, but Spartan, places, we were all expected to perform one small domestic chore before departing the following morning, such as washing up after meals. Normally, such a chore was of minimal inconvenience, but this time, we needed to make an early start, if we were to return again before darkness set in. We could achieve this only by volunteering for the least popular job - that of cleaning the porridge saucepans, a duty that could be carried out while the other hostellers were still eating their breakfasts. The following morning we went into the kitchen, where two huge pots had been left in the sink, very gummed up with thickened and burnt, cooked porridge. We got down to the task, and scrubbed away at a most unpleasant slimy mess of burnt oats, soaking in a pot of tepid water, attempting to remove the sludge from the bottom of the saucepans. With no rubber gloves, and armed only with a dishcloth and a wooden spoon to use as tools, it was not an easy task. No wonder everyone kept clear of that chore! But this messy exercise brought us down to earth, reminding us quite clearly of the domesticities of life that awaited us when this holiday was over. There would be no more kitchen or cleaning staff to look after us from now on. Anyway, we began our trek to Great Gable more than a half-hour ahead of the other hikers. On the trail, we met small groups of trekkers coming and going. But it was the only occasion when we saw people in numbers. Most of the time, we met no more than three or four hikers in a day, and on some days, none at all. The Swaledale sheep, bleating as they fed on the sparse clumps of vegetation, and the soaring and twittering birds that had ventured above their regular habitat, were more often our companions in passing, until we made our descent to the valley in the evenings. The route to the mountain turned out to be less arduous than we had expected, and we completed the round trip without difficulty - we need not have volunteered for the porridge-pot chore after all!

We came to the end of the final day of the vacation. It had been an energetic and enjoyable holiday. For eight hours that day, we hiked over the mountains, past tarns and screes, finishing up once more in the valley alongside Lake Ullswater. It was late in the afternoon, and the unusual heat of the day was beginning to lessen. As we walked along the shoreline towards the road, we came to a jetty with several rowing boats moored to it. There was a hand-printed notice pinned to a wooden post beside the jetty, inviting us to stop. "FOR RENT" it said in large red letters. This was the last opportunity we would have to accept such an invitation. "Let's rent one!" we said almost together and, for the next two hours, we rowed on the lake enjoying the most idyllic scenery, before continuing our hike in search of the Youth Hostel, where we were to stay for the last night of our trip.

That evening, we packed in readiness for an early morning departure on the train. Clean clothes and dirty, all got stuffed into the knapsacks together. We had acquired a few souvenirs on the way, and something had to be discarded to make room for new purchases. We inspected our RAF service shoes. They were no longer black and shiny, but brownish and dull-looking from many coats of Dubbin, the wax that kept them waterproof. The soles, despite, or because of, being reinforced with innumerable metal studs, were beginning to part from the uppers. They had lasted just long enough for our needs, and were about to disintegrate. There was no point in taking them home, not even to show our families how we had beaten the problem of hiking over the Fells. These shoes had been good and sturdy friends and, with a feeling of nostalgia, we reluctantly added the two pairs to the collection of garbage in the Youth Hostel's dustbin. We had said goodbye to our Service shoes, breaking one more link with our days in uniform. They had served us well.

Two months later, we joined our friend Joyce in London. The BBC Symphony Orchestra, after its forced evacuation to Bedford, had been back in London for some time. Joyce had found a flat, situated about ten minutes walk from the Albert Hall in South Kensington, where the Orchestra often performed concerts. So Barbara and I moved in, and we all set up house together. Barbara pursued her studies, and I registered at the Central School of Art in Southampton Row, Kingsway. We all found it a happy and satisfactory arrangement, as we each began to live a new phase of our lives in peacetime England.

It took very little time to realize that we were not the most talented of cooks. Trying to make the most of our rationed food, which was adequate but utilitarian and dull, was a difficult task. We resorted to unrationed commodities such as herbs and spices, which we added liberally to our tasteless meals. There were also other minor problems to contend with, one being a shortage of (coal-produced) gas during our first winter in the flat. We had only one method of cooking our food before the days of microwaves, crockpots, toaster ovens, etc., and that was on the old pre-war gas stove. For a few weeks, during a period when the gas pressure was very low, it became a long labourious job even to warm up a can of soup. We also relied on a small and inadequate gas fire in the living room for our warmth and comfort.

Soon we accepted the fact that we would have to think up some innovative ways of beating the gas shortage and our tasteless food. We devised a stock recipe for the evening meal, by putting curry powder into everything. Even the "M&V" - canned Meat and Vegetables (mostly vegetables in meat gravy!) - when spiked with curry powder, became quite tasty, and warmed our bodies to an acceptable temperature for a short time afterwards.

There were many evenings when, as we attempted to light the gas fire, the burning match would nearly scorch our fingers before the gas ignited. All too often, we would be given false hope, as the flame lit briefly, only to pop and splutter for a minute and then die out, leaving the room cold and smelling of gas. On those nights, we gave up and went to the local cinema, regardless of the programme, and sat through the performance, whether we liked it or not. The theatre was not heated either, but the fact that there were hundreds of people sitting in a confined space, generated sufficient warmth to make it tolerably comfortable.

The Art School was another problem, for it was cold there too. The normal rule was that the central heating would be turned on only when the temperature dropped below 55F. But these were not normal days, so it was not turned on at all! My fingers would become so cold and numb, that any attempt to work in the area of Fine Arts or Calligraphy was impossible. Then, driven by sheer necessity, I came up with an idea. Surely, I thought, the museums and art galleries have to keep some of their rooms at a constant temperature to preserve their collections of books and works of art. The Victoria and Albert Museum, being within walking distance of our flat, was my first choice. I looked into the possibility of studying its collection of old prints. To my delight, I discovered that the Print Room was kept at a steady 70F and, as far as I could see, very few people visited it. For over a week, I became an ardent enthusiast in the study of old prints, steel engravings, woodcuts, etchings and many other priceless works of art, which were available there. In their diversity, they all had one thing in common - they needed a temperature of 70F for their survival - and so did I! Despite the many problems, that period of my life is still a very pleasant interlude to look back on.

As time went by, we moved out one by one, as each of us in turn married, taking yet another step for-

ward in our lives, into a new and completely different future. But this time it was our own choice. Although we have only occasionally visited each other
since I moved to Canada, we have kept in touch,
and I look back on the good and bad times of the
war with both sad and happy memories, but with no
regrets.

www.ingramcontent.com/pod-product-compliance
Lightning Source LLC
Chambersburg PA
CBHW030249290526
45785CB00001B/27